MW01107994

THE GREAT
PHYSICIAN

A Plastic Surgeon's Confession

RICHARD DOMBROFF, M.D.

WESTBOW
PRESS®
A DIVISION OF THOMAS NELSON
& ZONDERVAN

WestBow Press books may be ordered through booksellers or by contacting:

WestBow Press
A Division of Thomas Nelson & Zondervan
1663 Liberty Drive
Bloomington, IN 47403
www.westbowpress.com
1 (866) 928-1240

ISBN: 978-1-5127-5290-8 (sc)
ISBN: 978-1-5127-5291-5 (hc)
ISBN: 978-1-5127-5289-2 (e)

Library of Congress Control Number: 2016913148

Print information available on the last page.

WestBow Press rev. date: 9/28/2016

For what shall it profit a man, if he shall gain the whole world, and lose his own soul.
Mark 8:36

CONTENTS

For Cynthia

"Fightin' Irish," our tireless paralegal research volunteer, is a truth-seeker sent to us of God. A woman who put her own life on hold, she showed up on our doorstep, ready to fight for justice. With the stubbornness and determination of her favorite Jack Russell terrier, Cindy painstakingly pored through tens of thousands of documents and, ultimately, convinced of our absolute innocence, thought it not robbery to grasp the torch of justice, which she still passionately and unapologetically bears to this very day for us, more than a decade later. She is a defender of liberty who saw injustice and tried to stop it, a legal professional of uncompromising integrity, a true believer and a woman after God's own heart.

FOREWORD

"THE MAN IN THE ARENA"

"Theodore Roosevelt"

It is not the critic who counts; not the man who points out how the strong man stumbles, or where the doer of deeds could have done them better. The credit belongs to the man who is actually in the arena, whose face is marred by dust and sweat and blood; who strives valiantly; who errs, who comes short again and again, because there is no effort without error and shortcoming; but who does actually strive to do the deeds; who knows great enthusiasms, the great devotions; who spends himself in a worthy cause; who at the best knows in the end the triumph of high achievement, and who at the worst, if he fails, at least fails while daring greatly, so that his place shall never be with those cold and timid souls who neither know victory nor defeat.

—Theodore Roosevelt
April 23, 1910

On this warm Independence Day Weekend as I observe our tumultuous 'national political scene, the words of Dickens comes to mind: "It was the best of times, it was the worst of times." I think about a great American, Theodore Roosevelt, arguably the father of the American exceptionalism movement. He, too, was a man of great contradictions. A great, unabashed warrior and hunter, he was also awarded a Nobel Peace Prize in 1906.

About a year after he left the presidency, Theodore Roosevelt addressed an audience at the Sorbonne in Paris and gave a long and brilliant speech entitled "Citizenship in a Republic." Much of it, predictably, was forgettable, but equally so, much of it was filled with treasures that stand today as testimony, albeit mainly forgotten, to the monumental intellect who uttered it more than a century ago.

TR liked to talk, but then he had a lot to say. The excerpt above, "The Man in the Arena," was merely one small paragraph, only 140 words from the middle of an 8,746-word speech, a tiny fraction of the words uttered that day, but like Lincoln at Gettysburg, it is this diminutive, concise nugget that has survived the ages. These 140 words are gold, and like all treasures made of this element they never rust or become moth-eaten with age. Wisdom is not meted out by the pound or by the yard.

It is a fact that every person has an arena in which he plays out his life, and the greater the man, usually, we find the greater the arena.

Interestingly, Theodore Roosevelt was perhaps the most serious man of faith to live at 1600 Pennsylvania Avenue. He was, I understand, a believer who espoused what became known as "Muscular Christianity." It was inspired by the example of the apostle Paul, who espoused a faith intermingled and manifested by a devotion to manliness, clean living, purity, and wholesome athleticism.

I suspect that for Roosevelt, the greatest arena was inhabited by an itinerant Jewish rabbi, the only "perfect" man in the history of the world, who walked the dusty roads of Palestine from the backwoods of Nazareth in Galilee to the cross at Calvary two thousand years ago. Daring greatly, to use Roosevelt's words, the Man of Sorrows' face "was marred by dust and sweat and blood" and at the Cross, just when all seemed lost, He snatched victory from the jaws of defeat, and an empty tomb is there to prove that final victory.

Arenas, like crosses, come in all shapes and sizes. For some, that arena may be a pediatric cancer ward. For others, it is the arena occupied by the military veteran, a young wounded warrior, a double amputee perhaps, being fitted for prosthetic limbs so he can one day walk his little girl to kindergarten and later, perhaps, down the aisle. Everyone's "arena" is unique, and the pain hurts just as bad. So are the moments of triumph that taste just as sweet in the end.

This memoir is, in fact, the work of a modern-day exceptional man in the arena, who "strove valiantly, who came short again and again, who strove to do deeds, who knew great enthusiasms and great devotions and who, when he failed at least he failed while daring greatly." And in the end, unlike the critic, he knew the taste of the "triumph of high achievement."

In fact, the author, in my opinion, exemplifies the concept of Theodore Roosevelt's "The Man in the Arena" more perfectly than any person I know. Perhaps that is because I know him very well, as we have been close for more than fifty years. I am intimately acquainted with all of his strengths as well as all of his flaws. Trust me; it is not easy to have close personal relationships with extraordinary people like this. They are statistical outliers. They are way off the curve. You experience all the exhilaration of their amazing triumphs and the excruciating years of pain when they fall short and endure the consequences.

Ultimately, though, it's not about trying and failing endlessly, over and over again, rebelliously and foolishly. Rather, it's about the willingness to change and grow. It's about redemption and healing. It's about transformation and renewal and how to get it. Whatever personal "arena" you may be in today, this book is written especially for you. Make it your very own playbook.

I did, and for me, someone who literally lived through most of it in real time, reading it chapter by chapter has indeed been an unexpected life-changing experience.

I promise that it can change your life in ways you never expected as well. Thus, on this special day in which we celebrate unique American exceptionalism and the throwing off of national chains of bondage some 240 summers ago, I proudly introduce you to this literary work and the unique human testimony which it presents as a fitting example of that exceptionalism.

Marc Dean Kaye
New York City
July 4th, 2016

In Thanks

I thank Marc Dean Kaye, both the genuine article and a genuine force of nature, my oldest and dearest friend for over half a century, who, when others, including family and so-called friends, turned their backs, averted their eyes, stopped taking my phone calls, slammed their doors in my face, sold me short, and walked away, has always been a true believer in me. My indefatigable cornerman and loyal "cut-man," he is constitutionally incapable of throwing in the proverbial towel on me.

When the world looked at me and saw only a human car wreck, merely a pummeled and soiled man of sorrows, battered and bruised, broken, bloodied and near defeat, little more than dirty laundry, yesterday's news, Marc always just took a steely-eyed hard look at me and simply saw "Rocky." Where the haters looked and reduced me to merely a caricature of a born-again, off-the-wall, Jesus freak-show has-been, Marc, somewhat quizzically at first, witnessed the profound changes wrought in my broken life and sensed fuzzily in his gut that somehow this peculiar childhood friend of his, now a nursing-home chaplain and international missionary, might well have latched onto "something real."

His generosity of spirit and substance, his unwavering support and patience with my foibles, and his integrity and encouragement have truly sustained and nourished this ministry as well as this important project. In short, Marc has been principally responsible for permitting me the privilege of bringing this testimony of redemption and healing to its fullest fruition and to a broken and hurting world.

And there is a friend that sticketh closer than a brother.
—Proverbs 18:24

SPECIAL ACKNOWLEDGMENTS

By this shall all men know that ye are my
disciples, if ye have love one to another.
—John 13:35

Whatever meaningful glory with which we may be blessed to experience as frail humans is often best evidenced on earth by the godly love that we receive from people who selflessly love and nurture us, in the rare instances, not because they want or need anything from us but purely because God has seen our need and has sent them into our lives to love us, expecting nothing in return. Take it from me; in this life, people like this are exceptionally rare. Thus, these are special acknowledgments because they recognize special contributions made by special people in my life to whom I must express my special gratitude.

I send my love to Chaplains Tony, Ralph, Rosemary, and Henry, as well as to all my other marvelous Chaplain's Association compadres who stood with me in the early times when I first came home to stay, brimming with optimism but also, as they no doubt sensed, somewhat dazed and confused—Pastor Sam Dickerson, who is singularly responsible for bringing me into the chaplaincy and helping me answer the "call"; Pastor Peter Conforte of the Assemblies of God Full Gospel Church of Island Park, a "man's man" who is always my port in the storm and my model for the best in Christian pastoral ministry; Pastor Lily and Brother Miguel Vega, my younger brother in the Lord, who has mentored me in the chaplaincy and never stepped away; Dennis, Al, Harry, Jeff and Nancy, Lourdes, John, Steve, Jordan and Kim, Tony, Aurelio, Jock, and my entire Assemblies of God congregation and Men's

Ministry, who provide affirmation, fellowship, and unconditional love and acceptance; and Frank Mignano, who came alongside me and gave me shelter when all I had in the world was empty pockets, a future, and whatever I could cram into a backpack. Finally, to Pavelle, who searched me out in prison when I was pretty much forgotten to the rest and reminded me of how much I was admired and respected by my surgical staff and the thousands of grateful patients who came to me from all over the world, so many years and a million miles ago.

To my marvelous editors at HarperCollins Faith division and the entire team at Thomas Nelson and Zondervan for their encouragement, belief, and expertise in bringing out the best in me as a writer. Pastor Mark Beavers and the entire congregation at the Soul Stirring Church of God in Christ, who took in this odd "white boy" wandering the hot streets alone that first summer, at the edge of the Atlantic, looking for his first church after he got saved and came home years ago. They cranked up the air conditioning that summer, put on sweaters, took up an extra collection for their electric bill, welcomed me with open arms, and made me feel instantly "at home." Rev. Robert Letalien, Deacon Bruce Daugherty, and all the other superb New York State Department of Correctional Services chaplains and staff "behind the wall" who nourished me spiritually as a baby Christian. To the amazing Kimberly in California for always gently reminding me who I am in Christ. To my spiritual parents, Hal and Margie, who always gave me a place to feel warm, welcome, and special on Thanksgiving and Christmas, quietly knowing that I had no place else to go.

I am quite certain there are other individuals, many of whom are probably unaware of how profoundly they have impacted my life. Please know that there is not a day that goes by that your angelic faces and deeds do not dominate my sweetest thoughts and daydreams, nestled warmly in the safe covering of your unceasing prayers.

The Lord has been so gracious and extravagant by bringing into my life such enduring human treasures. Truly, in the currency of love and acceptance by all of these special friends who came around me when the world recoiled, I am made profoundly wealthy and profoundly humbled, and I see the glory of His Grace. My cup truly runneth over. It is truly supernatural and, indeed, I call it the ongoing incarnation: Christ within us, our hope of glory. It is indeed that in witnessing how these saints live their lives that I know, all over again, that my Redeemer lives. And it is this knowledge that has made all the difference and the blessing for which I am most grateful. For it is in the divinely inspired caring of these special people that I have come to realize that the new birth is not an instant bounded by time and space, measured moment to moment but from faith to faith: a new life, beginning here on earth, stretching endlessly and gloriously out into Glory and timeless eternity.

> Think where man's glory most begins and ends,
> and say my glory was I had such friends.
> —William Butler Yeats

1

YOUR BLESSED LIFE NOW

THIS WORK, THE *MAGNUM opus* of my life, for better or for worse, is dedicated, as is everything else in my life, to the glorified God-Man, Jesus Christ of Nazareth, the living God and Savior of the world.

About a year after I was born again on December 27, 2004, in my prison cell in upstate New York, I was walking to my prison job, teaching other prisoners employment skills and preparing résumés for several thousand inmates. I had waited for several weeks to hear about my application for work release. I had always been approved by the superintendent (who used to be called the warden), but the Department of Correctional Services' central office in Albany continually denied my application for freedom after years in prison, without rationale. I think it had something to do with the fact that the system had offered me a slap on the wrist. I told the government, "No way," and I took them to the mat in a record-setting, seven-month-long white-collar financial trial, costing them (and me) millions of dollars. When you lose, you find out what they say about the payback.

As an aside, I conducted business for more than thirty years all over the world without even a whiff of impropriety, but for whatever reason, I was engaged in an on-again/off-again battle with a specific prosecutor's office for more than twenty years, dating back to the early 1980s. My firm crossed swords with this office when I was a young, brash plastic surgeon in a rural county in the boondocks of Long Island, New York, where we had a small outpost of an office. Curiously, the feds never bothered with me, and the famous white-collar unit in the Manhattan

District Attorney's Office, where I transacted about 99.9 percent of my nationwide business, never seemed impressed that my firm merited any negative attention whatsoever.

It seems that way out on Eastern Long Island, I was the proverbial big fish in a small pond, doing a huge amount of business and knocking our established competitors on their establishment rumps. In a protectionist move, the prosecutor's office there became my nemesis for nearly a quarter century. I might add also that the Suffolk County District Attorney's Office has been the subject of both federal and state corruption investigations for more than the last thirty years, continuing up to the present day.

They watched, salivating the whole time, as we garnered headlines and television appearances, as well as earning millions of dollars in fees, first in building a huge national network of cosmetic surgery centers that angered the local medical society and later by successfully arranging hundreds of millions of dollars in much-needed permanent financing for needy hospitals, nursing homes, hospice centers, and a variety of other industries. These were cash-starved health care facilities for the elderly, the terminally ill, and emotionally disturbed youngsters who had been redlined by traditional lenders due to exclusionary lending practices. Our financing kept their lights on when some of them were literally hours from having the banks close them down.

I must also mention my zipping around the country roads of horse country in Suffolk County, Long Island, in Rolls-Royces, Ferraris, and chauffeured limos. I could have kept a lower profile, to say the least. I've learned that the Rolls-Royce grille simply incenses some people, usually the ones who don't have such a motorcar. Of course, I always thought that's why they make Bentleys—because they're less showy. In my stupid immaturity, I liked these symbols of success. For better or for worse, in the old days, I never hesitated to step on the toes of the powers that be. I was reckless, brash, and arrogant; these traits were mixed with a potent tincture of greed.

Although we had a penthouse in Trump Tower, somehow somebody forgot to remind me that I wasn't "The Donald," and the world has an uncanny way of reminding us of our limitations, our overreaching, our fleeting delusions of grandeur.

Be that as it may, this time I worked my way into my own personal World War III, a losing seven-month trial, culminating in a long prison sentence. Although my attorneys advised that we were absolutely on the right side of the law, and they negotiated a plea offer that would have been nothing more than a relative slap on the wrist, I got stupid and stubborn and resolved to take the government to the mat.

I rolled the dice and lost. Big time.

It's a big mistake to underestimate motivated and ambitious legal adversaries, especially those who harbor an animus that goes way back. Even local prosecutors, though they may not be fancy, make up in experience and grit what they lack in flash and brilliance. It was a titanic struggle that consumed several years of my life, and when it was all over, there wasn't much left standing. Ultimately, I blew trial and got five to fifteen years in state prison. For all intents and purposes, my life seemed over. I was a broken man—rock-bottom city.

But it was the proverbial blessing in disguise, for this experience forced me to assume the role of the man in the mirror for the very first time in my life. Despite all the diplomas and accolades, I frankly didn't like the reflection. After being in prison for a very long time, it's hard to continue the charade.

Then I looked at all the setbacks in my life and connected the dots. The only dots that each and every disaster had in common were me, myself, and I. I had to face the inescapable conclusion that, despite the fact that life throws a certain level of real unfairness and persecution our way, there was something broken, and it was inside Richard. Ultimately, I surrendered all, decided I needed absolute truth, picked up a Bible because I was in solitary and had nothing else, and decided that it was a pretty good place to start.

The most unlikely thing occurred. This worldly, Ivy League, liberal Jewish physician and corporate financier gave his life to an itinerant rabbi who walked the road to Calvary in the flesh two thousand years ago. I spent the next several years behind the wall—or to be more exact, the fence line—immersing myself in the Word of God, twelve to eighteen hours a day, seven days a week, for years. It became a great adventure—the watershed, seminal experience of my life.

First, I came to trust Him. Then I came to know Him. Finally, I came to love Him.

Then He began to transform me, and I began to heal at "all the broken places," of which Hemingway wrote, "Life breaks everyone. But in the end, some are stronger at all the broken places."

I came to the personal conviction that despite the facade of accomplishment and brilliance I had constructed, I had squandered everything of value in my life: career, family, and reputation.

I had raced through life as a young hungry man, in a hurry to win the world's praise and approval—not to mention its riches. Lost and foolish, greed-driven and arrogant, I stumbled badly. I was broken and weak, and my humiliation was of Olympian proportions. In other words, I was perfectly qualified for the Cross. "But God hath chosen the foolish things of the world to confound the wise; and God hath chosen the weak things of the world to confound the things which are mighty" (1 Corinthians 1:27). I realized that I was foolish and weak but that God had been tugging at me.

Over time, the Lord made it clear to me that He had a larger purpose for my life than I could ever ask for or think. In fact, I finally accepted that all my egotism was born from fear. My whole life, I had actually sold myself short and settled for living at a very low (albeit opulent) level of existence.

But walking according to His purposes, I saw that I could finally have a life truly worth living. I could become the man I was intended to be from before the foundation of the universe, instead of an overblown Trumpian caricature of a twenty-first-century master of the universe, whose self-worth was wrapped up in an endless series of $25,000 wristwatches and $250,000 Rolls-Royces in the garage.

I began to lift my head off my prison-issue pillow that was drenched with anguished tears shed in the dark of night. I shed so many tears that God had to get another bottle to keep them. I began to feel alive again. My soul, no longer on ice, was on fire for the Lord, and it burned inside me. I yearned for freedom and another chance at life.

After serving several years in prison, I became eligible for early discretionary release but kept getting turned down. I later learned that the powers that be held a grudge, due to the fact that I exercised my right to go to trial. It was a lot more work for them than a quick plea deal. I thought it was water under the bridge, but these people never forget or forgive. Ever.

I applied and reapplied without success. Each time, I was approved by a series of facility superintendents who came to know me personally over the years, but an unseen, unknown someone in Albany had gotten the word and kept vetoing my release. Dejected, I didn't think I'd ever see the light of day, but I kept reapplying. However, it also forced me to just keep digging deeper into the Word.

I recall the turning point vividly. Fearful and secretly tense, I walked to the office of my counselor, who was also my work supervisor. I knew that one imminent day, she again would look at the computer screen on her desk, which had a direct connection to Albany, and tell me that my application was no longer pending, as it had been day after day, but was finally decided upon one way or the other. And that was when I would know whether or not that was the day that I was going to get another chance at life.

I was so apprehensive each morning and afternoon while walking to her office that I had taken to confessing under my breath while walking with other prisoners. I repeated Paul's words to Timothy: "For God hath not given us a spirit of fear, but of power, and of love, and of a sound mind" (2 Timothy 1:7).

After our lunch break, I returned to my work assignment, hung up my green state-issue coat, and my counselor looked up at me.

I was so tense that I could barely breathe. She looked up at me somewhat blankly. My heart sank.

"You got approved. You're going home," she said, breaking into a smile and congratulating me.

I need to say that the folks in Corrections, whom I've encountered over more than a decade, are, for the most part, very decent and very professional people. Caring human beings doing a nasty job. It can be dehumanizing taking care of other humans in cages and chains, but they were good people. I remember in the very beginning when I met my counselor, Mrs. Linda Pickering. The first thing she said to me after I sat down at her desk was, "Mr. Dombroff, our job-one is to get you outta here and home as soon as possible."

But now, after so many years of denials, delays, and disappointments, I knew that my nightmare was over. Though there were some rough speed bumps, setbacks, and comebacks ahead, that was the turning point of a very, very long struggle. I understood the meaning of being "weak in the knees" and, overcome with emotion, I excused myself for a moment and headed for the privacy of the inmates' lavatory.

Lightheaded, I made my way to the handicapped stall because there was plenty of room in there, and I was a little unsteady on my feet, naturally. I knew there was a cold, sturdy, modern brushed-stainless-steel railing for the disabled. I grabbed it and fell to my knees. I put my forehead on the rail and fell in silent meditation and prayer.

Sobbing silently with a mixture of joy, pain, relief, and gratitude, I spoke to Jesus as I had never conversed with Him before. I thanked Him for bringing me through this and told Him that however He needed to use me in the future, I was His. Period. I had never attempted to negotiate with Him in the sense that I had never formulated the proposition, "Lord, if you grant this dispensation, I'll do such and such." Making deals with the Lord never appealed to me. He already made the dispensation of every human need, two thousand years ago on the cross at Calvary, and I don't care to renegotiate it. I'll just receive it, thank you very much, and praise Him.

Having received this miracle in the bathroom stall, humbled by years of setback and in awe of His deliverance, I uttered this pledge:

"Lord Jesus, I dedicate my entire life to you, spirit, soul, and body."

It was everything I had to give Him. No, actually, it was the only thing I had to offer. In that toilet, kneeling at the altar-of-sorts, I made the proverbial living sacrifice.

That bright winter afternoon, just days before Christmas 2006, was almost ten years ago. It was on a Friday, I recall, and Christmas Day was on Monday. Typically, Friday afternoons in prison were melancholy and homesick times for me, but not that afternoon. It was the best weekend I have ever spent. The prison routine was always the same, but the load I had been carrying for years had been lifted.

Through trials and tribulations, even after that amazing day, I have remained steadfast in the commitment I made to the Lord that day. From time to time, the enemy takes a run at me and tries to buffet me by suggesting that perhaps tomorrow I might be wake up and lose all interest in the Kingdom and abandon the central commitment that gives purpose and meaning in my life. Then, of course, I realize he's nothing but a liar, and I kick the enemy to the curb and then do something like write a book.

It is then that Jesus of Nazareth, the Living God, speaks directly into my heart, reminding me gently, "Rock, what are you worried about? Didn't I tell you that I will never leave you or forsake you?"

Through suffering, redemption, and healing, I have ultimately come to the realization that it's not fundamentally about our commitments to Him at all because we have little or no ability in and of ourselves to keep our commitments. No, it's really all about receiving the reality of His commitment to us, for we know that it is not fundamentally about the fact that we loved Him but that He first loved us. And moreover, He loved us when we ignored or even despised Him.

I am drawn in my mind often, back to that moment in the spotless, cold prison bathroom stall. I can still feel that cold metal rail on my palms and forehead as I grasped it for support, on my knees praying in gratitude and humility. Actually, it was in awe of how He had turned my life around in the midst of such self-generated disaster and loss. By then, I had indeed lost everything. My wife divorced me when I went away; my family mostly turned their backs; my career, my home, my reputation—gone. Everything gone.

I recalled the words of the prophet Joel, words that have become the byline of my tragic existence: "The Lord shall restore the years the locusts ate" (Joel 2:25).

In the lives of so many of us, it seems we experience tragic loss and destruction, and looking back, it almost appears as if a huge swarm of locusts is cutting a swath of absolute destruction in our lives, measured too often in years.

Circumstances vary. For some, it may be sickness or disease; for others, addiction, legal entanglements, divorce, or one of a number of the many tragic afflictions common to man on earth. I learned from that devastation that when God is all you have, God is all you need.

That was almost a decade ago, but the vision of the swath that the locusts cut in my life and of my deliverance is still clear and the commitment that I made to Him lives. He and I sealed a covenant for life that day. And I offered him a sacrifice of my very existence, as it were, my "reasonable service."

Today, in that same service, with the same humble awe I felt on my knees in that bathroom, I offer Him this work of my heart as a sacrifice—a pittance of an offering, surely less than the turtle dove offering of the poor and downtrodden, perhaps. Nevertheless, I offer it as an unblemished sacrifice consecrated wholly to His glory, to His honor, and to His praise.

After all, He gave me everything: His name, His spirit, His mind, His faith, His righteousness, and His blood flows in my veins, as in all believers.

Just as Peter spoke to the beggar seeking alms at the temple, "Silver and gold have I none, but such as I have, give I thee" (Acts 3:6).

Like Peter, who was similarly delivered from guilt and folly by Jesus's extravagant love and forgiveness, I have nothing to offer Him but my testimony of His love. It is an offering that is, however, real and intact, pristine and unblemished. My testimony is the only thing of any true value that I possess, and, consequently, I guard it zealously.

Thus, as the title, *The Great Physician*, implies, this memoir is not ultimately about me at all, for my flawed but saved life is nothing but a backdrop to His perfect life.

No, this memoir is really all about Him—but make no mistake; it is not written for Him.

It is written for you. Yes, for you.

It is written for the broken and the lost. It is written for those who have lost a little and for those who have lost everything in life.

It is written for you, sick and suffering, alone and so desperately sad and distraught that your eyes are thick with burning tears, and you think you cannot make it through the dark night to another day.

Trust me; I know how that feels. I lived with that burden for years until I gave Him my burden, and He gave me His.

And He too knew suffering and humiliation better than any of us. He walked the dusty roads of Galilee, often denigrated and scorned. He walked the road up to Jerusalem with other pilgrims, often with no place to lay His head at night after a long journey. Ultimately, He walked the road to Calvary, rejected and alone. That is the walk that He asks us to take from the moment we are saved.

My greatest hope, therefore, is that by reading this, my testimony of His love, no matter what you may be suffering through, by this, a work of my spirit, soul, and body, you will come to know Him as a kinsman; that you will develop the thirst that I developed all those years in chains, to know Him better and to love Him more.

Here's the best part: yes, He's a jealous God, but at the end of the day, I found that He's a giver, not a taker. He needs absolutely nothing from us.

Anyway, all He ever wanted was my heart, and He's surely got that.

So this is my attempt to fulfill His final command on earth:

"Feed my sheep" (John 21:17).

It is my fervent prayer and expectation that in your own particular suffering, you will find the glorious healing of the Great Physician and that you shall experience in your own life's journey of pain and loss the absolute truth of His promise to "restore the years the locusts ate."

When I was a little boy in the 1950s, growing up in the synagogue in suburban Long Island, our beloved rabbi, a wonderful man, would end each Friday night Sabbath service with the traditional Aaronic priesthood benediction. It was the blessing that God himself dictated to His servant Moses and instructed him to tell his brother Aaron to likewise bless the people. Apparently, we know that Moses had the brains in the family but stuttered, while his brother, Aaron, was a bit of an airhead, but spoke eloquently to the nation Israel on behalf of Moses, servant of God.

Rabbi Charles Ozer was my parents' dear friend. He especially loved my father, but then, everybody loved my father. Rabbi called my dad "Benny." Today, my eyes mist when I hear that echo calling "Benny" deep in my soul.

Let's be clear: anything good and decent in me I got from my mother and father. The rest I messed up pretty much by myself.

That Sabbath Friday night, Rabbi looked resplendent and dignified, as ever, in his black robes, his kind face, his silver hair, his soft, loving demeanor, and his lightly Eastern European-accented voice. The high-arched sanctuary was modern, beautiful, softly lit, and peaceful. At the end of the service, Rabbi would step away from the pulpit and come to the very edge of the bema, or platform, and, standing straight and tall, would raise his arms, stretching his hands out in a traditional manner over the congregation, which was now somewhat sleepy and weary from the long week's grind and the late hour of a Friday evening. Still, they were devoted to hearing the Word of God.

Then Rabbi Ozer, at the climax of that evening service, would speak that ancient blessing of God over his flock:

> And the Lord spake unto Moses, saying, Speak unto Aaron and unto his sons, saying, On this wise ye shall bless the children of Israel, saying unto them,
>
> [May] the Lord bless thee and keep thee:
>
> [May] the Lord make his face shine upon thee, and be gracious unto thee:
>
> [May] the Lord lift up his countenance upon thee, and give thee peace.

And they shall put My name upon the children of Israel;
and I will bless them.

—Numbers 6:26

In remembrance, much in the same way, today in my own pastoral
ministry now as an ambassador of the Gospel of Jesus Christ, I close
each service with this same ancient Hebrew benediction, just as I learned
it from that wonderfully kind and gentle old rabbi in my breezy boyhood
hometown near the ocean's edge.

And, beloved, in that same manner, infused with faith and with blessed
assurance, as you read these words, at this very moment I raise my hands
in prayer over you, reading these words. At this very instant.

In the kingdom, however, time and chronology is meaningless. Thus,
right at this moment, as you read this, with one foot on earth and one foot
in the Kingdom of Heaven, together in timeless eternity, my hands are
ever so lightly forming a crown over your head as I, like Aaron, a fellow
eloquent airhead, pronounce this ancient powerful blessing over your life.

Receiving a blessing is a good way to start any journey. Especially when
it's a journey to a new beginning in life. A journey on which your life
depends. Thus, brother and sister, blessed of God, with your Bible at
your side, you are invited to finally turn the page on the past.

Let us embark together on the most exciting journey of your life. A life-
changing journey of discovery, redemption, healing, and Love, Himself.

And all God's people said:

Amen!

2

IN THE BEGINNING

IT'S A FUNNY THING, but one can discern a lot of love—no, literally a tremendous amount of love—in a dank state prison visiting room. Much more than one would think. It's palpable. Like a beating heart.

On the flip side, there is also a huge amount of tangible anger, resentfulness, accusation, anguished betrayal, fear, shame, humiliation and, most painful of all, the bitter realization of irretrievable loss and searing hopelessness. On both sides of the visiting table.

I would come to rediscover this over and over again throughout the next ten years. In excruciating ways.

I watched my twelve-year-old sandy-haired son, my namesake, devour the microwaved buffalo hot wings he'd purchased from the visiting room vending machine for us, seemingly oblivious to his surroundings, as only kids are capable of.

I remained glued to my seat as I was instructed to do, gripping my cold can of Diet Coke, and was invaded by a totally unexpected amount of love for him and his sister, as well as for their beautiful mom, who was sitting across from me. I felt as if I was playing the role of a terminally ill person being catered to by his visitors in a hospice. But it was twisted and tragic in a way that I sensed but could not fully comprehend. In a strange kind of way, I thought the tenderness I was feeling would ease my way through this living nightmare, and we would emerge from it a closer and more devoted family.

Until after they stopped coming, not too many months later. I am very naive.

I was dressed in "state greens" because I was the one they'd come to see. New York State Department of Correctional Services, DOCS, inmate number 03A4961 printed on my forest-green shirt and pants on a white heat-sensitive label and affixed to the fabric for the duration. It was brand new, crisp, and deep green at the time. By the time I was finished with it a decade later, it was a faded and frayed, somewhat threadbare mint-green cloth, so falling apart that had become to me a daily devotional of sorts, a relic with sacred spiritual significance. As it changed with time and brokenness, so did its occupant. The fabric became silky soft and comfortable in a familiar sort of way, and along the way, my heart became tenderized.

A heart of flesh.

The duration, by the way, was fifteen years, or to be more exact, five to fifteen years. Not an atypical indeterminate sentence levied for a typical white-collar financial offense but much, much longer than I was offered if I had not gotten stupid and stood on principle and had been willing to take the plea deal. Clearly, I was not living a prayerful existence at the time. To say the least.

It was much longer than most; the average confinement was less than two years. The ugly part was that under New York State statutes, I could be home in a little as twenty-six months or as long as fifteen years, with everything else in between at the total and complete discretion of faceless bureaucrats sitting behind computer screens in the DOCS central office in Albany using a mysterious calculus. There was no such thing as a guarantee, and there was no way, contrary to popular belief, to earn your way out of it. This was not a merit system; there was no such thing as being a "model inmate." That stuff is all for the movies and television. You went home when they decided to let you go, and there was absolutely no algorithm governing it. The law has a term of art for this kind of irrational decision-making non-process: "arbitrary and capricious."

Mostly, it's very scary, especially when you're inside.

These folks handed out additional years like they were handing out candy. They were decent people, I suppose, with a job to do, and they didn't even think in terms of months. They doled out denials and extended holds of years at a time. It took a while for me to get my hands around that concept, and it still gives me shivers.

I remember once, years later, when I was first approved for early release by the superintendent of the facility where I was imprisoned at the time. The "analyst" in Albany overrode the warden's decision the next day and denied my release. I was invited to reapply in twelve months.

As was my right, they included in the denial envelope a form on which they afforded me the right to appeal their denial to the director of work release. I did so, and a week later she politely wrote me back, denying my appeal and extending the time for my next eligible release application date from the original one year to two years.

Obviously, I never, ever again exercised my right to appeal a denial. They apparently took it personally, and it simply made a bad situation worse.

The time for "lawyering up" was pretty much in the past. Any rights I had were of a purely theoretical nature. They held all the cards.

In the words of one of my white-collar buddies, an ex-attorney, Frank "Veal Chop" Gangi, "Richie-Dee, we're in the hands of the Philistines." I soon discovered that I knew I was in state prison when I realized that my earliest release date was many years after the expiration date stamped on the can of tuna that someone gave me at the time as a "welcoming" present.

But as I sat there in the visiting room in the early days, a "new jack," still close to the beginning of my sentence, still definitely in a relative state of shock at my new "home," I marveled at how close-knit I felt that my family had become as a result. I had a bright but very unrealistic notion: "Wow, this is really bringing us closer together as a family and as a married couple."

I almost felt that this was going to be a blessing in disguise. As it turned out, I was indeed blessed by it, but in a way I could not have predicted or even imagined.

So my family-togetherness fantasies that day, as I very soon came to realize, were unrealistic, and a year later my loving, attentive, beautiful blonde wife of twenty years, who was fifteen years my junior, unceremoniously divorced me.

A little later, figuratively speaking, so did my kids.

Looking back, it is apparent to me they were probably there out of some sense of duty, which was not entirely bad, but in time they would walk out of my life and never look back. I became the man who used to be their father.

I came to accept that they viewed my existence as tragic, the way people view a car wreck or terminal cancer and have to stay away or have to look away. Frankly, I can't blame them. Adopting a victim mentality gets you nowhere, and it was never my long suit. Losing one's wife and kids is, as the state prison saying goes, "All part of the bid." In reality, regardless of anything else, they're "doin' the time" as well. And they hurt bad as well, probably in ways that I will never know.

But at that moment in time, I knew nothing of that and felt totally above it. Similar to the way a wild animal must feel the instant the trap snaps shut but before the realization sets in that it isn't getting out of this. The next instant, the panic becomes real.

Ultimately, the love that was flying around the visiting room for me, at least in those early days, turned to heartbreak and all the other nasty things before too long. It got a lot worse before it got better.

I remember being in the supermax facility, Downstate Correctional Facility, very early on. Downstate was an orientation and reception facility where most New York State prisoners, who are from the metropolitan area and are destined for "upstate" sentences, are received into the system, examined, tested, poked and prodded, marched, clothed, and indoctrinated, and finally given a security classification relating to many factors, including how violent they were or weren't and, most important, how long their sentences are.

Imprisonment is based on three concepts from an institutional point of view: the three C's of correctional science—care, custody, and control—and the whole process begins in reception. The "control" part is the senior partner that modulates everything else.

My sentence structure, because of its relatively long yet indeterminate duration, fell into the higher-security range, but my nonviolent nature indicated a minimum security level. What I did not understand at the time was that the label "sophistication" was affixed to all my security classifications and thus, I would never be eligible for relatively cushy jails, where I could go outside daily as part of a group and do community service, such as painting firehouses and so forth.

Rather, I would spend all my confinement at seriously locked down maximum security B or medium security A "joints" that housed murderers, sex offenders, and the full gamut of street criminals.

It was a nice mix of sociopaths.

In other words, there were to be no "country club" or "Club Fed" type jails in my future. For that matter, even among minimum security facilities, there are no "country clubs" in the New York State prison system. Anyone who says there are is either lying, doesn't know what he's talking about, or is in serious denial. I've encountered all three, especially in inmates.

Ultimately I learned what "upstate" really meant. Growing up and spending most of my life in the New York metropolitan area, we always thought "upstate New York" was where you went to sleep-away camp as a youngster. Like up in the Catskills, ninety miles from midtown Manhattan. Lakes and rolling hills, Grossinger's and the Concord Hotel (now long gone).

In fact, that is just where Sing Sing is located in Ossining, New York. But I soon came to realize that going upstate would mean something entirely different for me. I found myself on a prison bus, hands shackled and in leg irons, going five hundred miles to the north. Shackled ankle-to-ankle to your new best friend, the man sitting next to you, for ten hours. In the event you had to use the bathroom on the bus, homeboy was going with you. Or vice versa. So far away that even a few miles farther would have put me out of the country altogether, into Canada—a hop, skip, and a jump from Ottawa.

There, stretching hundreds of miles across the northern border of the United States, New York State has constructed a virtual "gulag archipelago," to borrow Alexander Solzhenitsyn's term, establishing a vast, anonymous string of high security prisons extending from the extreme western end of New York State by Lake Erie all the way up central New York through the Saint Lawrence Valley to the northernmost tip of New York by Montreal and the border of northern Vermont.

All of them built with the sale of triple A-rated New York State Dormitory Authority Bonds. Triple tax-free to investors and a public who thought it was supporting higher education for fresh-faced college kids. Typical cynical government lack of transparency employed to fool the electorate regarded as too stupid to be entrusted with the truth. This is the kind of brilliant municipal financing scheme that has given the United States the highest prison population in the world.

Generally speaking, as a bonus, Corrections throws off lots of jobs that support the local economy, which has seen the complete collapse of the manufacturing sector over the past fifty years.

So much for the Catskills. Just a fleeting memory. I passed the maximum security facility, Clinton Correctional Facility, in Dannemora, and as the bus rolled endlessly north, I knew I was headed for the American equivalent of Siberia. As I was to find out, in the winter months, the tundra up there was so Siberian it would have stopped Hitler's Wehrmacht in its tracks.

I was on my way to the land of ice fishing and hunting lodges. Next to Corrections, the only other industry was dairy farming. In fact, from the prison yard on a warmish early spring day, in the thaw, I can still, years later, smell the aroma of aging manure. But let's not romanticize this unnecessarily.

However, during those few glorious and warm delusionary minutes in the visiting room at Downstate, I was still feeling the love, so to speak. As a prisoner, I sat on one side of the square Formica-covered table directly facing the officer on a raised platform at the front of the room. My wife and kids were already seated, and all our eyes locked as I entered the room from the search area.

I had been searched before entering the room but not nearly as thoroughly as I would be after the visit was completed. It was a full strip search with full visualization of the body cavities and folds, including the mouth and anus.

I remember the very last time Tricia visited me.

I was given one phone call the very first time I arrived upstate and was in the reception population at Downstate, the supermax just north of New York City. She was so genuinely excited and delighted to hear my voice for the first time in about a week that I was instantly filled with warmth and hope.

But over time, reverse "climate change" became a reality, and the frostiness on the phone was becoming a constant theme. She had supported my earlier decisions and believed in my innocence staunchly throughout the entire three years prior to my conviction, even to the point of telling me there was no reason I should ever agree to take a plea. Suddenly, after the roof fell in, there was palpable resentfulness and blame.

I had founded an amazingly successful boutique firm that specialized in arranging otherwise nearly impossible financing for health care facilities and other specialized businesses. Structuring and closing these kinds of complex transactions was something for which I had a gift, and throughout the 1990s I became "the man to see" in the United States if the bank or a bond trustee was foreclosing on a hospital or a nursing home. I was compensated very well for it, and I had earned millions of dollars in fees for my services.

After my years at the highest level of plastic and reconstructive surgery, I combined my health care delivery expertise and experience with my financial acumen, and for a period of two decades, people beat a path to my door in search of financing for projects the banks had red-lined, such as nursing homes and hospices, which Wall Street bond funds traditionally did not view as acceptable credit risks. We taught them differently.

Bottom line was that my team successfully arranged hundreds of millions of dollars of badly needed financing that literally kept the lights on at hundreds of facilities all over America. We saved the beds and homes of thousands of elderly citizens and other vulnerable folks living in facilities that were targeted for extinction by banking institutions that were only interested in A-credits. It was kind of a subprime situation but in a highly specialized area of corporate finance that only I and a handful of other individuals fully understood and could translate to the capital markets.

This was not without many controversies that arose over fees, which our attorneys advised us we had earned but that the government later felt were unfairly retained. I played hardball with my clients and everybody else. Truth be told, there was more than enough greed to go around.

The fact was that we personally arranged successfully well over a hundred million dollars of financing out the door to cash-starved nursing homes and hospices for the terminally ill, and at the end of the day, I was brought down by a brouhaha over fees, disputed refunds, that totaled less than 1 percent of the total amount for which we successfully arranged funding. The small fraction of fees we refused to return over nearly ten years, totaling about a million and change, compared to $125 million funded to our needy clients, was the sole gravamen of the case. A pathetically insignificant banana peel to slip on.

In truth, I was always on the wrong side of the political equation in a rural county where crooked crony politics ruled supreme. But as I've stated, there was more than enough greed, arrogance, and selfishness to go around.

There certainly was on my part.

Years later, speaking with my daughter from prison, I apologized to her for causing this mess and by refusing to accept a sweet plea offer. She said, "Stop that, Daddy. You stood on principle, and we're proud of you." She learned something about the abusive potential of government power, and she's now a staff attorney with the public defender's office, doing amazing work for some of society's most vulnerable. I had inculcated in her the unpopular understanding that it is in the area of criminal justice that there is the greatest danger of an overreaching government abridging the rights guaranteed to the citizenry in the US Constitution.

The defense bar knows that this is true. It's not in question, and the reason the government gets away with it is that nobody cares about the accused. The basic prejudice is, "They're all garbage, so let's lock 'em up and throw away the key." Quite honestly, I know quite a bit now about criminal justice and correctional policy in the United States, and it has been my observation over the past decade or so that, at least in New York State, that probably 90 percent of those men and women serving time in state prison for nonviolent offenses could be well-handled in highly supervised community settings, where they could be helped to rebuild their lives in the right way while they contribute to the welfare of their families and their communities.

It's just easier to incarcerate them.

If I had it to do over, I probably would take their deal and forked over the million or so of refunds that was in controversy. If I had chosen that path, this would have been over in a few months instead of fifteen years and I would have been the same multimillionaire. It was not to be. I was living a Godless existence and was busy worshipping my own success. Frankly, I was constitutionally and spiritually incapable of coming to grips with my own profound character flaws and limitations. In short, I was still believing my own press clippings and once again served myself up on the proverbial silver platter laid on the altar of self-love.

Although my daughter, the lawyer, was proud of me, it seems as if once I was shipped off, my wife distanced herself from me, ultimately to the point of seeing a divorce lawyer. After that, it seemed as if Tricia somehow needed to put voice to blame in order to generate the hostility needed to move on with a clear conscience. Either way, her commitment ended abruptly. Amazingly, that was something I never anticipated because I saw us as irreversibly devoted to one another.

I can be so pathetically naive at times. Actually, it was denial grown out of fear.

Truth be told, in 90 percent of instances comparable to mine, the wife-left-behind files for divorce within the first year or so of the husband being incarcerated, unless it's a Mafia-type family, in which case the long-suffering wives seem to stick around. It seems that *la famiglia* actually means something to these folks, and I've always admired that. Of course, Dad is a professional career criminal, so they're used to enduring this kind of occupational hazard. It's part of the fabric of their lives. I'm sure Mom's not happy about it, but it is what it is.

My own brother, who in earlier, happier years would hang out with his family during vacations on my Hatteras Yacht, moored in Palm Beach over the winter holidays, actually once sent me a handwritten note while I was in prison. In ten years just once. I was glad that our mother wasn't alive to read it.

I used to write my brother regularly. I never received a reply or even an acknowledgement until the final few months of my imprisonment after ten years.

I had mentioned in my letter to him that he and I were really the only family we had left from growing up. I didn't belabor the point; I just mentioned it to emphasize that I valued the relationship, as distant as it had been. In all fairness, he had been extremely generous over many years of my travails, so I thought we had a good chance to build on that goodwill. I was working hard to keep things upbeat.

A few weeks later, I was amazed to get a letter from my brother, a famous Washington, DC, attorney, handwritten on a sheet from a yellow legal pad. I was overjoyed to finally get a response—until I read it. He affirmed that we had the same parents, but beyond that he could not see what I thought we could possibly have in common. I was so totally crushed and was left speechless. It was a body blow.

I recalled the times, many years before, when we would meet, me in medical school at Johns Hopkins in Baltimore and my brother, Mark, in Washington with the Justice Department. We were proud of each other, and secretly, he was my hero. He still is. He is a great and respected man.

His letter broke my heart, but I let it fly and continued to write to him. What he wrote might well have been true, but even today, I wonder how a sensate human being could put that kind of denigrating sneer on paper and actually put it in a mailbox.

I suppose I let him down.

It took all the Jesus in me not to respond in kind and, as I said, I was glad my mother didn't live to read it because my wonderful mother would have been incensed. Yes, incensed but, sadly, not surprised. She knew my brother better than anyone in the world, of course, and she loved him. She also knew how cruelly cold, impersonal, and judgmental he could be, especially when circumstances called for emotional intimacy, warmth, and acceptance. It was just something of which he was incapable.

My father fell sick with a tragic, ugly form of presenile dementia, beginning when I was about seven years old; he was only about forty. My mother leaned on me for emotional sustenance over the years of his gruesome decline, and we were soul mates in that regard. She was my mentor.

My mother used to say, "If you're angry at someone, and you want to tell him off in a letter, then by all means go ahead and write it. Then put it in a drawer for a week or two. Then take it out of the drawer and reread it. Then throw it out."

I can honestly say that in all my life, I never witnessed my mother being unkind to anyone. She wasn't a Christian, but she and my father had us in synagogue every Friday night, hearing the Word of God. It was the Torah and the rest of the Old Testament, of course; I didn't know what the New Testament was until I went to prison, but the Word must have taken root. No surprise, because we know,

"Faith cometh by hearing and hearing by the Word of God" (Romans 10:17).

Loyalty is a touchy subject with me because loyalty is like a close cousin of faith. Like faith, loyalty is not a feeling. It's a spiritual force. Loyalty, like faith, is not about what we see with our eyes or hear with our ears. It's not about what we even believe with our "heads." It's more often what we choose to believe with our hearts.

The thing about loyalty is that it demands self-abnegation. That is a difficult thing for most of us, so consumed by self-love. Worse still, people who have trouble exercising loyalty also have trouble exercising faith, and that is a sad thing indeed, because it is the underpinning of our eternal salvation.

With respect to my expectations of brotherly loyalty, though, even Whitey Bulger, the notorious Irish gangster from South Boston, had a loyal brother, William Bulger, the president of the University of Massachusetts–Amherst, who testified to a Senate subcommittee investigating organized crime, which had subpoenaed him, "Hey, I love my brother." Then he politely refused to answer any more questions, basically telling the senators where to get off.

That's loyalty in my book. However, despite what happened between me and my only sibling, I can honestly say now, "Hey, I love my brother, and you can take the rest and let it fly."

Unfortunately, I've found little loyalty and it is a rare and precious commodity in my life. Honestly, that's the part that made me question my own character and my heart the most when I ultimately got saved and was able to be brutally honest with myself. The isolation and the abandonment I experienced made me face the revelation that despite all the surface accolades, diplomas, media attention, money, Rolls-Royces, and Ferraris, perhaps I wasn't exactly Mr. Wonderful after all.

Hey, I did some amazing work in healthcare and closed tons of critical transactions in business that helped a lot of folks. I didn't expect a Nobel Prize, but when I badly stubbed the toes of my "feet of clay," I also didn't expect to get destroyed.

As I've said, I can be extremely naive at times. Perhaps disingenuous as well.

The other thing I've learned, painfully, is that often the seeming loyalty and attentiveness of people around you, even those who say they love you, usually extends only as far as the size of your checkbook. This is not cynicism. It is sadly a biblical truth that I have had to accept, as almost everyone special to me has turned their backs and walked away as if I were dead. Solomon, in the wisdom of the Lord, figured it out ultimately.

"Wealth maketh many friends; but the poor is separated from his neighbor" (Proverbs 19:4).

"The poor is hated even of his own neighbour: but the rich hath many friends" (Proverbs 14:20).

Bible wisdom, I have found, can be pretty rough-and-tough love. I've also experienced the very cold truth of these verses in my own life, as family members, siblings, kids, and a whole array of "friends" don't take my phone calls anymore, now that the yachts and the limos, the parties and the pools, the tennis courts and the private jets, the Louis Vuitton house accounts, the Trump Tower penthouses, and fat, juicy bank balances are gone.

I am saddened by the sobering string of personal abandonments, perhaps more than anything else that I have lost, because I am left to conclude that in the past, people who attached themselves to me perhaps did so out of what I could do for them, as opposed to who I was as a human being. I was defined by what I did for a living, my worldly erudition, my status in society, and what I could tangibly produce. When all of those indices tanked, they did the math and walked away. Unfortunately, that is the way of the world. I am sorry to say that even in the church, among members of the body of Christ, that seems to be the calculus all too often.

So I have learned to lean on the wisdom of the scriptures, which I've found to be uncannily prescient, particularly with respect to my own life.

"It is better to trust in the LORD than to put confidence in man" (Psalm 118:8).

Thus, predictably, as time went by and phone calls from prison became frostier, Tricia stopped coming altogether.

Then, about a year and a half into my time upstate, I was called unexpectedly to go to the visiting room one Sunday afternoon. Generally speaking, people don't just stop in for visits to state prisons that have been deliberately built hundreds and hundreds of miles from the New York metropolitan area to discourage frequent visiting.

"I'm not expecting a visit from anyone," I told the officer. "Are you sure it's not a mistake?"

That is the wrong thing to say to an officer. "Listen up, Dombroff. The woman's been waiting. Get going."

There were no women in my life, other than Tricia and consequently, I had a sinking feeling in my gut because I knew instinctively something wasn't right. I doubted that she had driven ten hours in the middle of February because she missed me or wanted to wish me Happy Valentine's Day. No way. That wasn't happening today.

Well, sometimes I tend to veer to the negative and jump to mistaken conclusions, but not that day. I was unfortunately spot-on, because as I entered the visiting room after getting searched, I connected with Tricia's eyes, and I immediately knew it was over. Twenty years done.

I sat down. She was blonde, blue-eyed, and bosomy beautiful and, of course, she told me she had filed for divorce. She came up to tell me personally so that I would hear it from her and not just get the papers.

I thanked her for her thoughtfulness and kind consideration. The anointing of sarcasm was coming upon me, but I kept it in check and pretty much shut up. Anyway, I was in shock, and I had such a bad attack of cottonmouth that I could barely speak. Interestingly, I never thought it would come to this.

I fell totally crazy-in-love with her from the first moment we met, twenty years earlier when she was nineteen. Truth be told, today, so many years later, I still am crazy about her. Of course it's been over for a long time. In a loyal heart some things never waver and the bitterness fades. That's what happens when Forgiveness, Himself, lives inside you.

"Trish, you know that I love you and the kids. We could put our life back together after this. I think you're making a mistake, but I'm not going to argue with you about this. Certainly not here. You're short-selling, but it's your decision."

Prison visiting rooms are not great places to work out profound family issues, so I punted. Trust me; in another time and another place, I would have made a last stand, but that was neither the time nor place to do so.

When I look back on this, I think that it was a good thing that I was saved just a month or so before because I probably would not have had the power to receive this buffeting with such equanimity. It wasn't me being calm. In looking back, I realize that I was operating on full Holy Ghost power, because in the natural, internally deep in my soul, I was coming apart at the seams.

If I sounded cool and collected, I wasn't. I was dazed and although I was devastated, I wasn't going to go to pieces. Not there. I kissed her lightly on the cheek, motioned to the officer that we were done, rose, and she walked out first.

While I was waiting to get the usual mandatory post-visit strip search, an officer called me over and asked, "Dombroff, was that your wife?"

"Yes," I replied weakly.

"My compliments to you. She's a really beautiful woman. Good for you. You're a lucky guy." He couldn't realize that the lucky guy was the one waiting for her in the car in the prison parking lot. The officer saw the blood drain from my face, and he immediately added, "No disrespect intended."

"None taken, sir. I appreciate the compliment."

I really didn't need to hear it at that moment, but the poor fellow had no way of knowing what had just transpired.

As I waited my turn to be searched before going back to the block, my mind was numb, and I did something utterly careless and stupid that I'd never done before and haven't since. I wasn't thinking too straight, and in prison, one needs to "stay on point" and generally not run off at the mouth.

The officer who was assigned to perform the pre- and post-visit searches had been a little grumpy when I first came to the visiting room, so I turned to the inmate immediately in line ahead of me, who I did not know at all, and whispered to him, "That officer is a real creep." I regretted letting those words out of my mouth immediately, because I generally feel that no one dressed in green in state prison is to be trusted. Nor believed.

He said nothing and went in when "Officer Grumpy" called him into the curtained area for the strip search.

Five minutes later, it was my turn before being cleared to go back into general population.

"I heard you think I'm a creep, Dombroff," the officer said bloodlessly, putting on his specially padded, light-blue leather beat-down gloves. He was getting set to "tune me up" a little bit.

My heart sank, but I didn't deny it. I still cannot fathom how another inmate would be such a miserable rat to repeat something like that to a cop. Misery loves company, I suppose. So much for my big mouth. It wasn't the first time it put me into a nasty jackpot, and although I was just a baby Christian, I immediately remembered a very relevant Bible verse:

"And the tongue is a fire, a world of iniquity: so is the tongue among our members, that it defileth the whole body, and setteth on fire the course of nature; and it is set on fire of hell" (James 3:6).

"I apologize, sir. My wife just came up unexpectedly and told me she was divorcing me. Havin' a bad day overall. No disrespect intended, sir."

This officer look quizzically at me at first. He wasn't used to honesty from convicts. One thing he did understand, because he was a professional, was the kind of real-life drama that percolates just beneath the surface in a prison visiting room.

"None taken. Go back to wherever you lock," he replied, taking off the gloves and stuffing them back in his uniform pants pocket. Real *mano a mano* stuff.

I suspect he also knew that he was a creep as well.

Frankly, dealing with what they have to deal with every day of their lives in places like that, getting grumpy becomes an occupational hazard. Anyway, he turned out to be a real standup guy, and we respected each other to the point that over the succeeding years, we became friends of sorts.

The cavity searches and the humiliations of complying with an officer's commands to "Pick up your junk" in order to search my groin became routine, and over the years I came to expect it, but it is never something that one "gets used to." Truth be told, however, in all the times I was strip-searched over the years, as uncomfortable as it was for me, I always felt infinitely worse for the officers.

After Tricia left and I went back to my dorm, feeling raw inside, I crawled into my bunk, put a state green towel over my head, crawled under the covers, and wept bitterly for a very long time in the dark. I just did not see how I could recover from yet another body blow. I leaned on the Lord, and He spoke into my heart these words:

"Weeping may endure for a night but joy cometh in the morning" (Psalm 30:5).

Having given my life to Jesus of Nazareth just a month or so before this, on December 27, 2004, I must admit things had been going well, and I kind of looked forward, in baby-Christian optimism, to smooth sailing. Obviously, we're never promised a rose garden here on earth, even as heirs of salvation.

He does, however, tell us tenderly that from here on in, He will never leave us or forsake us, come what may. We learn what this means as the storms of life come rolling on in, as they invariably do in one form or another. Indeed, in looking back, I know now that it was actually in the midst of this very painful trial, the first after I was born again, that I began to discover the true nature and miracle of the new birth and the Christian life. It is life lived under the force field of the anointing.

That is literally the meaning of the term *Christian*. It is an exact translation of the Greek word for the Anointed One and His Anointing. No longer do we walk alone, having to rely on our own power, for the power of the Holy Spirit is in us. The Holy Spirit Himself lives inside of our human spirit and possesses us in loving tenderness as our Groom and we as His Bride.

Oh, the enemy will throw people at us, and events to seek to engulf us, but those in Christ under the anointing are literally "sealed until the day of redemption," and nothing—absolutely nothing—can separate us from Love, Himself.

After he was saved, the apostle Paul suffered more than most of us can imagine. It is meaningful, especially to me personally, that he suffered through the personal betrayal by those closest to him, as well as suffering imprisonment, but he was still able to write most of the New Testament, including the following from the eighth chapter of Romans:

"Nay, in all these things we are more than conquerors through him that loved us. For I am persuaded, that neither death, nor life, nor angels, nor principalities, nor powers, nor things present, nor things to come, Nor height, nor depth, nor any other creature, shall be able to separate us from the love of God, which is in Christ Jesus our Lord" (Romans 8:37–39).

So for me, tears endured for a night, but joy did come in the morning.

Oh, maybe not the next morning per se, but I was sealed and under the blood of the Lamb for the first time in my life, and the joy of the Lord sustained me in this very first trial after I was saved, as it has during countless trials over the next ten years. For we know that "the joy of the Lord is our strength."

But this leads us to a larger issue. Divorce, abandonment, or betrayal, even when we have had a hand in bringing it on ourselves, is terribly painful. Social isolation of this nature, particularly in restricted settings such as in nursing homes, hospice care, the military, and certainly during imprisonment, is especially frightening to the human organism because we are designed by our Creator God to dwell within a loving, affirming family unit.

The reality for most human beings is vastly divergent—most go through life as best they can, dazed, lost, cold, and with little love.

The sense of betrayal and alienation generated in the wake of the abandonment by those we consider dear to us can send many people over the edge into severe depression, both acute and chronic. In fact, much of the world suffers daily from depression brought on by the social isolation and alienation inherent in our modern society, in which the family is increasingly fragmented by divorce, dysfunctional gender roles, economic pressures, expectations and identities, as well as other destructive forces.

In walking alongside me all through the unique and painful experiences of my life, much of which I brought on myself by rebelliousness, the Lord has graciously kindled within me a wonderful spiritual burden for those similarly afflicted. Through the new birth, He has begun a supernatural transformative process in me. He has brought me through dark nights of the soul. He has given me "beauty for ashes," and despite all that I have lost and all those who have walked away, He has anointed me with the "oil of gladness."

This is good news for everyone because the Lord is no respecter of personage.

Regardless of how soiled or dysfunctional a past we may have or how we may have humiliated ourselves over and over again, when we finally come to Him, He gifts us extravagantly with the realization that, from the moment of our new birth, Love Himself is living inside of us. We will never have to walk through the fires alone again, and "because He lives, we can face tomorrow."

3

THE POSSIBILITIES OF UNCONDITIONAL LOVE

Graduation Johns Hopkins, 1976

The dork in the middle is me.

ACTUALLY, IT'S PRETTY OBVIOUS, and I can say with great affection and respect that we were all pretty dorky at that point. Of course, most of the brilliant dorks around me, including the other ninety or so you don't see, went on, over the succeeding thirty or forty years, to become incredibly famous and accomplished physicians and surgeons who saved the lives of countless men, women, and children all over the planet, changed the world, and made it an infinitely better place in which to live. To know them, to live with them, to study and to work with them was a great privilege and a blessing.

It was the red-letter day of my young, seemingly charmed life, at least up until that point. No, actually that day was probably at the top. Over the top. It was perfect—very heady stuff, and it felt good. It was good.

Personal achievement based on the singular, tireless dedication of one's talents and boundless ambitions can be, in itself, an admirable thing. But there is a double-edged sword to every human striving that can cut both ways. Depending on the context in which it is exercised, it can be for good, but it also can have a corrosive effect on one's life, even in a delayed sense. This is especially true when the striving to do good deeds in the eyes of other people occurs outside of a personal relationship with God, in which case, it is always about self-glorification. Invariably, this only serves to intensify the corrosive effect of self-love.

In looking back, I see that I paid a great personal price. The very early overwhelming success changed my character and personality in many ways, some good, some not so good. Up until that day, everything seemed charmed, but it wasn't. Seemingly the rest of my life, with endless blue-sky potential and only goodness, appeared to lie ahead, but it didn't.

May 25, 1976. Baltimore, Maryland. Graduation of the class of 1976 of the Johns Hopkins University School of Medicine. Elite. Authentic. The genuine article. The stuff dreams are made of. Legendary. Like playing for the New York Yankees. Pinstripes and all. Except you don't ever get traded, the afterglow lasts a lifetime, and almost everybody has a good shot at Cooperstown.

I began taking college-level science courses at Columbia University as a high school student at the age of fourteen. I commenced full-time premedical studies there at seventeen, and after two years in the Ivy League, I was recruited by the wise men at the Johns Hopkins Medical School and earned my MD there, with honors, at twenty-four.

At that point in my life, I was batting a thousand and pitching a perfect game all at the same time. I was a young man in a hurry, with a ton of talent and drive to make things happen in my own power and for my own glory. Of course, I didn't see it that way at all. I was just doing what came naturally. That, of course, was the problem. It was all "in the natural."

I remember that graduation day vividly. It started early, with an unaccustomed breakfast with my wife and her parents and my recently widowed mother, all visiting from New York.

As an aside, the last time my mom had visited us was about a year earlier. Nice little visit for the weekend, and my wife, Pam and I put her back on the Metroliner at the old Baltimore railroad station. In those days, horse-drawn fruit wagons were driven by elderly black gentlemen, who sang songs for passersby to hear as they slowly navigated up and down the streets of old Baltimore.

The Inner Harbor was still on the drawing boards. Jim Crow and segregated lunch counters were still a vivid memory. The Orioles still played on Thirty-Third Street with Brooks Robinson at the "hot corner," and Johns Hopkins Hospital was referred to as "mecca," as it was regarded as the seismic epicenter of the medical universe.

Everything on that Baltimore list of attractions is changed today, except for the last. Brooks resides in the Hall of Fame, Baltimore's got an African American mayor, a very nice woman as well. The Orioles now inhabit the converted Camden train yards just outside of downtown, and the Inner Harbor has transformed Baltimore from the "Armpit of the East Coast" to Disneyland on the Chesapeake, so to speak. Only Hopkins goes on and on the same way as it has for over a hundred years.

On the first day when the doors were opened, it was the finest medical and surgical center in the world. It was designed that way by its founder, a very righteous Quaker merchant, named Johns Hopkins. He was never a slave owner; he believed in equal opportunity for women in the professions; and even in the intolerant, arrogant, politically correct, anti-white privilege revisionism of today's liberal academia, the old Quaker is still rightly admired and revered. It is simply the epitome of medical excellence against which every other hospital and medical center in

New York, Boston, Los Angeles, London, or anywhere else in the world continues to be measured.

We were preparing for Monday morning when the phone rang in our seventy-five-dollars-a-month, highly roach-infested efficiency apartment across the way from the hospital. It was, as expected, my mom calling upon her arrival back home. She sounded different, however.

My mother told me that my father had died over the weekend, and she just had received the call from the hospital where my father had lived for several years. It was late on a Sunday night, and my nose was buried in one of my medical textbooks at the time. I put it aside.

I don't remember feeling much of anything at all. Other than shock and relief. I am not ashamed to admit it. That sounds unusual and mean, but it wasn't. I loved my father and respected him totally. Interestingly, I regret that I cannot specifically remember ever telling him so.

My father had died for us a long time ago; for about twenty years, he had been part of the living dead. As a young husband and father, he had developed the true, vicious form of presenile dementia that the famous Bavarian neurologist, Alois Alzheimer, described in 1906. In Dr. Alzheimer's study, he presented the case of a fifty-one-year-old patient with unexplained short-term memory loss, leading to his institutionalization and ultimately to his demise, totally demented.

As a brilliant young Manhattan lawyer and business leader in his forties, my father had experienced gradual and insidious loss of his legal career, his personality, his mind, and, eventually, his life over about a two decade period, beginning when I was about five or six years old and ending when I was a senior in medical school at the age of twenty-four. It was a living nightmare for him as well as for us. Only in the past few years have I fully faced the toll that it might have exacted in my life.

My brother, Mark, was five years older, and he went off to college in Washington, DC, in 1963, about the time our father's deterioration began to be so noticeable that we could no longer ignore it. It was a necessary escape for my brother, I suppose. Understandably, my brother stayed in Washington, and we rarely saw him after that. I am certain that Mark suffered greatly as well, although he has never spoken a word about it. However, being older than me, he knew my father well as he really was and in a way that I never got to see him—dynamic, handsome, articulate, loving, and highly accomplished.

One of the nice things I vividly remember about my father during those good times was the smell of his freshly laundered, crisply starched white business shirts as I, a three- or four-year-old little fellow, lay with my head on his chest in the evening—he held me as he reading the evening newspaper—somewhere in the 1950s. There are one or two other nice memories I ponder in my heart of a loving, tender, decorated war hero, so prototypically emblematic of the "greatest generation."

To make this family nightmare even more ugly, my father died as the broken shell of a man, beaten to death mercilessly at the hands of a nameless someone in the Veteran's Administration Hospital at Northport Long Island. Whether it was by a staff member or another patient, I never learned. I never wanted to know. And I have never asked or made any inquiries. This is just something that I cannot go near, and we finally buried all this with him with honors at the Pinelawn National Military Cemetery on an mild April morning in 1975.

As a family, we were devoted to each other, but we had "buried" my father a long time before, when he was alive but no longer even a shadow of the powerful, dynamic guy we all idolized, including my mother. We felt nothing but relief and a blessed release for him and, admittedly, for us as well, from this long bondage to this still incurable destroyer of human beings.

Trust me; there is a huge difference between what we speak about as Alzheimer's disease today, as opposed to how it was spoken of forty or fifty years ago. This was before human disease became big business and a lucrative financial vehicle with which to raise billions of dollars on Wall Street. This was before our present era of the drug companies, or "Big Pharma," as well as the not-for-profit charitable sector with its executives who pull down multi million-dollar annual salaries.

In my father's time. Alzheimer's was defined as true presenile dementia, or dementia occurring in otherwise healthy men and women in the prime of their lives, as opposed to the senility that occurs in the later seventies or eighties age groups. Then, it was considered a rare disease of unknown etiology and very incurable, with no known treatment. Hardly the kind of rare disease that could capture the general public's attention enough to stimulate the sales of zillions of dollars of useless drugs or empower big government to dole out billions to universities for research that over the past forty years has yielded next to nothing useful. Certainly as a rare disease, it could not support huge foundations, with their never-ending appetite for gobbling up money by the boatload, big expense accounts, fraud and other abuses.

Nothing got rolling until the best and the brightest of the medical-industrial complex figured out a way to bring this rare, almost unheard of disease to the big time. It was at that time just an ugly little disease.

The solution was simple. Just expand the diagnosis to include every single man or woman who developed some memory or cognitive loss in their sixties, seventies, or eighties. Now you're talking about millions of patients a year and its perception as a widespread public health issue. A pandemic demanding and consuming billions of dollars annually, lining corporate pockets richly. Tons of television spots hawking worthless wonder drugs.

Frankly, it's all turned out to be a lot of hype, with next to no results. Truth be told, we know next to nothing more definitive about its cause or its treatment today than we knew when the neuropathologist, Alois Alzheimer, described it clinically and microscopically in 1906. After hundreds of billions of dollars have been spent and continue to be thrown away, we have drugs being peddled by the major pharmaceutical houses that do absolutely nothing to alter the progression of the disease, inexorably to death. Look up the latest journal reports. Look at the drug package inserts.

Read 'em and weep. We did.

I remember taking my father to a famous Columbia-Presbyterian neurologist in 1969. He did the whole neurological exam and then cheerfully told me that my father had this rare disease called Alzheimer's. He matter-of-factly told me that there was no treatment for it, that I should take my father home, and that we should try to make things as nice for him as we could.

By that time, he had lost his ability to even hold a low-level job as a telephone clerk. Forget about the legal profession. That was gone more than ten years before. Now, I cannot even remember what my reaction was to the doctor's news, other than confusion. I was 17 at the time. I cannot recall why my mother was not with us, but frankly, I suppose that she just couldn't handle any more at that point, and she needed a break.

I was clearly in over my head and in way over my level of maturity, but that kind of yeoman service is often demanded of a child charged with the care of a chronically sick parent, not to mention having to support the other parent who is greatly suffering as well. I didn't have time to think about fear, anxiety, and loss, and I was too ashamed to discuss it with anyone who might have been of some help to me. I just did what was necessary to get through it and kind of buried the feelings for many, many years. Isolated, I ignored the damage as well.

Today, there are all kinds of support groups and counselors, and open communication is encouraged. That is a good thing because this disease extracts an immeasurable toll on the families. Fifty years ago, there was nothing but shame and humiliation, and we suffered in isolation and stoic silence, not to mention experiencing near poverty. Had it not been for my mother getting a teaching position at the local high school for the next sixteen years, we would have gone under.

These are things that I rarely thought about or confronted coherently until the last few years, having buried these memories deeply in the pain of shame and guilt. I cannot explain why I felt this way, but I have since learned that it is not unusual in this kind of dysfunctional family dynamic. Fifty years ago, for instance, the word cancer was not discussed in polite company, and it too was shrouded in similarly irrational shame, fear, and embarrassment.

I hate to use the word "dysfunctional" when describing my family growing up because it does not do my parents justice. We had a great family. My parents were both attorneys. They were amazingly wonderful, decent, and loving people. My father was a charismatic civic leader, and in 1957, he built a large synagogue along with a group of other WWII veterans, which flourished and became the center of our spiritual and social lives. It is still going strong today and is one of the oldest and most respected reform Jewish synagogues in the world.

It stands as a monument to my father's vision and guts. I include intestinal fortitude because he and a small cadre of other men, patriots, none of them wealthy and all of them with growing families, stepped up to the plate and personally signed and guaranteed the construction and mortgage note.

That is not a small thing. As someone who has arranged hundreds of millions of dollars of facility financing, I can personally testify that nobody—but nobody—signs huge commercial loans personally. It is very rare and precious when it happens, and when it is grown out of faith, God honors that kind of sacrificial giving.

> Bring all the tithes into the storehouse so there will be enough food in my Temple. If you do," says the LORD of Heaven's Armies, "I will open the windows of heaven for you. I will pour out a blessing so great you won't have enough room to take it in! Try it! Put me to the test!—Malachi 3:10

To build a synagogue was considered even in Bible times to be the act of a righteous man. When the Jewish leaders came to Jesus to ask Him to come to the aid of a man whose son was deathly ill, they were sure to tell the Lord that the man, though Gentile, loved the Jewish community and actually built them a synagogue. When they told Jesus this, it clinched the deal in our Lord's mind:

"For he loveth our nation, and he hath built us a synagogue" (Luke 7:5).

It was not until I came to love the Lord and His word, many years after my father's death, that I realized that this verse from Luke was, at last, a fitting tribute and epitaph for my father's life.

I can only believe that calling me to faith in His Son was the divine blessing that God had promised to pour out of the windows of heaven into my life in remembrance, as it were, of my father.

In that sense, like Isaac and Jacob, I too, a second son, inherited my father's blessing and became the child of promise. Perhaps that too explains why my relationship with my older brother, the first son, has come to grief, in the manner of Ishmael, who despised Isaac, and Esau, who despised Jacob.

My parents were utterly clean and decent people who, as far as I knew, led naturally sanctified lives. Divorce was unknown in our family; I'm sad to admit that I've been divorced three times.

Trust me; today many folks would drop their spouses like a bad habit if forced to go through the chaos and brokenness of a mate who was slowly, over decades, losing his or her mind, with all the attendant behavioral disturbances.

Divorce never occurred to my mother, and I never heard her utter the D-word. She kind of adopted the only half-joking maxim for which Billy Graham's devoted wife, Ruth, became famous, when asked in an interview whether she ever considered divorcing her husband during the hard times associated with Reverend Graham's travel and the crushing demands of his ministry.

She thought about it for a few seconds and then calmly answered, "Murder, yes; divorce, never"

Growing up, I never heard the word divorce, and I am quite sure I never heard any four-letter words in my house. I also am also quite certain that I never heard the N-word or any other ethnic or racial slurs spoken by either of my parents. To this day, I cannot bring myself to utter this slur, and I cringe when I hear someone else use it. Ours was an honest, wholesome family. But it was a family that harbored a inexplicably shame-filled secret of unspeakably horrible disease.

Suffice it to say that I never grieved for my father, and as I've looked back over the paths of self-destruction I've trodden in my own life and tried to examine their roots, I've come to several understandings. There exists a secret scourge on families and kids that is still well hidden and seldom talked about—chronic illness in a parent and its effects on kids who have to grow up really fast in a family in crisis; kids who have to be parents, often to their parents.

We know a lot about the kids of Holocaust survivors. Books are written, movies are made, lectures are given, talk shows and so forth have put that phenomenon out on Jump Street, and that is a healthy thing.

But for most of my life, from about age eleven onward, I bore a silent burden of shame because each day, little by little, my father, my hero, my pal, was literally and noticeably disintegrating as a human being, his intellect disappearing one pixel at a time until we could no longer care for him at home. This occurred in full view of the neighbors and friends, as well.

He was still a relatively young man when we reluctantly placed him in a VA hospital, where he was put in diapers and spent most of his time in restraints, tied into a rolling highchair of sorts, drooling and staring aimlessly and, ultimately, vegetating. Innocent prey for some raging violent predator.

My regular visits to him are still indelibly seared into my thoughts, lifelike images from the worst horror movie ever made. This all led inexorably to the coup de grace, having to visibly identify him on a cold slab at the Suffolk County Coroner's Office before his autopsy, as his death was a homicide.

My brother, Mark, was a rising Justice Department attorney and had come up from Washington. We stood in front of a six-foot-long horizontal glass window, and two canvas curtains opened upon the push of a button by a morgue attendant. Of course, they had the right guy.

My father, a gaunt, almost unrecognizable sliver of what we remembered as kids, lay there with his head supported upright on a steel block and the rest covered in a body bag. He looked uncomfortable, I remember thinking. I looked away quickly but to no avail because even that split-second glance haunts me to this day when the lights are off.

In searching the corners of my mind for answers to the puzzle of my own life problems, that scene and others has replayed often. But as the mind heals, the affective component—that is, the pain—has attenuated over the decades and the memories rest safely and securely in a healed but hidden part of my mind today.

I cannot help but believe that fear has a lot to do with our human emotional problems, as it is the polar opposite of faith. And fear can only thrive in the darkness and ill-lit corners of our lives. And there were plenty of those when I dwelled in the darkness of my own broken adult life for so many years, even when I was surrounded by the trappings of worldly honor and success.

For many, many years, I actually lied to people when the topic of conversation might turn benignly to how someone's parent had died. I even told examining insurance physicians that my father had had a heart attack and died suddenly, because I was too overwhelmed with inexplicable undeserved guilt and shame over what had really occurred.

I still cannot explain my shame over my father's affliction and ugly death. To paraphrase that line from *Good Will Hunting*, "It wasn't my fault." But then, inexplicably, I could not process that for decades.

It disarmed me emotionally for years, contemplating the nature of what this very, very decent guy had endured, quietly and as gracefully as someone—a superstar of a man—could have been expected to have endured. His decline transpired over a very long time in the prime years of his life, and it pains me to confront the fact that my father was undoubtedly cognizant of his disintegrating intellect. Honestly, though, I never heard that old soldier complain or get bitter. He just became more and more confused.

And everyone was acutely aware of it as well. I remember, as a youngster, picking up the phone to call a friend, unaware that my mother was talking to my grandmother on the phone. Before I had a chance to politely put the receiver back in the cradle, the first thing I heard was my maternal grandmother, Grandma Betty, who had loved my father dearly and genuinely, ask my mom, "How's the zombie today?"

I recoiled with shock and anger and still feel a tightness in my gut, fifty years later. I never told my mother that I heard this. I stopped resenting my grandma years ago because I suppose she was just struggling with this tragedy as we all were—most of all my mother. Sometimes gallows humor helps to break the mood.

I resort to black humor even today to lower the stress of a situation, but the sheer horror and thoughtlessness of that remark echoes in my mind, and it makes the little boy inside me want to cry the tears I never, ever shed for him.

So behind my seemingly charmed young life, there existed an ugly backdrop of sickness and disease, of secrets and lies, of inexplicable, unwarranted shame and humiliation, and of irrational fear and guilt.

So my father, a great man, was removed from the family scene so many years before by presenile dementia, and he never saw his son graduate and receive his MD. At breakfast that morning, when I looked at my mother across the white-clothed table, a foggy sadness hung over our pancakes and eggs and dampened our buoyant celebration.

My mother, a doctor's daughter, had seen to it that I had been groomed for this coronation day since the day I was born. I was literally the fulfillment of everything she lived for.

I'm fine with that.

First order of business was the graduation ceremony at the School of Medicine and the Johns Hopkins Hospital itself, which is located in a poor, working-class neighbor called East Baltimore. It is their equivalent of Harlem, Bedford-Stuyvesant, or any number of crime- and disease-ridden urban areas that were fully capable of generating the constant supply of gunshot wounds, stabbings, and horrendous medical problems indigenous to poor folks, particularly in the South, four decades ago. As we young healers arrogantly and inhumanely termed it, they were "cannon fodder" for our medical educational needs.

In addition to my diploma, I also picked up the prestigious Research Award from the Johns Hopkins Medical Society for groundbreaking cardiovascular surgical research in which, as a medical student, I was a principal investigator in the famous cardiac surgery research laboratories, where, years earlier in the 1940s, Dr. Alfred Blalock, with his famous African American assistant, Vivien Thomas, virtually invented open-heart surgery.

At the time, I worked day and night in the cardiothoracic research lab, simply because I thought it was fun. It wasn't about glory, and it sure wasn't about money. As I flourished years later in plastic and reconstructive surgery, it wasn't until decades later that I learned from others that the advances we made in 1976 had directly contributed to the lengthening and saving of the lives of literally millions of men, women, and babies undergoing needed cardiac surgery, procedures that were so complicated as to render them unthinkable before our work made it possible.

Today, the procedures refined in my laboratory in 1976 are in standard use every day by 98 percent of the cardiac surgeons worldwide, and the work of our team has been mentioned from time to time, I understand, on the informal short list for a Nobel.

All in all, it was a memorable morning that set the stage for the main university graduation on the Homewood campus, up near Memorial Stadium on Thirty-Third Street.

After all the graduates had assembled at a staging area behind the thousands of seated guests, the processional began in a traditional formation, with each graduating class from the various schools that made up the university marching slowly in a long serpentine line, two by two, that was seemingly endless. That was where it happened.

As the line entered into the shadows of an elegant, university-style Georgian portico, just before snaking down a set of brilliant white marble stairs to the huge quadrangle, where the ceremony was to be held, my stately, elegant mother caught my eye, and she was beaming proudly just alongside where I passed.

Six inches away, she had wormed her way in through the throng of people. Nothing was said by either of us, but nothing needed to be said. It was one of those moments that passes between a mother and her child, bone of her bone, flesh of her flesh. All was understood. It was as the oneness of a single-celled organism.

Ten years later, when the world was caving in on me, I marched in another processional, this time very different in nature but a processional nonetheless. And that day I was not just one of many, but I was literally the star of the show—or a circus, depending on your point of view.

The coffee and doughnuts had been laid out in great supply for the television news cameramen and reporters from all over the nation who had come to witness and report on the carefully orchestrated takedown of perhaps the most famous and rich young plastic surgeon in the world—indeed, a Hopkins graduate—by a local prosecutor's office in a rural county on Long Island.

No doubt politics were involved, everyone agreed, but the accusatory instrument was filed, the downfall was complete, public humiliation was the order of the day, and the very public stoning was to begin.

As the court officer yelled to the assembled press out a second-story window, "Here he comes!" cameras were raised and microphones were leveled as I stepped out of the district attorney's office with my hands shackled behind me and led before the press on my way to court to be arraigned.

This was the moment every nameless prosecutor lives for. The infamous sensational "perp walk." Regardless of how the case is disposed of later on, charges dropped or whatever, on this day it's "Macarena Time" in the DA's office, and they savor it every time their name gets mentioned in the paper.

Even if the case lasts for years, the prosecutors will never have another day like this. It's organized to be their ace in the hole. It was a perp walk in a case that was so sensational that it was made into a television program, and periodically I catch myself on TV when I least expect it. It makes me nauseous, but women say I look sexy. "Bad boy" complex, I guess.

Dazed by the lights and shouting reporters and not really aware of what was going to happen next, I was simply led slowly through the throng in an eerie mental reprise of the graduation processional ten years earlier in Baltimore. But as I was about to dismiss that thought from my mind, I glanced to my immediate left and made familiar, soothing eye contact with a nice lady standing there, watching from the sidelines.

My mother, looking worn, deflated, and older, stood there, just as stately as years earlier, inches away from me. I was not in cap and gown that day, as before, but in handcuffs and a two-thousand-dollar suit. She was beaming painfully but proudly, as she had years earlier on a better day for us both. No words were exchanged between us. None were needed. All was understood. The time, place, and circumstance didn't matter. I was flesh of her flesh and bone of her bone, and, from where she stood, the rest was just a whole lotta shoutin'.

On both days of my life, the happy triumphant day years before and this one, my mother, I am quite sure, could not possibly have loved me more. But here's the part that gave me a glimpse of divine love. On that terrible day of defeat and utter humiliation, in my terrible imperfection, I saw that my mother did not love me less.

In bondage to self-love and still so lost in my sin at that time, when God was still a stranger to me, I learned something profoundly life-altering about the possibility of unconditional love on that unhappy day so long ago. I am now absolutely certain of this: that although God was a stranger to me at that time, I was not a stranger to Him. He knew me before the foundation of the universe. Before I was born, He saw how I would rebelliously work my way into that awful day and other terrible sin in my life. I was still blind and lost, and He knew that I would not be able yet to see His glory, as it were, to receive the full revelation of His radiance, but He could use any circumstance to reveal to me just a glimpse of His nature. As I stood with my face like Moses in the cleft of the rock that day, in the eyes of my mother I saw His back as He passed by, or in the literal original Hebrew, "the after effects of His radiant Glory."

It was on that horrible day, in the unconditional love of a parent, that I glimpsed the nature and the promise of His radiant glory. In the fullness of time, He would yet reveal Himself to me completely in the Personhood of His Son.

I learned that unconditional love can be exemplified in the world by many wonderful things common to man, such as the unconditional love a mother has for her child. God really outdoes Himself when it comes to a mother's love. For we know that long ago and far away, in a dusty little Jewish village in ancient Palestine, the Lord used the tenderness of a young maiden's heart to magnify and focus the components of His essence which is love, His light, and His life into a threefold cord that rescued a broken and hurting world:

"And Mary said, My soul doth magnify the Lord" (Luke 1:46).

Modeled after God's kind of love, which "bears all things, believes all things, hopes all things, endures all things," this was what the apostle Paul wrote from the horrendous depths of a first-century prison: "Love never fails." That is the kind of selfless love that carried me through terrible times. If you will take a chance and open your heart just a sliver to Him, He will fill that void with a kind love you have never known.

What's more, it was a heart full of that kind of love that created the universe.

It was ultimately only years later when I learned that this kind of love, *agape* love, is not at all a feeling. It is a Person. The second Person of the Trinity. Yeshua ha Moshiach. Jesus the anointed Savior of the world, who I came to know intimately as family. As we Jews would say in Yiddish, we're *mishpucha*; that is, "We're family. We're kinsmen"

Even when I didn't know God, He knew me, and He was telling me my whole life, in one way or another, that He would "never leave me, nor forsake me." He can manifest this through a mother's selfless love or a multitude of other ways.

The Lord was there too, standing resolutely on the sidelines of my life, loving me always without expecting anything in return. Love given freely to me. Loving me just as I am. Unconditional love. Perfected love that casts out all fear.

For in all of this I learned about the infinite possibilities of unconditional love. Moreover, it is in the seasons of our utter brokenness and weakness that, if we allow the Great Physician to come in, the infinite healing power of His love can be exquisitely magnified and perfected at every broken place in our lives.

4

The Making of a Plastic Surgeon

I AM GOING TO let you in on some inside plastic surgical stuff. Some spicy tidbit of surgeons' locker room conventional wisdom. Brutal truth you won't hear on Dr. Oz or Oprah.

To begin with, there was a nasty little saying among young surgical residents heading toward plastic surgical training, which we used to cynically mutter to each other, always out of earshot of others. It became a comical mantra, actually: "A Lear in a year."

It was always followed by a wink and a smile, a knowing smirk, and the mutual secure acknowledgment that after all the years of sacrifice and suffering in medical school and general surgery training, followed by a years in plastic surgical training, there was a sure pot of gold at the end of the long-travelled road. And for plastic surgeons, that pot of gold was cosmetic surgical practice, where the dough-re-mi would roll in, in such quantities that the proverbial "Lear (jet) in a year" came to symbolize some twisted materialistic version of a promised land.

Hyperbole, of course, but I have to tell you from personal experience, once you get used to being flown around in your own private jet, closing deals in four cities in one twenty-four-hour period, it's awfully tough to go back to a commercial airline.

My former colleagues mostly never got the jet, but it became a particularly powerful and insightful metaphor nevertheless. It is a humorous exaggeration, to be sure, but as the saying goes, there is a nugget of often-ugly truth buried within even the most outlandish black humor.

That's a fact. The dirty little secret that nobody else will tell you is that a vast and overwhelming number of young, formerly idealistic young doctors detour their altruistic childhood dreams of healing and head toward cosmetic surgery for one reason: to find refuge and deliverance in a cushy lifestyle after so many years of lack.

They hit the figurative ejection switch and bail out of "real" medicine and surgery for the glitzy allure of societal prestige, fashion, and the relative ease with which money can be rapidly accumulated as compared with other heavy-duty surgical specialties, such as cardiac surgery.

As with all generalizations, I suppose there are exceptions, but these are statistical outliers. Totally off the curve.

To witness brilliant, respected, highly trained surgeons peddling skin cream and snake oil on late-night TV infomercials is a pathetic, sickening sight. It's about trading sacred blood-stained and sweat-stained scrubs for a blue wool Paul Stuart blazer, gray slacks, and Gucci loafers, perhaps with a stethoscope poking out of a side pocket. Purely as a fashion statement.

It's sad to say, but in a very real sense, compared to a heart surgeon who saves lives, toiling in the operating room often in the middle of the night, there's a cute little term for what a cosmetic surgeon really is: a "Gucci Loafer." (I've earned the right to make those value judgments, and if the truth hurts, so be it. They'll get over it.)

I know this from personal experience as well as close observation over the decades of hundreds of other young men and women in cosmetic surgery. I recall particularly the comment of one young colleague, a fellow Johns Hopkins Medical School classmate and a dear friend, who graduated near the top of our class and who engaged in some amazing cardiac surgical research.

He seemed destined for a glorious career as a famous heart surgeon. After arduous general surgical training at Columbia-Presbyterian, he burned out, abandoned his first love (heart surgery), bailed out into plastic surgical residency, and now is cozily ensconced in a thriving cosmetic surgical practice in tony Westchester County. Nothing wrong with that. It's simply instructive as to how surgical training seems to winnow out those looking for a cushy-cashy existence and those who are more than ready and willing to drop their idealism like a bad habit and go for the fast buck.

After many years of not seeing him, I remember being shocked to see Tony at our first day of plastic surgery residency. He was, in a way, my role model because he was so capable and had achieved so much in cardiac surgery research in medical school. For me to see that he had thrown it all aside, as had I, and bailed into plastic surgery was jarring for me. I pushed the feeling aside.

I recall a phone conversation years later, a few months after we entered cosmetic surgery practice. We were discussing no more grueling schedules, no more eleventh-hour life-or-death titanic struggles in the operating room, no struggling with insurance companies. With more moola flowing in from cosmetic surgical practice than we knew what to do with, my brilliant friend, who formerly had so much to offer men, women, and babies with sick hearts, whispered his confession quietly over the phone line for my ears only: "What a racket this plastic surgery thing is, huh, Richard." I chuckled in assent, somewhat ashamed but in agreement.

This is not an isolated case and in fact is much more the rule than the exception. It certainly was in my life. Oh yes, I hear all the insistent protestations: "What about cleft lips and palates? What about the Smile Train, hand surgery, free flaps, burns, and skin grafts? That's why we become plastic surgeons."

To quote Shakespeare,: "Thou doth protest too much."

Any successful plastic surgeon who is honest will quietly admit it's all ultimately about building a huge cosmetic surgery practice, and all the rest is a sideshow. The cleft lip and palate clinics in Africa are but a public relations canard to camouflage the fact that it's all about cushy-cashy cosmetic surgery, and that makes it all about the money.

Ultimately, modern cosmetic surgeons don't even want to do any more surgery because they'd rather simply build a big enough reputation, appear on as many society pages as possible, sit with Oprah and Ellen enough times to be able to simply parlay that reputation into peddling skin creams and other snake oils, retire to Palm Beach, and sit on their sixty-foot Hatteras yachts. I suppose there are exceptions. I just never met one in forty years. The only difference is that most are not talented enough to ever make the transition from plodding practitioner to superstar.

In the past twenty years, cosmetic surgery has degenerated more so than ever into a cash-dominated medical industry. A circus of beauty cream peddlers composed, for the most part, of effete but incredibly brilliant men and women, armed with publicists. The best and the brightest who have sold their souls and sacrificed their childhood dreams and ideals as healers on the altar of materialism. Trading in their aspirations to alleviate human suffering for Botox injections and the lure of luxury shopping, jettisoning their surgical research journals for the *Robb Report* and *Town and Country*.

I hear the protestation, "Oh, he's just sour grapes!" Perhaps, but that doesn't change the truth. At worst, it just explains why I'm exposing it. No doubt those grapes got soured a long time ago. I don't worry about sucking up to people anymore. I stopped being interested in being a people-pleaser a long time ago. So now that we've dealt with that, let's continue.

Plastic surgeons as a breed, generally speaking, are by no means an inspiring group of men (and women). Allow me the indulgence of parentheses simply because back in the day, it was largely a male-dominated province, as were all surgical specialties, even ob-gyn. Not anymore.

I remember an eminent New York Hospital–Cornell Med School professor of plastic surgery, who admitted a patient for a breast augmentation. I was the chief resident, working under his tutelage. I called the professor in the evening and reported to him that the gal's routine lab results were all out of whack. She was a model who had been starving herself to stay rail-thin.

"Hey, Dr. Schwartz, sorry to wake you up. Ms. Bloom's pre-op chemistries are way off. It seems she's totally dehydrated from anorexia bulimia. You know, she one of those model types who throws up ten times a day. We better cancel the surgery, discharge her, and send her for a medical consult, right?"

"No way, Richard. She paid me a big fee, and her check already cleared. You get her tuned up. Intravenous potassium supplements all night. Whatever you gotta do. Just get her ready for surgery in the a.m. Sorry, buddy boy, the fee's already in the bank."

I could tell he was only half kidding, but the fact was that he wanted that surgery done in the morning, no matter how much surgical prudence dictated its postponement. Well, I did as I was told, infused about two liters of fluid and heaven-knows-how many milli-equivalents of potassium chloride, and she was perfect, electrolyte-wise, by eight the next morning. She did fine, and she looked much better for it. Her face really filled out from all the fluid replacement, but I'm sure she was teed off when she got home and started abusing water pills again, like poor Karen Carpenter.

The fact remains that it was reckless for the attending plastic surgeon, a full professor, to insist on operating on her before things got straightened out in a proper fashion instead of in a mad rush in the middle of the night. I'm still ashamed that I didn't stand up to him.

She did okay, but it was all about money and greed, and in a very subtle way, I was changed for the worse. She could have died, but that greedy attending knew he had one amazing Bellevue Trauma Service-trained surgical resident on call to retrieve a totally messed-up situation. In the final analysis, we were lucky, and it gives me chills, thirty-five years later, to consider the reckless greediness that was in play. That was the system I learned to be part of, and I always learned my lessons well. Too well.

I remember Dr. Robert Robertson, the highly reputed chief of plastic surgery at a local university-affiliated hospital in suburban Long Island, finishing up a purely cosmetic rhinoplasty one morning. The great Dr. Robertson was one of the most esteemed plastic surgeons in the nation at that time. I had assisted him as the Plastic Surgery Senior Fellow. Knowing it was my job to dictate the operative note for him, he whispered to me, "Dick, dictate a septal reconstruction on this lady's operative note. Let's help her out with the insurance."

In other words, "Let's falsify the operative note because we're going to hide the fact from the insurance company that this is a purely cosmetic nose job, and you're gonna do this by dictating a procedure that we did not perform. Dick, you and I are gonna commit fraud and grand larceny this morning, a C felony, punishable by three to nine years in state prison." Of course, I went ahead and did what I was told and falsified his operative note as usual. It was my job. I was in awe of these older role models, and I modeled myself after them perfectly, right up to the larceny. It was institutionalized long before I was institutionalized.

These were just a few of my eminent plastic surgery role models. I was all of twenty-eight years old, and that was the system I learned to emulate. I said nothing and dictated the operative note. The suggestion that I was just following orders was as fallacious then as it was for the "man in the glass booth" of an earlier generation. It was moral cowardice.

Had I lost my moral compass? I don't know. I don't even think I had a moral compass. When we do not have a personal relationship with our

Creator on a minute-to-minute basis, when the Bible is nothing other than a quaint relic we use to press autumn leaves, then we just make things up as we go along, doing what we think is right in our own eyes or at least taking the path of least resistance and rationalizing it all. That's the effect of today's moral relativism, as it has been for thousands of years. It's an old story, and my life became a cautionary tale of this insidious form of "stinkin' thinkin'." Pilate expressed it well when he looked at Jesus and asked, "What is truth?" and then proceeded to wash his hands.

"There is a way which seemeth right unto a man, but the end thereof are the ways of death" (Proverbs 14:12).

The top plastic surgeon where I trained at a great New York medical center was Dr. Philippian Souza. His peers called him Philli. We called him Dr. Souza. He was about five feet tall in Cuban heels, of Lebanese extraction, very nice to all the residents and students, and totally inappropriate to other senior plastic surgical attendings on staff—gossiping behind their backs about them, criticizing them in an adolescent Trumpian manner, bullying them, and generally encouraging an attitude of disrespect toward anyone but him.

Despite that, I kind of loved Philippian Souza and was grateful and loyal to him, particularly when the new chief of surgery at Cornell, the powerful and legendary Dr. Tom Shires, was imported from Parkland Memorial Hospital in Dallas, of Kennedy assassination fame.

It seems Shires and his whole staff, which he brought with him from Dallas, basically thought Souza was an unstable, idiotic, embarrassing clown and needed to go so they could bring in a chief plastic surgeon with real academic credentials.

They were correct about Souza. He was a total lunatic. But he was our lunatic, and moreover, he was a scrappy little New Yorker and wasn't about to let himself get kicked outta Dodge by some Johnny-come-lately hillbilly rednecks from Parkland Hospital in Texas, sporting five hundred dollar Luchese cowboy boots and green surgical scrubs.

He fought back, and I helped lobby for him, quietly and behind the scenes. All of the residents did, as well as Dr. Laurence LeBeaux, the associate professor of plastic surgery who shared Souza's office suite. Larry was my favorite, and he was responsible for bringing me being back to Cornell after I left to do two years of general and trauma surgery at NYU-Bellevue. Those were amazing, super-high intensity years for me, but I was burned out and needed to seek refuge in plastic surgery back at the more genteel "country club" atmosphere of the New York Hospital–Cornell Medical Center. It was a busy, big-city university medical center, to be sure, but compared to NYU-Bellevue, Cornell was totally "Upper East Side." A gentleman's service, as it were.

Souza was sure to repay his protégé, Larry LeBeaux's, loyalty by ridiculing him behind his back every chance he had and generally making a clown out of him. In fact, Souza was the embarrassment that we all had to cover for, including Larry, who was totally loyal to his mentor until the end. It was like a totally dysfunctional family. I had never seen anything like it, and, eventually, I was sorry I had ever left Hopkins in Baltimore.

The end did come when Souza mercilessly rode Larry so hard and poisoned the atmosphere so much that Larry, ever the courtly gentleman, looked elsewhere and took the chief's position offered him by the Geisinger Medical Center in Pennsylvania, which was a respectable step up for him. It was occasioned by the totally unprofessional treatment and bullying by Souza, who despicably used one of the residents, Jerry Mullaney, to needle Larry and humiliate him behind his back. A more inappropriate and unprofessional display I have never witnessed, whether in academia, medicine, or in business and industry. Real degenerate behavior.

Souza, back in the disco 1970s, acted strung-out half the time, was hyperactive, and never focused seriously on anything. But he was saved by the fact that, instability aside, he was an extremely facile and deft surgeon. He had, as we say, "good hands." In his day he was the best of the best. A top gun. Our chief, as unorthodox as he was, was one of the world's great plastic surgeons.

Larry LeBeaux was a totally decent, sober presence, but he was a mediocre surgeon who operated with uncertainty and whose hands shook noticeably as he carried out even simple surgical maneuvers. He was, unfortunately, an easy target for ridicule. I could never understand how Larry had become Souza's protégé in years past. But I suppose Larry LeBeaux played the role of Souza's sycophant at one point, doing his bidding and helping Souza ascend to the throne at the New York Hospital–Cornell, one of the world's most prestigious medical centers.

The crowning blow came after Larry announced he was leaving. Souza moved him out of his office prematurely and ultimately installed the Harvard-graduate Mullaney, who was returning from a microsurgery fellowship in Miami, as his new protégé. Frankly, these two creeps deserved each other. Mullaney, a shameless careerist like all of the others, utilized his reconstructive surgery credentials simply to gain leverage for quick advancement and left academia a few years later to go into his own cosmetic surgery practice. In the end, it was all about the dough. He was more interested in picking out new drapes and carpeting for Larry's old office than he ever was in microsurgery.

We all covered for Souza and kept our mouths shut. Once, when the American Society of Plastic and Reconstructive Surgeons got wind of some "problems" with Souza's program at Cornell, they sent an esteemed professor of plastic surgery to conduct a site visit and report back. That was a total sham. Souza was so nervous on the inspection day that he actually showed up in a shirt and tie to look respectable to this academic, straight-laced surgeon from out of town. Peoria or something. It was the only time I saw Souza in a tie, and back in the 1970s, that was radical.

Unfortunately, he looked only half respectable because his button-down-collar shirt was so stained and filthy it made me so furious. I took his personal assistants aside and totally reamed them for not taking better care of him. I asked them "Do I have to dress him too? I'm the chief resident, not his valet. Listen up; if we lose this program, guess what? He won't need personal assistants. That shirt he has on is so filthy he must have found it rolled up in a ball under his bed or something."

I actually think that was indeed where he found it.

I apologized later because I knew they were upset as well, and at that point our diminutive chief was impossible for anyone to keep on balance.

We all towed the line for him because we loved the poor little twit. We respected what he had been and weren't gonna rat out our chief. He might be a bum, but he was our bum, even when he reached a new low and ordered us to fill the previously unused plastic surgery research laboratory room with scores of lab animals and literally create a fraudulent stage setting, portraying a busy, productive academic experimental surgery lab.

As it turned out, the only research work that was actually being conducted in the lab was my project, testing the effects of embryonal nerve growth factor on peripheral nerve injuries. I had been awarded a prestigious research grant from the American Society of Plastic Surgeons' Educational Foundation. I was working with one of my junior residents, who was assisting me. We had a few guinea pigs, but the Boss needed a stage setting that appeared a lot bigger and busier. Still, we passed with flying colors.

I suppose the site inspector suspected something, but he covered for the famous Philippian Souza as well—Souza knew everyone around the country, and nobody wanted to rock the boat. Everybody who knew him knew he could be vicious if provoked.

So we took Dr. Peoria or whatever his name was out to dinner and then packed him off to wherever he came from, and we carried on.

At the time, I thought it was somewhat humorous watching Souza's survival Kabuki dance, but over the years I've become deeply ashamed of it.

But that was the system that I chose to be part of. I suppose I sold my soul along with my integrity. After being part of a groundbreaking research team at Johns Hopkins that developed lifesaving techniques, in use by 98 percent of the cardiac surgeons in the world today, I settled for the circus cult of personalities in a big-city, top-rated plastic surgery program. What a waste. I just wanted to finish my training and get out into practice so I could support my family and have a reasonable, decent life, or so I rationalized it.

Unfortunately, this kind of behavior was not limited to Cornell; it was pandemic. This was standard procedure. That was in the 1980s, and, sadly, it is standard procedure today as well. The salient point is that this corruption was not idiosyncratic to my life or to one institution or even to one period in history. It is systemic, and it was a system in which I made a conscious decision to take part. I devoted all my talents, all my giftedness, and all my blessings to push it to the Herculean max.

Personal experience over years tells me that plastic surgery is, today as always, a largely a money-oriented, greed-driven industry. It is populated, almost to a person, by extraordinarily brilliant and capable people. People who are often motivated at their deepest level by a full measure of greasy effete pseudo-sophistication and worldly greed not generally seen in other major surgical specialties, such as cardiac surgery.

For a multitude of reasons, there is a general type of person who gravitates into plastic surgery. I can hear the roar of condemnation of self-serving generalizations rising, but while generalizations are often not totally accurate, general "understandings" can be valid, particularly when they arise from a lifetime of personal and high-level professional experience, observation, and retrospection. As the maxim states, "Through the 'retrospectoscope,' hindsight is twenty/twenty."

Farm boys, blue-collar type guys, middle-of-the-road plain Jane-types generally don't become cosmetic surgeons. They populate the real, heavy-industry-type, lifesaving surgical specialties such as cardiothoracic surgery and vascular surgery. To be sure, the heart surgeons are at the top of the heap.

Cosmetic surgery is populated by brilliant fancy boys. Effete fops who self-style themselves with slick hair and three-thousand-dollar suits, and whose idea of being "well-published" is appearing in yet another pathetic puff piece in *Vogue* or *New York* magazine. Sad but true.

Why is this so, and how does this come about? Certainly, there are exceptions, but over the decades, certain valid understandings have emerged as to the forces that shape a young surgeon's professional worldview, irrevocable career decisions, and accurate portrayals of the personality types and personal values of the individuals and the hungers that drive and shape their expectations.

Surgical training, which begins in medical school, lasts for many years and is the most physically and arguably the most emotionally rigorous of all the specialties to which young doctors in training are exposed. It is qualitatively and quantitatively a vastly different experience than is the training of an internist, a pediatrician, or other types of physicians, and consequently, plastic surgery selects out for certain personality types. There is much evidence for this.

I have observed in my peers, even beginning in the early years, that twenty-four-hour work days that melt foggily into the next and unrealistic workloads begin, within a few years, to wear down the idealism of the vast majority of many young surgeons. They are worn down by the demands of their crushing professional responsibilities as interns and residents, including matter-of-fact life-or-death decisions foisted upon these young surgeons in training at 3:00 a.m. or in the middle of bathroom breaks. There were constant beepers going off (or now, I suppose, cell phones summoning them for all manner of interventions), as well as the demands of a young spouse and children in many cases. This is complicated by the constant shortage of money and the means to meet the requirements of big-city life. It begins to wear down the sharpest edge of idealism of even the most incipient adamantine personalities. To be sure, this happens in many surgeons in training, and there are exceptions, but in general, these are exceptions.

Beginning in medical school, in a class of one hundred or so of the most brilliant and dynamic medical students in the world, the selection process separates those destined for surgery. Perhaps for many this migration begins far earlier, in early childhood. It certainly did for me.

My maternal grandfather, Dr. John Adam Glassbury, was a respected surgeon in New York City for many years, and some of my earliest memories were of my sleeping over at my grandparents' apartment, which was filled with one of the world's most important collections of ancient Tibetan art.

Many a middle of the night was interrupted by phones ringing from answering services, hushed voices in Grandpa's study, followed by the rustling of closet doors and wardrobe drawers sliding open and shut in the dark, followed by my witnessing, through my fog of sleepy child-eyes, the vision of my grandpa, medical bag in hand, padding out the door into the cold, dark Manhattan night to the hospital to attend to a sick patient or to make, heaven forbid, a house call. He was, for lack of a better phrase, my real-life hero, and growing up in his shadow shaped the early course of my life.

It was a life course that in retrospect, six decades later, I know—and I say with not a little regret—that I should have stayed. My grandfather was old school; he was a quiet, unassuming professional and served unaffectedly as an ideal role model, a role model that in no way has been idealized through any lens that time and bitter experience could have certainly distorted but did not. My memories, like most of those from childhood, are vivid and accurate. Dr. John Adam Glassbury was a dedicated, selfless physician. He was the genuine article in that regard.

In an earlier, simpler time of modest fees, Dr. John Glassbury had, like most physicians, a "charity list." He was at once a society physician and one who treated the poor and indigent with equal devotion. I think there were many physicians like him in the last century.

There was no Medicaid or Medicare, and patients with insurance coverage were few and far between. He employed no reimbursement revenue-enhancement consultants, and there were no rich HMOs or big drug company payoff schemes that cut fat monthly checks. Simply put, patients were human beings who needed care, and he cared for them first, and whatever they could reasonably pay he graciously accepted.

This was in Manhattan, and to be sure nobody paid him with a bushel of wheat or live chickens, but I remember that more than one office visit was concluded by a grateful patient removing a bundle of Garcia y Vega cigars tucked under an arm while sitting across from him in his office and presenting this treasure to him. This simple gift, worth at the time maybe three or four dollars, was both given and received with genuine love and appreciation, and nothing more needed to be said.

Looking back, it was inspiring. Humorously, despite the fact that Dr. Glassbury suffered from what used to be called *angioedema*, or terrible allergic facial and cervical swelling triggered by cigar tobacco. Even his adoring nurses could not pry his prized cigars out of his grip, although they tried mightily out of love, concern, and dedication to his well-being. He was Dr. Marcus Welby in real life.

To be sure, it is an understatement to admit this was not the way cosmetic surgery was practiced on Park Avenue. But of course it is easy to rationalize it by acknowledging that medical economic realities have changed radically over the decades, and I was by no means unique in this regard. However, for the life of me I cannot fathom where and how such modeling and inspiration was so pathetically dissipated by me. It breaks my heart more than anything to contemplate how I wasted such an early exposure to professional purity and idealism.

As an aside, despite Saint Paul's admonition to not become mired in past failings, I am drawn into the examination of this for the simple reason that my life experiences have been so extreme and radical. Huge accomplishments and triumphs have been punctuated and eclipsed by self-generated tragedies and abysmal failures. My very storied existence has become a cautionary tale for others.

As such, my life can serve as a guidepost to others in different professions, who will most certainly meet the similar challenges and temptations. It is only by looking back dispassionately and objectively at these past events that I have been able to visualize things clearly. Importantly, I learned that the real plan for my life was never mine to begin with. I thought it was all about my plans and my desires, but I was wrong.

As the Old Testament prophet Jeremiah was inspired by God to write almost three thousand years ago, when we yield to Jesus' plans for us, we are not destined to live out Thoreau's "lives of quiet desperation." God has a greater plan than ours, and only when we discover His plans for us can we truly become the men and women that He intended us to be, even from before the foundation of the universe:

"'I know the plans I have for you,' says the Lord. 'They are plans for good and not for disaster, to give you a future and a hope'" (Jeremiah 29:11).

This is no small thing, discovering the answer to the age-old question, cleverly reformulated by Pastor Rick Warren: "Why on earth am I here?" In my life, that revelation did not come until after many years of darkness and bitter tears .

It did come, albeit after great pain, and I learned personally the literal meaning of what the psalmist wrote: "Weeping may endure for a night but joy cometh in the morning" (Psalm 30:5).

I grew up seeing firsthand how a highly respected, loved, and devoted surgeon—my grandfather—conducted his life. Even as a very young child, I was hooked from day one. So for me, the separation process and migration into life as a surgeon commenced long before I walked in the footsteps of the famous William Halsted and all the other surgical ghosts who haunted the hallowed halls of the great Johns Hopkins Hospital in Baltimore in the 1970s—Doctors Alfred Blalock and

Denton Cooley, the great cardiac surgeons; Frank Spencer, the real-life model for Trapper John McIntyre of *M.A.S.H.* fame; Harvey Cushing, the brilliant neurosurgeon; and A. Earl Walker, the neurosurgical giant who inspired the likes of Dr. Ben Carson and so many others.

In fact, I remember my grandpa saying fifty years ago, "All the medical schools in the world are pretty much the same, except, that is for Hopkins, which exists in a class by itself." It was certainly true then, and this pecking order arguably hasn't changed a whole lot today.

So as the years pass in medical school, each student begins to "choose sides." That is, they eventually make the all-important decision as to which field of the medical profession they will devote their lives. Surgery begins early to have a magnetic attraction to a very certain personality type.

To be sure, the vast majority of surgeons I trained with were extremely brilliant and talented, but they most decidedly were not "eggheads." Anti-intellectual, really—I never knew a surgical resident who used a pocket protector. Brilliant, yes, but not geeks.

We were guys who kind of swaggered around hospital wards, literally taking matters into our own hands. Because this is the essence of surgical practice, personalities that were bold, bordering on arrogance, were *de rigueur*. When you are at the operating table—whatever the specialty—and the patient is under general anesthesia, a multitude of decisions need to be made continuously. Course corrections need to be employed almost unconsciously, and there is no time to have leisurely medical-staff conferences to get a consensus on the right next maneuver.

Not only does surgery demand the highest level of intellect and skill, but it also demands utter self-confidence (often breeding arrogance and egotism) which is a surgeon's most indispensible weapon. That is, however, often a two-edged sword that can cut both ways. It is not a self-confidence that is born of some misplaced bravado but rather from years of training and thousands of hours of the most inexpressibly grueling experiences of taking care of grievously sick and horribly injured men, women, and children.

It is very much like being a highly experienced fighter pilot who flies by instinct and experience. I was told this by a colleague of mine years ago, when we were both in surgical training at Bellevue.

Dr. Storm Claussen, who is now a wonderfully respected cardiac surgeon, flew fighter jets, A-6 Intruders, off carrier decks during the Vietnam War before he went to medical school. At breakfast after morning rounds and before we went to the OR, Storm used to regale us with his experiences as a naval aviator.

He equated trauma surgery at Bellevue to flying a fighter jet in combat. He was a bit older and light-years more experienced than I was, and I used to listen to him with rapt attention. He was the closest thing to a role model I have ever encountered. I'm not ashamed to say I idolized the guy. I kinda still do. And he was the absolute opposite of the personality type that drifts into cosmetic surgery.

To be sure, surgical training is rigorous training, much like marine boot camp, but surgical-resident training alone can go on for the better part of a decade, and this endurance testing is the most successful and time-proven way of turning out surgical iron men. Simply put, it works, and it's going to continue. It has been made somewhat softer and gentler in the last thirty years, as society itself has become more effete, government regulations have limited the number of hours young doctors in training can work, and supervision of surgeons in training by senior attendings has improved.

However, over time, young surgeons in training not uncommonly begin to bend and change in character under the weight of such relentless metamorphic pressures. The inevitable result is that they can often succumb to burnout at the age of thirty—cynical, money-hungry, and uncaring. I surely did, although it took me decades to admit it.

RICHARD LAWRENCE DOMBROFF

Anything, even the most noble of professions, can become corrupted. This corrosion is evident to anyone who has been shuffled through the medical-care system in America or who has witnessed the explosion of medical and surgical negligence litigation.

It is not money that corrupts, but as the Bible says, it is "the love of money" that corrupts. And to paraphrase Machiavelli, speaking of power, "Love of money corrupts and it corrupts absolutely."

It certainly happened in my life. We see it elsewhere in contemporary society as well—eminent titans of industry and political leaders who fall from high positions because of flaws they have hidden from the world and, worse still, from themselves. This is not an educational problem, nor is it a character problem, because our characters are already corrupted from the Fall.

It is, first and foremost, a spiritual problem. It is rank idolatry, worshipping at the altar of self, of money, and of everything else under the sun that has the potential to feed our egos—power, family, toys, prestige.

Money is a wonderful tool, but it just makes a lousy god.

Judas Iscariot did not set out to betray to the death the Savior of the world. His first sin was just a "little" sin, comparatively speaking. He was the treasurer of Jesus's ministry, the chief financial officer of the biggest ministry of its time.

People keep saying Jesus was a poor man. Let's clarify. He was not a poor man. He chose to live a simple life, unencumbered by the usual trappings of royalty and power, but he was by no means poor. In fact, Jesus had a treasurer, Judas, and it is often overlooked by so-called pious believers that there was a lot of money going through that ministry. Just imagine the offering taken up from five or ten thousand congregants at a time. Poor people, no doubt, but even the widow's mites add up.

- 68 -

Judas's initial sin was dipping into the accounts, a little here and a little there, no doubt because he rationalized that he was underappreciated, working harder than the others, and entitled. In his mind it wasn't stealing; it was his fringe benefit. He rationalized that he had found a "loophole." He was probably burned out from the demands of ministry as well. Nevertheless, his guilt was total.

The power of self-delusion is amazing, and I am reminded of the *Seinfeld* episode where Jerry, a relatively straight-shooting guy, consults with his best friend, George Costanza, a congenital liar, on how best to craft a socially necessary lie he needs to tell to lubricate a messy situation with an acquaintance.

"Jerry, my young friend, remember this, and you'll do fine," George says. "It's not a lie, Jerry, if you believe it."

So along Judas went, as do we, believing his own lies. Ultimately, there is no such thing as a little sin, because corruption and sin anywhere in our lives opens a portal for the enemy to enter and take us captive in every area of our existence.

Thus, Judas graduated from sticky fingers to selling out our Lord for thirty pieces of silver. The probability is that Jesus would have prospered Judas beyond his wildest imaginings if he hadn't insisted on taking things into his own hands. Judas was a minister of the gospel, and he served the Jehovah-Jireh, the God who provides. Even today, the Lord supplies extravagantly to those who love Him and are called to His purposes. Even a godly janitor can have a jet, if said janitor is an evangelist who needs to preach the Gospel in six different cities over a weekend.

But when we take any noble human endeavor, such as medicine, law, public service, or ministry, and we twist it to our own purposes and make it about the money, we build an altar to silver and gold that never leads anywhere good. It might not lead to state prison, as it did in my life, but it leads to other forms of imprisonment, bondage, and strongholds. We paper over our greed with the best of intentions—family, kids, humanitarian service—always twisting our motives until, hopefully, a time comes when we are honest with ourselves and remember the words of H. L. Mencken, who wrote: "When someone says it's not about the money ... it's about the money."

With cosmetic surgery, in all too many cases, even today, I am sad to report, the words of the editorial gadfly of Baltimore still apply, "It's about the money." That is, I can assure you, no way to live a life. It was for me, rather, a promising and brilliant professional life wasted.

To be sure, there is nothing wrong with having a Learjet. Learjets are morally neutral, climate change carbon footprints notwithstanding. And flying in a Gulfstream G6 is even less objectionable. Trust me; private aviation is a great and wonderful blessing.

It is a great gift. Private jets are great tools. They just make terrible gods, as we have pointed out.

But in seeking these gifts, my head got turned around, and my world, like that of Saul of Tarsus, got "turned upside down." Much bitter disgrace and many painful years have confirmed a central truth: my error came when I sought the gifts instead of the Giver. I followed my self-conceived, self-actualized purposes instead of making my life about His purposes.

But let's be clear about this: the purpose of everything I have related is to reveal the nature of the professional contexts in which I personally made a series of conscious decisions to sell out to the dark side. I am not judging others. Other people have different experiences and make different decisions.

They can write their own memoirs.

But I have sole ownership of the disasters of my life. Like Adam, my eyes were open all the time. Blame-shifting and denial are poisonous currencies in which I cannot afford to deal anymore.

The good news is that our sinfulness, no matter how much we destroy in the disasters that ensue, need not be fatal because His grace is inexhaustible. His mercies are renewed day to day. He heals the contrite and the broken-hearted. He saves us even in the midst of the sin-stained wreckage of our broken, tattered lives.

Ernest Hemingway wrote something to the effect of "Life breaks everyone, but in the end we're stronger at all the broken places." Sadly, Papa never lived to see healing take place in his own life. With all the adulation and rewards the world can bestow on a man who was gifted with talents beyond compare, Hemingway's life ended in a self-inflicted shotgun blast to the head. Another lost soul, with all his brilliance and gifts.

I can surely understand that cautionary tale, and before I found the Lord, I am not ashamed to admit that I too was not far from that end. The currency that I deal in today is praise and gratitude to Him for how He saved me from similar self-destruction.

Sadly, we have no evidence that Hemingway ever sought the face of the Great Physician, who can take us and wash us "whiter than snow." He takes the wreckage of our lives and makes it into something new and beautiful. Despite the worst that we've done or the worst circumstances that we may have brought crashing down around us, our Lord can heal us at "all the broken places," no matter how badly we have crashed and burned, for

He tells us,

"I make all things new" (Revelation 21:5).

And He does, in fact, make every part of our lives new. When He moves in, He doesn't just renovate. He doesn't just freshen up or update the premises. The Cross pulls down the walls and floors. Calvary kicks down the doors and changes everything. The Lord is not slack when He remakes us into new creations.

The Savior of the world meets us each exactly at the intersection of His grace and the personal point of our need, and He does this while we are still on our own particular Damascus Road.

Just as we are.

Just in time.

Just like it never happened.

5

TRICIA, MANHATTAN, C.1986

FRANK ASKED ME, "SO, Richard, are you seeing anyone? Any ladies in your life?"

I was separated, heading for divorce from my college sweetheart, my first true love, Pamela. I was lonely and missing my home. I was then living in Delmonico's on Park Avenue and Fifty-Ninth, at the crossroads of Manhattan and the world, twenty-one floors above Regine's, at that time the most fashionable club in the universe.

"Naw, buddy, honestly, I'd love to get back with Pamela and see if we could put this thing back together. She's always been the only love in my life, despite all the craziness. But she's not feeling it, and I don't think it's ever gonna happen. I blew it all up with Claudette."

Claudette Flambois was the cutest little French Canadian from Montreal who had come to work in one of my plastic surgery centers in New York. After her divorce, she was living with her married sister in Huntington Bay not too far from our Long Island cosmetic surgery center out in Suffolk County, Long Island. Claudette's sister was married to a famous hockey player, a revered goaltender who had held the Stanley Cup aloft a few times. Nice, genuine, simple people who opened their home and their hearts to me right up front. They were country folk and had none of the guile of the people that usually came in and out of my life.

But it was funny how it all started.

We were finishing our eleventh surgical procedure of the day and I got the usual call from my wife, Pam, about four in the afternoon. I always loved to hear from her, and she was totally low maintenance anyway, so it was a nice break from the action.

Big Joe Slaska, one of our chauffeurs, my personal guy, was waiting downstairs with the engine running in one of the big stretch limos, ready to take me over to New York Eye and Ear to make evening rounds on our post-op patients, and then we were going home to Long Island. I was looking forward to settling back with the cold Amstel Light that I knew Big Joe always had on ice for me for the ride home. I was still in scrubs and as I threw on a crisply starched long white coat with my name embroidered in blue on the pocket, I took the call from my wife.

"Hey, baby, how're you and the kids doing?"

I was standing in the corridor outside my office operatory and figured I'd get the low-down on the kids' day at school or the work that was proceeding at the house, a ten-thousand-square-foot new postmodern on a seven-acre horse farm out in West Hills in Long Island. This place was amazing, but it was draining me pretty good, with no end in sight.

"Richard, you are never gonna believe this, but I just interviewed the most amazing girl to work out here in the Huntington office." Pamela raved on and on, and it was clear she thought highly of this new employee, a recent export from Canada who had some "cosmetology experience," I was informed.

"Richard, I tell you that you are just gonna love her," Pamela said, presciently.

I listened absentmindedly because I had about ninety-two other things on my mind that had to get done, plus a pocketful of call-back messages that was gonna keep me occupied all the way home and then some.

"Whatever you say, Pam. From what you've said, I'd go ahead and hire her."

"I already did," she replied. "Is that okay?"

I said sure and told her I was gonna be at the Huntington office in the morning, so I'd meet her then.

Let's back up a bit.

Things were beginning to unwind in just about every area of our lives at that time. I was immature and blind as to what was really going on, but I sensed that I was losing control over everything I was worshipping— my marriage, my family, my practice, and, ultimately, myself. But I was so clueless it was pathetic—through the "retrospectoscope," of course.

I was relatively young at the time, thirty-four, to have built so much and to have so much under my control. Frankly, the practice of surgery alone is enough of a responsibility for any one man to shoulder, even in one lifetime, let alone the stresses of "empire building" on top of that. For me, it spelled disaster, and ultimately everything came tumbling down. That tends to happen when we aspire to build towers up to the sky.

Suffice it to say, at the time I was living the life of Tom Wolfe's prototypical "Master of the Universe," as he had termed the 1980s species of "uber" man in his epic *Bonfire of the Vanities*.

When my wife introduced me to an amazing Canuck, what did I do? Like a real dummy, just like she innocently predicted, I fell in love and in lust with her and blew out what was left of my marriage. Ultimately, Claudette became my "transitional person," the poor unfortunate soul who got me out of one faltering relationship, only to find the new one didn't last long. Claudette loved me purely, and I treated her poorly in the end. It was all about me.

In the end she split for Vancouver because she saw the freight train heading straight for me—but not before, in a distraught, jealous rage, she did some deadly serious damage to me behind the scenes that changed my life forever.

As they say, "Hell hath no fury …"

I moved out of the horse-farm manor house into an apartment at Delmonico's on Park Avenue, a short walk from my office over on Madison, where I lived alone, fantasizing about and longing to put my family back together, not realizing it was splintered forever. Pamela did not want hear about marriage counseling. I had regret with a capital "R." She wound up on *Regis and Kathie Lee* one day talking about how "wonderfully liberating divorce can be." That was the result of one of the high-powered publicists I paid for every month.

Night after night, I would go out with Nicky Salvatore, the "Preppy Don." Nicky was originally a patient with a big Italian nose who was forever in awe of me because he thought I transformed him into a handsome man. Talk about the power of self-delusion.

He had become variously an admirer, confidant, consigliere, leech, hanger-on, and, in a twisted kinda way, a dear, wonderful friend at a time when I was alone and needed one.

I remember one night when Nicky and I were eating the amazing lobster rolls at Bill Hong's on East Fortieth Street. Nice place. Classic Chinese, old school. White tablecloths and napkins. I was facing the door, and in walked one of the regulars, the mobster John Gotti, followed by Sammy "the Bull" Gravano and his whole crew.

I looked at Gotti like I was starstruck because I'd only seen him in the newspapers. I blurted out loudly like a rube, "Hey, Nicky, there's John Gotti! Somethin', huh!" I must have sounded like a real tourist.

As the boss of bosses and his party was led to their booth, way in the back, I turned back to Nicky and was stunned to see an empty seat where he had been seated moments before.

"Nico, where'd ya go … where are you?"

He had vanished.

At that moment, out of the corner of my eye, I spied Nicky with a starched white napkin draped over his head and on all fours in his dark Armani suit and Gucci loafers, crawling out the front door of the restaurant.

Later, after we left, he took me aside and told me, "What is wrong with you, Richard? You numbskull with a big mouth. Don't you know that guy would just as soon make you dead as shake your hand?"

Well, at the time I didn't know that, and Nicky never explained why he hit the deck when Gotti walked in. I never pressed him. I just figured that maybe there was some kind of stupid beef between him and the mob boss. This was just a few weeks before Gotti had the big boss, Joe Castellano, gunned down by Sammy "the Bull" in front of Spark's Steakhouse. After that, I understood why Nicky did what he did that night.

John Gotti was definitely not a person with whom you wanted to have a beef.

Nico was really just a fringe mob character, as my criminal defense attorney, Sam Dawson, later told me. I knew his uncle was the actor George Raft, and his godfather was the "real" godfather, Aniello Dellacroce. I'm talking the seriously real godfather. I thought he was just a nice old Italian man, but Sam, a former federal organized-crime task force prosecutor, later assured me that Aniello Dellacroce was the most powerful Mafia boss of all time.

Compared to him, John Gotti was a minor leaguer who, on his best day, couldn't shine Aniello's shoes. Gotti was good at getting his face plastered in the *New York Daily News* but he made a lot of problems. Dellacroce was old school. He didn't make problems; he made solutions. John Gotti got himself locked up and died in prison. John Gotti was a colorful thug in a two-thousand-dollar suit. Aniello Dellacroce was a businessman, but nobody knew what he looked like, except maybe the FBI. He made billions of dollars for himself and his "associates." He died in his bed of extreme old age, with his great-grandchildren at his side.

There's a definite lesson there about keeping your mouth shut and your head down as a good business strategy. I wonder if they teach that at Wharton. I certainly didn't learn it until the world gave me a couple of good headshots. Way too late.

We went regularly to the Surf Club on the way Upper East Side near Elaine's, where my limo waited downstairs with Joe Slaska, fully uniformed behind the wheel and sporting Ray-Ban Wayfarer sunglasses at 2:00 a.m. Just like George C. Scott in *The Hustler.* Joe waited while we drank and danced with society girls. Thoroughbred fillies. Eighteen- and nineteen-year-old debutantes from famous families. Nieces of senators and presidents who found the thirty-four-year-old plastic surgeon dazzling. I briefly dated a Senator's blonde niece and she liked me, but in my inimitable fashion of that crazy time, I messed that up too.

Nothing ever came of that compulsive running around, as I sank deeper into loneliness and longing for what I had thrown away. It was literally the first time in my life that I experienced the blues. Situational to be sure, but until then, having lived what I considered a charmed existence, it was a novel experience for me. I found that I spent a lot of time sighing, like some pathetic cartoon character.

Predictably, an emptiness set in that I could only try to fill with activity, money, women, and everything else in the created world.. And I mean everything that went with it. Two-thousand-dollar suits from Bergdorf's, two or three at a time. And in those days, I don't mind telling you, two "large" for a suit was real money. I couldn't burn through money fast enough.

I dabbled in alcohol and Valium and phenobarbital, but beyond facilitating really poor decision making, it was never directly evident to anyone. Of course, how would I know? My reality testing was zilch, and I was surrounded by sycophants who would never level with me anyway because I was "always right." When someone tried, I banished him or her to Siberia.

Of course, I learned that denial's not just a river in Egypt, and all the substances ever did was make a really bad situation even worse. And it made me even more blinded to reality than I already was—and I was totally in the dark, bumping into the furniture and everything, figuratively speaking.

When you're in that nastiness of your own making, it's frankly the only way you can go. Otherwise, you'd have stop, realize you're headed for disaster, and take ownership. And I was absolutely not about to do that. It was still about what everyone else was doing to me, about everything I wasn't getting, about the respect that I deserved, and how I was the victim in all this.

"No, Frank, right now there's nobody in my life. I wish there was."

Dr. Frank Veteran was a close friend of mine. A fellow plastic surgeon who was on my staff and with whom I had bonded over the years. A quarterback in his days at Harvard, Frank had graduated from Columbia Medical School, and he and I had ultimately trained in plastic surgery at the New York Hospital–Cornell Medical Center, where we were both chief residents. Later, he had come to work for me at Personal Best, my network of cosmetic surgery centers that I had founded around the country, including my flagship in New York and the fledgling centers in Palm Beach and on Rodeo Drive in Beverly Hills. Frank was a fine surgeon, a man of high character and a good friend.

"Listen to me, Richard. You don't need any more entanglements at this point. Wanna get back with Pamela? That's fine. But don't be stupid. Get some temporary companionship. Call this number. She's the friend of one of my nurses. I was going to call her because I hear she's very nice. You go ahead and call her."

As we hung up, I wasn't sure I knew what Frank was talking about, but I deflected it.

In those days, New York was becoming the place where I could get anything delivered—I mean anything. Regine's downstairs would send up full-course meals, complete with escargot on a silver platter and fine china. The crazy-expensive Japanese place on Park Avenue, where I regularly chitchatted with Andy Warhol while we waited for our meals, as well as all the other "beautiful people," would send up full platters of sushi before anyone dreamed that could be done. I had imported my personal trainer from out on Long Island to work out with me in the apartment at Delmonico's and in Central Park; my laundry and cleaning were shuttled up and down the elevator by my personal valet, or *assistant*, as he liked to be called.

The moment I had taken down the number, although I had acted diffidently on the phone with Frank, I knew that I was going to call, and I did. I don't remember how long went by before I did. Actually, I think it was the next afternoon that I called.

Some days later the doorman called upstairs to me on the house phone. "Doctor, there's a young lady here to see you." Well, I was never big on blind dates but Frank assured me she was "a very nice girl." What an understatement.

"It's okay, Jimmy. Send her up." I was sporting an eight-hundred-dollar crimson-red cashmere robe from A. Sulka, and I suppose some slacks and black velvet opera slippers when I opened the door and saw the prototypical blonde, blue-eyed, nineteen-year-old Irish lassie, a knockout with a fifty-megawatt smile and a peaches-and-cream complexion, dressed conservatively but beautifully in a white silk high-collared shirt, black skirt cut for the office, white stockings and black patent pumps with a tasteful heel that was high but not too high. Just perfect.

Cut to the chase. I was bowled over. An eleven out of ten on the Richter scale, with a sweet and genuine personality to match. I was toast; it was love at first sight, if such a thing exists—and it did that night. It was supposed to be just a meet 'n' greet, but something occurred between us that lasted for two decades. She called home about two hours later and said, "I'm going to spend the night over at a friend's house."

A few hours later, Tricia told me that she grew up in the lower East Side in a three-room, one-bathroom apartment with her elderly grandparents. In a few weeks she would be twenty. After graduation from a highly respected high school, she worked at an architectural firm in Manhattan. Although she'd graduated with honors and had been guaranteed acceptance into a great college with a full scholarship, she just wanted to get out into the world and didn't have any desire to go to college. I was mesmerized by her simplicity.

She was engaged to a young cop. Pat something. She said that he kept putting off the wedding, and I could tell she was desperate to get out of a dreary, cramped apartment in those red-brick projects by the East River.

A week later, just before she moved in with me, she told me the big Irish cop cried when she gave him the ring back. It bothered me even then, and I had a premonition of what she might do to me in the future. I never could understand how she could just drop him like a bad habit and take up with me, seemingly without batting an eyelash. Although I found out many years later, I was too much in love and lust and way too selfish to care about anyone else, so I put it out of my mind.

After the worst happened between us, and she divorced me when I was in prison, I was always reminded of the story about the guy who finds a lost baby rattlesnake and nurses it back to health and adulthood. Out of the blue, one day as the man was caressing the creature, his beloved pet reared back and bit him. As he was dying from the effects of the poisonous venom, the man asked his pet snake, "Why did you do that? I thought you loved me!"

"Why are you so surprised?" replied the rattler. "You always knew what I was." It's a mean parable.

Tricia also liked to shop and had a big credit-card balance due at Saks Fifth Avenue, which bothered her. Mainly because, periodically, she had to stop shopping. All in all, I thought we were the proverbial match made in heaven.

She was the prototypical "It Girl." A nerdy guy came up to her on the Long Island Railroad one day when she was coming back from the city, a few weeks after we met.

Mr. "Pocket Protector Guy" sheepishly handed her a love note he had scrawled on a scrap of paper during the ride in from Manhattan. As he handed her the note, he said, "This is for you. I'm sorry. I wasn't sure how many D's there are in goddess."

That night, that particular goddess was too good to be true. But for me, she was true. And at that moment, in my very troubled life and for a long, long time after, she was the main thing I believed in—the *only* thing.

We talked and talked all night, until daybreak, listening to the *Quiet Storm* on WBLS and the sound of Shirley Murdock's soulful croon of illicit love, "As We Lay":

> *It's morning,*
> *And we slept the night away.*
> *It happened,*
> *Now we can't turn back the hands of time.*

I wasn't a Christian at the time. I understand that the wonderful R&B artist Shirley Murdock became a Christian sometime after she recorded this beautiful song about the consequences of adultery. Before I had Jesus in my life, I saw only the lure of the lusts of the flesh. From time to time, when I happen to hear this song now, more than anything else I see the pain and destruction that it produces inevitably in everyone connected with it.

No, we sure couldn't turn back the hands of time. We both knew it. Especially Tricia. She was a simple, decent, and wonderful person. Honestly, I think she has always had trouble handling the particular circumstances of our first meeting, and it became a barrier we could never breach, even after decades. I think she pictured a different beginning. I know I pictured a different ending.

In the end, I think our first meeting bothered her so much that it destroyed us.

But I turned to her in the gray of the Manhattan predawn light—this perfect, sweet, and beautiful angelic teen—and I saw tears forming in her eyes.

"Baby, what's wrong, sweetheart? Why're you crying. Everything's gonna be good."

She whimpered as I dried her salty-tear eyes with my lips. "I know it is," she whispered, "but you're always going to remember how we met, like forever, and I can't ever make that go away. Even as long as we live."

I told her she was being foolish and as I wrapped her in my arms, kissed her slowly, and pulled our bodies together yet again, in a way I would come to repeat ten thousand times over the next twenty years.

I whispered to her, "Forget about the past, baby girl. You're with me now. Tricia, how we met doesn't matter to me, and it never will." She had come off initially as a real wild child, but I discovered she was actually an old-fashioned Catholic girl who had the proverbial heart of gold and just wanted a stable family life. I'm not idealizing either.

And it didn't matter. Really. Not even thirty years later, after raising a family together, after family vacations and PTA meetings, after silly fights and passionate make-ups, after Christmas presents and jack-o'-lanterns, and after my having to endure bitter betrayal and heartbreak.

Even after the storms of life came in, and we went our separate ways, even then it really never mattered to me at all.

Even now it doesn't matter. I'm still crazy about her, thirty years and a million miles later. She was the best woman I've ever known. She was heaven-sent, and I totally blew it.

Just like everything else.

6

PERSONAL BEST

"HAVE A SEAT, RICHARD. How're you bearing up?"

Sam Dawson, my criminal defense attorney, laid a hand on my shoulder as he came into his office, where I was waiting for him. On his wall was the colorful pastel Associated Press artist's renderings of Dawson before the court in various famous federal trials, in which he had gained stardom as "the man to see."

"Thanks, Sam. I'm doin' okay, given the lousy legal situation I'm in."

"Well, maybe it's not as bad as you might think," Sam countered.

Samuel Dawson was arguably the most powerful and feared criminal defense attorney in New York in the mid-1980s and had represented all kinds of defendants, from suburban tax cheats to the leader of one of the mob's "five families" in the famous Mafia Commission prosecution, a real trial of the century. Sam was a former assistant United States attorney in the Eastern District and had prosecuted tons of organized crime figures but had made his real reputation as an ace-beaucoup defense attorney, who beat the government over and over again. He initially was not my first pick, and when I first smelled danger, I retained for a few weeks an excellent Long Island attorney, the great John Case, a sole practitioner who was referred to me by my pal, "the Preppy Don," Nicky Salvatore. Not only had I operated on Nico's big Sicilian nose, but later had resculpted the Italian profiles of both his kids. They looked great, and they thought I walked on water as a plastic surgeon. As a result of how much they were pleased with the results, Nicky, a long-time resident and member of La Costa Spa in California, sent me tons of patients from La Costa, and I became the unofficial plastic surgeon at the Spa and at other famous spas all over the world in the 1980s. The plastic surgical establishment—in other words, my competitors—were incensed and jealous at how much this young upstart was gaining attention. I suppose they felt I should wait in line. Really what panicked them was the fact that we brought down costs by upwards of 50 percent, and that hurt them in their fat wallets. It had nothing to do with quality or professionalism. They ignored us until we started advertising on television, making medical care more affordable, and emptying out their waiting rooms. On any given day Personal Best was doing a huge percentage of all the cosmetic surgery in New York.

I took it as a compliment but didn't realize the daggers they were sharpening for me until it was too late.

I never charged Nicky and the other friends and colleagues because it was always my belief that doctors don't charge family, friends, or other doctors and their families. I learned that from my grandpa. Go try to find a doctor who does that today. I viewed it as a compliment when those who knew me entrusted themselves or their loved ones to my hands. Unfortunately, the level of genteel professionalism in medicine today is so low and venal that professional courtesy is considered a quaint relic of the past.

Nico was adept at working his way into the lives of the rich and famous, and he certainly did into mine. He had become a friend, and later I gave him a job in the office doing God-knows-what. I still can't figure out what work he did, but I do know he wore nice suits, and I signed his check every week. I guess he was kind of a figurehead, and he had lots of friends in Hollywood who made the pilgrimage to my operatory throughout the 1980s. With all the media attention, such as the cover story in *Newsweek*, *Regis and Kathie Lee*, *Redbook*, and others, the medical establishment was going crazy at the mere mention of my name.

I suppose I used Nico just the way he used me.

Nick was a colorful fellow. As Sam Dawson told me, he was a minor mob "fringe" character and informer and one of those guys who could manage to walk between the raindrops. Because he buddied up to both sides, he rubbed elbows with saints and sinners, as he was fond of saying. He was consequently protected by the cops, who traded favors for his information. By that time, Nico still had never been charged in connection with anything, despite the fact that he was, for many years, one of New York City's most infamous fences of stolen property. As I later found out, he regularly bought stolen jewelry and artwork from robbers, burglars, and thieves of all descriptions in New York. In fact, we were in his apartment East Fiftieth Street one evening after I'd had a particularly long day in the operating room, and we were watching television. Years earlier, before everything blew up, I would tell Big Joe Slaska, my driver, to stop the limo at Nico's for an hour or so. It was convenient because it was right at the foot of the Midtown Tunnel, so I could skedaddle out of Long Island really quick without being reported MIA and still get home in time to eat with Pamela and the kids.

Nico Salvatore was a real Damon Runyon character. The genuine article, and I thought he was a hoot. I later learned that he was present at the El Morocco when the Mafia boss of bosses, Frank Costello, coined the phrase, "Tough guys don't dance." He told me the story himself. Later, Norman Mailer reprised the line and titled a best-seller with it. The difference was that Nicky heard it firsthand and told me the story himself, and I know he didn't steal it from any writer—because Nicky never read a book in his life. He couldn't barely read, even the phone book. Maybe he was dyslexic, poor guy, but one thing—he was a natural dancer. No, Nico was a great dancer. I saw him cut a rug on the dance floor out at La Costa one night. He was amazing, all five foot six of him, dancing like Fred Astaire with a tall blonde starlet and everything.

As we watched television, the news report on the Jennifer Levin Central Park murder case came on. A young prep school grad, a tall pretty-boy punk druggie named Robert Chambers, had been arrested and charged with felony premeditated murder of a beautiful young girl who had followed this creep into the park after meeting him at an Upper East Side hangout, Dorrian's Red Hand, which had been the favorite of the young-and-beautiful set. The tabloids had dubbed him the "Preppy Strangler." I had known Jen from pro football player Doug Flutie's restaurant in the South Street Seaport, where this delightful, sweet young kid was a hostess. When I found out what happened, I could've strangled that little creep Chambers with my own hands. I would've taken that rap gladly. A lot of people in New York felt that way.

"I know that guy," Nicky said absentmindedly as he ate a bowl of cereal. "I buy swag from him all the time. A lot of jewelry, mostly. Sometimes there's a lot of blood and hair on it. He's a violent bum. He robs all the Park Avenue apartments." Then he muttered with a mouthful of Cherrios, "Kid's a total psycho. This doesn't surprise me. He's a major dope addict. I guarantee he strangled her and robbed her, probably the poor girl's jewelry. No doubt. That's his M.O."

Nick turned out to be right. He surely knew that kid's *modus operandi* because not only were they left with a dead girl's body, choked to death and beaten, but they discovered later that her diamond-stud earrings were missing as well. Poor Jen—raped and strangled and left dead in Central Park with the two empty holes in her tender little ear lobes. What depravity. I'm sure she actually liked that bum, but she was so innocent and so trusting she never had a chance against that predator.

Shocked to hear about the bloody jewelry, I was silent in disbelief. I kind of thought he was making it up because he was an inveterate liar, a real Sicilian master at it, but I later found out he was telling the *emis* on that one. By the way, "emis" is Yiddish for "truth," as in the Hebrew "emeth."

Nicky grew up in Brooklyn, where the Jews and the Italians lived on top of each other. In fact, Nico's mom was a nice old Italian lady who went upstairs on Friday nights to light the stoves for the Jewish moms because it was the Sabbath, and the old school Orthodox Jewish families were forbidden to do any work on the Sabbath. They called her "the

Shabbos Goy," or the Sabbath Gentile. It's a beautiful old tradition that proves that different cultures can get along once they assimilate and get comfortable with each other—just as long as one of the "cultural groups" doesn't demonstrate a fondness for suicide vests, AK-47s, pipe bombs, or world domination as a means to an end of their religious expression.

I grew up as a Reform Jew, without the rituals. We worshipped in "spirit and in truth," and we thought most of the old-line traditions were "whacked."

So when I first got in legal trouble, Nicky and I went to meet with his lawyer friend, an attorney out on Long Island, who was very nice and seemed serious and competent but who, I decided later, was simply not up to the huge prosecution that the medical cabal, together with the Suffolk DA, were cooking up to drive me out of business.

I think he wanted out because he realized that his one-horse firm was not up to what the DA later termed as the "crime of the century." Of course, I came to realize that everything they prosecuted was their idea of the crime of the century, especially when it involved a great white defendant.

Further, I knew that I needed an attorney who would go no-holds-barred against the DA, and it stood to reason that no local-yokel lawyer, no matter how competent, was about to rip a local prosecutor or a judge a new intestinal orifice, if the opportunity arose, given the knowledge that he, in all likelihood, would go before that court again and again on future cases.

So we interviewed attorneys who were so far out of that sphere of influence that they could use the "nuclear option," if and when opportunity arose.

In Sam Dawson, Esquire, we hit pay dirt.

Over several decades of painful, personal experience with the criminal justice system, I've come to appreciate that the vast majority of local district attorney's offices spend 99.9 percent of their time prosecuting poor black and Hispanic defendants accused of low-level street crimes, and they toil in miserable obscurity for most of their careers. Of course, when they get the rare golden opportunity to take down a rich white defendant (or a cop) they can't contain themselves, knowing that they will get their names in the newspaper and their faces on TV, all for their mommies to see. Best of all, that kind of publicity leads to big fat jobs in private practice later on, when they go over to what they call, the "dark side," or private criminal defense practice. It also helps when they run for Congress.

But I really respect criminal defense attorneys because the reality is that the criminal defense bar is the last firewall defending the basic liberties of all Americans, simply because those accused of crimes are the subset of citizens most reviled and vulnerable to the powers of an abusive government run amok. This is one of the many things that makes America exceptional. It's called "due process."

I am always amused when an elected political leader gets indicted for a crime and starts screaming about his "rights" and "prosecutorial misconduct." These are the same guys who spent their lives running roughshod over the rights of thousands of other private citizens who, unfortunately, fell into the deadly crosshairs of an out-of-control prosecutor's office.

So we engaged briefly an uber-famous defense attorney, Tom Puccio, of Abscam fame, as well as the guy who, with Alan Dershowitz, the Harvard Law professor, turned it around for Claus von Bülow. He, however, turned out to be a big zero.

Puccio was a nice guy, quietly unimpressive. Actually, he was self-impressed, if anything. At the time, he was a partner at Stroock, Stroock & Lavan, in charge of white-collar cases. Frankly, I usually don't trust ex-prosecutors-turned-defense-attorneys, particularly guys like Puccio, who was a big showboat as a prosecutor. That Abscam situation, with FBI agents dressed up as Arab sheik-bribing-congressmen was a total circus. It was nothing other than payback for how the Congress embarrassed the Bureau after Watergate.

Puccio blew a whole lot of smoke at me and bragged about how he liked to "prevent" indictments. I guess that predated the Prevent Defense later adopted by football's Denver Broncos in Super Bowl XXXII. The trouble was, Puccio wasn't preventing anything.

Frankly, his brief involvement in our case just juiced up the prosecutors more because they figured with a big name like the great Thomas Puccio on the case, they would get a lot of headlines. Right out of the box, he handed off my case to a junior varsity associate the day after he took my retainer. What teed me off was when I found out that instead of going out to talk with the Suffolk County DA himself, as he'd promised me he would, he sent the no-name JV-squad underling instead. Can you imagine the chutzpah of that guy? I fired him quickly.

So much for Puccio's vaunted "Prevent Defense." Clearly, it worked better for the Denver Broncos than it did for me.

Ultimately I wound up in the office of Samuel Dawson, a quiet bulldog kind of man, who had developed a fierce reputation for defeating the government in celebrated cases like this. In fact, in legal circles, he was considered by his peers—including defense counsel, prosecutors, and judges—as the attorney you want when you're in seriously deep.

Very recently he had given the Suffolk County DA's Office and a certain county court judge out there, William O'Shea, the judge in my case, a real spanking on a celebrated case, so I settled on him. This judge, Sam told me, was a real crumb-bum, and Sam had wiped him out. Totally embarrassed him so that the judge had to recuse himself, which was exactly what Sam wanted. Sam knew his way around a courthouse, no matter where in the nation it was. But he really knew Suffolk County.

I look back now and believe that my crossing paths with Sam Dawson was totally a "God thing." I wouldn't be born again for years, but I know now that Jesus, the "Hound of Heaven," was with me even then, when

I was oblivious to Him. It was still all about me and my wonderfulness, and, sadly, I would remain that way for a couple of more decades. Self-impressed, blaming everybody else, and hopelessly lost.

But after Dawson came on the scene, the whole chemistry of the case changed. He was not a man to be trifled with, and he struck quiet fear and respect in the hearts of prosecutors as well as judges, who, for the most part in rural counties, were political hacks in black robes. There are exceptions, most notably State Supreme Court Judge Arthur Pitts, a judge I stood before decades later and who I found to possess the epitome of judicial integrity and temperament, fairness and conscientiousness. Despite the fact that I got spanked pretty bad by him, I still hold him in the utmost respect, and I have actually kept in cordial contact with his office over the years. His Honor has assisted me in helping to put my life back together. He is an extraordinary jurist and a very decent man.

When Judge O'Shea found out that Dawson was my new attorney, he literally dumped the case from his docket into the lap of Ken Rohl, one of Dawson's favorite judges out there. I was totally blown away with the fear factor that Dawson possessed, and I gladly gave him the $150,000 retainer he requested. It seems that in a prior case, Dawson dug up some dirt on O'Shea, a real bum of a judge, which linked him financially with one of the other parties in that case, creating an embarrassing conflict for O'Shea and, subsequently, when O'Shea saw Dawson coming down the path, he ducked for cover. Sam told me on day one that his first strategy was to get Judge O'Shea out of the case because, as Sam said, "O'Shea is a lazy ignoramus who doesn't even read defense motions before he denies them, so I gotta get this case outta his courtroom so we can exert some control over the outcome."

And Sam did just that in dazzling fashion.

For years I had been on the wrong side of Suffolk County cronyism and politics, and the old-line medical-surgical establishment-type guys didn't like losing patients by the hundreds to my Personal Best Centers, the expanding cosmetic surgery centers I had founded. Spending upwards of $75,000 a week on television, radio, and newspaper advertising, Personal Best literally drowned our competition and threatened them with extinction. In addition to the advertising, we employed the top-drawer public relations firm headed by Howard Rubenstein, the dean of media hype. Seventy-five thou' a week was a ton of dough to put into local television back in the '80s, and it's not too shabby today either. Especially because what we were advertising, cosmetic surgery, was in a class by itself, and we had the media and the airwaves totally to ourselves. It was a once-in-a-generation economic phenomenon. A perfect storm, and I blew it.

My wife, Pamela, a smart, beautiful, decent girl who had been a commercial actress, starred in the spot, a basic, clean, talking-head situation, and it was a thirty-second sensation. Really, it was just "Television Commercials 101," but it worked. Everybody in the country was talking about it, and we were getting calls from patients booking surgeries from all over the world.

Cover stories in *Newsweek* and interviews with Bryant Gumbel on *The Today Show*, appearances on *Regis and Kathie Lee*, as well as write-ups in *Redbook*, a photo spread by the legendary Mary Ellen Mark in the premier edition of a major national magazine, and a zillion other placements didn't hurt either. For a while, until the wolves descended on us, we were getting unbelievable ink, and my senior colleagues in plastic surgery were beside themselves with fury. I mean, they were totally inconsolable. Furious.

People from all segments of the population and from all over the globe came streaming into our network of centers, from working-class secretaries to Hollywood superstars whose names you'd recognize if I told you (but I won't), from blue-collar factory workers to Wall Street-types, having come out of the shadows and secrecy surrounding cosmetic surgery. They saw our tasteful commercials, shot by the best Hollywood directors on quarter-million-dollar Panaflex cameras, and run on television, radio, and print, twenty-four/seven.

Folks realized that cosmetic surgery could be accessed without shame or secrecy and without having to take a second mortgage on the family farm. As our tagline stated over and over again, "Personal Best. We're on Park Avenue, but only our address is expensive." We used actual letters in our ads from happy and satisfied patients, of which we had amassed thousands, and that really irritated the medical societies because testimonials from actual patients are immeasurably powerful and fueled our growth. They are like neutron bombs, and the medical society hated them.

Of course, the competitors found the relatively few dissatisfied clients and fed them to the DA. The reality was that it was a tiny percentage of all our patients, less than one-tenth of 1 percent. A batting average of .300 gets you into Cooperstown, and although our firm was batting .999, all it brought me was a "one-way ticket to Palookaville," to quote Marlon Brando's character in *On the Waterfront*.

Cosmetic surgery often is sought by patients who are dissatisfied with something in their lives, and it is often connected with their appearance. Even the top professors of plastic surgery have unfavorable results. I know because I saw them in my office regularly but never piled on or encouraged the patients to sue my colleagues.

Unfortunately, the same cannot be said for our competitors, who used every chance they could to undermine our reputation and stir up lawsuits against us. And they were certainly adept at that. In reality, even a real numbskull could have seen it coming, but I was gonna do what I wanted to do, and nobody was gonna tell me otherwise. I was a real hot mess in those days. A toxic cocktail of brilliance, high-intensity self-love and godlessness.

In particular, I remember I was seeing new patients in the Personal Best Center on Park in Manhattan one day, and a man was ushered in, a Larry something or other. He had had a handsome, very recognizable face because prior to his plastic surgery elsewhere a few months earlier, he was one of the top, highest-paid television commercial actors in the nation.

Unfortunately, since his surgery, he could not get a job simply because the "top plastic surgeon in New York" who had performed his facelift had so disfigured him that his handsome, All-American boyish face was now hideous. I am not exaggerating this. This was the worst complication I had ever seen after a supposed "ordinary" face lift. Hey, there are no "ordinary" surgeries. Only "ordinary" surgeons. That's Surgery 101.

After he related his story, Larry told me that he had been operated on by James W. Smith in New York. Jim Smith was probably the most skilled and respected plastic surgeon in the world at the time. He was a full professor of surgery at the New York Hospital–Cornell Medical Center in New York, and I had been his chief resident. I had operated with him a hundred times on facelifts and everything else. I thought he was a solid, adequate, careful surgeon, but Smith had the same "feet of clay" that everyone had, including me.

"Larry, I know Dr. Smith personally, and I can tell you that he is a superb surgeon. Every one of us experiences unfavorable results in cosmetic surgery, and it's not always a matter of fault. I suggest you go back to Dr. Smith and try to work with him. I do feel that things will improve somewhat with time, but I appreciate that you're losing huge amounts of income."

This poor guy's cheeks were filled with horrendous welts and depressions where Smith's subcutaneous sutures had caused inflammation and were being extruded, leaving his complexion hopelessly pockmarked and filled with craters. No way was this guy ever going to be able to get before a camera again in his life, except maybe in a Mickey Mouse costume.

A year or two later, when I was being vilified by competitors and in the media, I got an unexpected telephone call one afternoon at home, the seven-acre horse farm on Long Island, from none other than my old plastic surgery professor at New York Hospital–Cornell, Jim Smith. I don't even know how he got my home number because I hadn't spoken to him for years, not since I was chief resident and senior fellow. But I didn't care that he called me at home. I was fine with that. I knew why he was calling.

"Hiya, Richard. How are you? I hear you're having a little bit of a hard time."

"Hi, Dr. Smith. It's nice to hear from you. What can I do for you, sir?" I knew immediately that he was calling about that disfigured TV actor.

"Listen to me, Richard. I don't like what they're doing to you. You're a top-flight guy. I've seen your fine results, and I want you to call me if there's anything I can ever help you with. The gentlemanly and professional manner in which you handled that patient of mine with that bad complication is something that I will never forget. He's back under my care. Obviously, we're in settlement discussions with his counsel and our malpractice carrier, but frankly, because of the way you spoke with him, it is not going to be an adversarial process. That's the way all these unfavorable results should be handled. These guys are out to get you, and they are stirring up dissatisfaction all over the place over trivial things with every patient of yours they can get their hands on."

"Dr. Smith, you have no idea how much I appreciate your taking the time to call and affirm me in this way."

I got a handwritten note from him, encouraging me to stay strong and ride out "these wild, baseless allegations," but we never spoke again. We didn't need to. The bond was there.

I remember during that time, when I was getting dragged through the mud daily, I was cheering myself up, buying a shirt in Bergdorf's on Fifty-Seventh and Fifth. The young pretty girl behind the counter looked at my credit card, recognized me, and said something I shall never forget.

"Are you the Dr. Dombroff I see on TV all the time?

I said I was and smiled and braced myself for an earful.

"Dr. Dombroff, don't feel too bad. My dad's a surgeon just like you, and he always complains that he has 98 percent of his problems with 2 percent of his patients."

I smiled broadly and thanked her, thinking, *From the mouths of babes and sucklings* ...

So in the early 1980s, Personal Best was a revolutionary medical juggernaut. Our timing was impeccable, and it was a "perfect storm" that blew away the competition. It was a case study in pioneering, a new American industry. Unfortunately, in time it became a dark, cautionary tale as well—a textbook case of pride, ego, arrogance, jealousy, and every other kind of sin of the flesh, getting in and messing up an otherwise great human endeavor.

Unfortunately, I was too busy working day and night to notice or care what frightening economic damage my jealous "colleagues" were experiencing and how negatively they were reacting and plotting our demise. People close to me tried to alert me, but I believed in the free market, and, together with a good dose of arrogance and a tincture of greed, I went full speed ahead. I also was not of a mind to listen to anyone anyway.

I remember one stodgy, bloated, self-righteous leader of the plastic surgical establishment stating critically, "Plastic surgery should be sought, not sold." Whatever that meant.

Well, the world was indeed "seeking it" at a Personal Best Center like nobody's business, as I mockingly noted in a *Newsweek* cover story at the time. On any given day at our center in Manhattan, we experienced a line-up of patients snaking from the reception desk to literally outside the door onto the Park Avenue and Eighty-Sixth Street sidewalk. That is no exaggeration. It became ridiculous. Our surgeons were so experienced that they were doing more cosmetic surgery procedures, with 98 percent satisfaction rates, in a month than most competitors did in a decade.

At the vast majority of plastic surgical practices, the surgeons suffer from a cosmetic surgical overcapacity. That is, they're lucky to get even 10 percent of the total cosmetic caseload that they could really handle; thus, they have to spend much of their time dredging up non cosmetic stuff at clinics and ERs in the middle of the night. Simply put, we had it, and they wanted it.

I became apprehensive with the pent-up demand that I had unleashed. Finally, I had to dial down the advertising. I didn't appreciate it at the time, but it is an extraordinarily rare phenomenon in economics when all the market conditions are right for a single player to totally pioneer, cultivate, and then dominate a particular market. It's happened a few times in our lifetime in the digital arena, and a hundred years ago, a guy named Rockefeller did it with Standard Oil, but never in health care delivery has there been one single dominant player. Health care was always termed "the biggest small business in America," and I, in my naiveté, was going to change that.

No doubt, though, at that time we were perceived as posing an existential threat to traditional single practitioners and small groups, and they were just not gonna let it happen. I was oblivious to what was going on around me until events occurred that grabbed me by the scruff of my starched, monogrammed, white, 100-percent-cotton, braided-buttoned doctor's coat and changed my life forever.

Overnight, we had changed the rules of engagement by overturning the traditional way that cosmetic surgeons obtained their patients and grew their practices. They toiled through lean years of cultivating referral lines with local physicians, often employing quasi-legal kickbacks and fee-splitting schemes, lavish gifts, and other gray-market ways of currying favor.

Nobody—but nobody—advertised. I was totally out there. It had been illegal for physicians until 1980s, when I went out into practice. Even after the rules changed, the state medical societies frowned on it and literally ostracized any foolish individuals who dared to advertise in newspapers, radio, or TV.

The only thing for which they left you alone was the dopey Yellow Pages. Yellow Pages never has been a primary form of advertising. At least, not for me. Sure, I took full pages but only as an adjunct to mass media, so that when people were flipping through the Yellow Pages, trying to figure where to get their breasts enlarged, for example, the consumers would see a full-page ad from Personal Best and say, "Oh yeah, I know that place. That's the Personal Best girl I see on TV all the time. I'll call them."

Nobody had the guts to go on television but us. In 1983, that was the equivalent of "jumping the shark," and it changed forever the world of health care and even pharmaceutical marketing. Today, it's commonplace, but then, it was subversive and revolutionary. I really didn't care about their unspoken rules and regulations, and certainly I eschewed traditions. I was a product of the sixties, and I was determined to make my mark.

Hey, I never expected to win a Nobel Prize for it, but I also never expected to get crucified for it either. I just wanted to pioneer something new and different from what had come before. Good intentions, but then my mother always told me, "The road to hell is paved with good intentions." I never really knew what that meant until years later, after the locusts ate a swath through my life, twenty or so years wide. In other words, we do beastly things in life to satisfy our appetites, and then we paper over it with a thin layer of so-called good intentions, thinking that it's all justified. It's not. It's the height of hypocrisy. I had it by the truckload.

But Personal Best did cut patient fees for typical cosmetic surgical procedures, often by more than half. Our centers chauffeured patients to and from their appointments in stretch limousines with uniformed chauffeurs and, most important, accepted insurance assignments. That's all pretty common now. Thirty-five years ago, it was revolutionary and unheard of by established cosmetic surgeons, who demanded their whole splendid fee up front and generally catered to the carriage trade

The net effect of the Personal Best juggernaut was to hugely expand the cosmetic surgery market nationally, as well as to devastate long-established practices. We neatly transferred to us millions of dollars from the pockets of senior plastic surgeons. Unfortunately, these were the guys who controlled the State Medical Society, the Medical Malpractice Insurance Company, and the credentials committees of literally every single hospital in the region, as well as having powerful influence over county government, including the highly politicized Office of the District Attorney of Suffolk County.

This particular prosecutor's office was notorious and had been cited for years by numerous New York State civil liberties and judicial watchdog groups for a panoply of corrupt practices and prosecutorial abuses, most notably the misuse of the all-powerful prosecutor's office for financial gain.

Today even it's still under investigation by the Justice Department for corruption in dozens of cases that it has brought against the citizenry.

Indeed, the federal and state governments had requested court-appointed special masters to oversee the running of the prosecutor's office in Suffolk County, which had earned the nickname the "Wild West" because of the lawlessness that had characterized their shady practices and wanton police-state tactics. These included, most notably, a long documented record of illegal search-and-seizures, particularly of luxury BMWs, Mercedes, and other high-end cars from the citizenry for the ultimate personal use and enjoyment of staff attached to the District Attorney's Office, including ADAs, detectives, and others.

These dedicated civil servants were apparently dedicated to their expensive taste in cars, and they used seized funds from businesses and personal bank accounts to buy jewelry for themselves and to take "continuing legal education" junkets to Caribbean resorts. They were racketeering, plain and simple, and in the 1980s, straight up until around 2002, it was literally out of control on Long Island. It still is today.

An investigation was conducted by the *New York Times* and other media outlets just after the Personal Best prosecution. They blew the whistle on the tradition of prosecutorial misconduct infecting the Suffolk DA's office throughout the 1980s and 1990s, right up until the chief offender, DA James Catterson, was kicked out of office in 2002:

> *Seized Assets Disappear as Prosecutors and Police Profiteer Off Forfeiture Program*
> by Brenda Grantland, Esq.
> F.E.A.R. Chronicles, Vol. 1. No. 5,

> Suffolk County, New York: October 2, 1992, the *New York Times* reported that Suffolk County, New York, District Attorney James M. Catterson, like prosecutor Bissell in New Jersey, has asserted complete control over the assets his office confiscates through its forfeiture program. Until Long Island's *Newsday* brought it to their attention, Suffolk County officials knew nothing about Catterson's handling of the forfeited assets. Catterson drives a BMW 735i that was seized from a drug dealer. He spent $3,412 from the forfeiture fund for mechanical and body work on the BMW, including $75 for pin striping. Also, from the fund, he bought a $300 watch for a retiring secretary, and spent $3,999 for chairs, among other things. Catterson told the *Times*: "By my view, I really don't have to ask anyone else's permission to spend monies that come to me." The county has not audited Catterson's office since 1981.

> Asset Seizure Is Questioned in Suffolk,

by John T. McQuiston,
New York Times, 10-2-92, page B1.

So at that point, in 1987, unbeknownst to me, idiot that I was, we were sitting ducks for the Suffolk DA. To make matters worse, I was too stupid and self-absorbed to contribute money to any of the political bosses who kept demanding it. I wound up on the wrong side of the politics out there, especially with the powerful medical establishment lined up against us.

Ultimately, they manufactured a case with wild, laughably false allegations they had cooked up and fed to the press about chauffeurs doing surgery, and we were charged in a seventy-eight-count indictment, in which they threw in everything including the kitchen sink. Unfortunately, people love to listen to salacious stuff, and the dream was over as the nightmare began.

I remember visiting with former United States Attorney General Ramsey Clark to consult with him about the charges. He was in private practice in New York City, having acquired a reputation as a radical anti-establishment attorney with an extreme distrust for the government and a powerful insider's bird's-eye view of just how abusive to individual rights the government can be.

The radical attorney William Kunstler was cut from the same cloth, but Ramsey Clark had been the consummate insider, a member of President Lyndon Johnson's cabinet, whose nomination as Attorney General occasioned the historic stepping down from the Supreme Court by Ramsey Clark's famous father, Supreme Court Justice Tom Clark. Kunstler and guys like him were never regarded as anything but troublemakers and media hounds because they had never been in the highest corridors of power, as had Ramsey Clark.

Ramsey, who first worked for Jack Kennedy, helped get the South straightened out during the era of Jim Crow laws. He was the archetypical example of the insider turning on the establishment, and because of that he had always resonated with my slightly antisocial, countercultural streak. Consequently, I had always idolized him.

My association with him began with a strange, anonymous call in my office about a week after the criminal indictment was handed down in Suffolk County Supreme Court. My perp walk in my two-thousand-dollar suit from Bergdorf's was covered in every newspaper and every television and radio station in New York and many around the nation. Instantly, I had been chopped down to size, as one competitor quipped. But the ladies loved me, as I later found out from a girlfriend, who told me, "Wow, you looked great on TV." I laughed at that heartily and thought that it was the electronic-age equivalent of, "I don't care what you say about me in the newspapers; just make sure you spell my name right."

One of my receptionists told me there was a call for me from another doctor interested in my case.

"This is Richard Dombroff. To whom am I speaking?" I answered the phone call.

"Dr. Dombroff, it's not important what my name is. I know you, but you don't know me. You don't need to know me. But I've known everything that was planned about you. Just let's say I'm a fellow physician who thinks you're getting beat up unfairly, and I have information that can assist you. Listen carefully to me. I cannot be directly involved in this, but if you call Mr. Ramsey Clark in his office at this number, he can help you." He spoke in an Indian or Pakistani accent, and I still don't know who the mystery caller was, but I had sure heard of Ramsey Clark.

I said thanks; I was interested and amused but perplexed by the intrigue and secrecy. I went into the operating room and thought little about it until later, when I called the number and made an appointment to see the famous man, a legendary figure of the 1960s. He was one of the heroes from my revolutionary college days at Columbia, where I had a personal role in shutting down the Ivy League campus in the wake of Nixon's invasion of Cambodia. I avoided a nightstick to the head but was detained briefly in handcuffs by the NYPD, who later put their gloved hands on me a bit and tuned me up before they kicked my Ivy-covered bottom down the steps of Low Library. Then they lectured me and let me go back to my dormitory. They weren't a bad bunch of guys, actually. Ever since taking care of them as the senior resident on the trauma service at Bellevue, I've had a soft spot in my heart for cops.

A few days later, sitting in his office in downtown, I handed the indictment that seemed a hundred pages long to the tall, lanky Texan. He put on his spectacles and read through it breezily. Clark looked just like the pictures I had seen a million times. He was dressed just like a Kennedy-era Justice Department guy in a medium gray off-the-rack suit, white shirt, and nondescript tie. Something out of *Mississippi Burning* or an Oliver Stone film. He wore heavy Florsheim Oxford shoes, and I swear I saw a hole worn through the sole of one of them.

As he read, I noticed an amazing photograph of him, showing Clark standing tall, his back to the camera, presumably as attorney general, talking with J. Edgar Hoover. Just Hoover's piercing eyes could be seen peering malevolently and menacingly over Clark's shoulder at the photographer. The photo has, to my knowledge, never been published anywhere, but it was so eerie that I've never forgotten it. I was always amazed that the photograph had even survived Hoover's paranoia, but there it was, the sole photograph on this famous man's wall, to my recollection.

Suddenly, I looked away from the photograph, which had mesmerized me, because I heard Clark laughing. After leaving the Justice Department, Clark made a career of defending the most unpopular and most reviled defendants in the world, a real rogue's gallery, who were the subject of, in his view, a tyrannical government run amok. Branch Davidian David Koresh, Slobodan Milosevic, even Saddam Hussein at his show trial in Iraq before they neatly separated his head from his torso at his eventual execution—the more unpopular you were, the more he wanted to stand up for you. This guy was the genuine Atticus Finch meets Abby Hoffman.

He fanned through the pages and laughed.

"I did a little checkin' around 'bout you, Doctor. You got mighty impressive credentials, and mah friends tell me you're a mighty fine surgeon too. Ha-ha-ha! No two ways 'bout it, son. You're a threat to the fat cats. Yep, and they think they gotcha good too," he said in a Texas drawl.

"But don't worry 'bout it too much, son. The lawyer you got, I know him, and he's very good. With him in the mix against that DA's office out there, it ain't a fair fight. Besides, this indictment ain't worth the pound of paper it's printed on. A real waste of natural resources. Ha-ha-ha." He was real neighborly, like we were discussing an upcoming cattle drive.

"I'll give your lawyer a call, and maybe we'll get this straightened out. Keep your head up tall, and keep heapin' it on the establishment. Those bums deserve it. They had all the business for themselves since year one. Now you young'ns come along and hit 'em where it hurts. In their fat wallets. It'll be a little rough sleddin' for you for a while but we'll getcha through it." He gave me his hand and a big, warm, reassuring smile.

More than trusting him, I knew I was in the presence of greatness. This was one of the most genuine men I have ever met. He was everything I expected.

Interestingly, he never asked me for a cent. I recall that I asked what I owed him. He just waved his hand and said, "For what? Just a little friendly conversation? Call it professional courtesy. Have your attorneys call me."

We stood up, we shook hands, and I left, thinking, *This guy's amazing, the genuine article. He actually gets off sticking it to the government. Really pokin' them right in the eye.* Clark was definitely a one-off, the consummate insider who's inveterately countercultural because he knew firsthand how abusive government power can put a citizen's lights out. He had wielded mighty government power personally. If the government and the establishment hated you, he was for you. Period. That old Presbyterian knew we were all sinners, and he hated the hypocrisy of dangerous self-righteous political correctness. I totally dug him.

He was my kind of soul mate: an old-school stand-up guy of the first order. I didn't always agree with his various political statements later on, but I always admired the fact that he stood for justice and that if you were unpopular, he was ready to help. That is the essence of grace. It was the unmerited favor that I experienced later on when I asked Jesus into my life and learned about the possibility of unconditional love.

"I got a call from Ramsey Clark the other day. He was very helpful," Sam Dawson said quietly. "I didn't know you knew him."

"I didn't until a few days ago. I got an anonymous call advising me to speak with him," I replied. "Was that okay, Sam? What'd he say?"

Sam sat back in his chair and pondered for a bit what to share with me. It was obvious there was some insider lawyer-to-lawyer stuff going on that was critical to my case, but it was not something that needed to be revealed to me.

"He seemed to know a lot about the case."

"Well, I gave him the indictment to read," I replied.

"Oh, that's all DA propaganda. The D.A. gets headlines with that indictment. No, Clark knew inside stuff. Anyway, I'm glad you came in today. I met with the prosecutors and the judge after I spoke with Ramsey Clark. We all met in Judge Rohl's chambers. Totally off the record stuff, but we busted their case wide open."

For the first time in months, I saw some daylight and kept my mouth shut, listening intently. Sam Dawson was not a guy to be interrupted.

"You shoulda heard this crazy nut from the prosecutor's office, the ADA, a real zealot on a mission to bring down a young, white, Jewish doctor. She actually started telling Judge Rohl this was the "crime of the century.

"That old clam-digger of a judge actually laughed at her. I told the judge, 'Really, Your Honor, what are we talking about here? A few hundred bucks of insurance claims?' A technical violation of the education law because you used foreign medical graduates from the hospital as medical assistants in the office? Just like every other prominent plastic surgeon in the city? 'Your Honor,' I said, 'this case is bogus.'

"The judge was still laughing when he looked at the ADA and told her directly, 'You know I'm inclined to toss this case out of court. Seriously, you know that search warrant was falsified. Don't push me on this. I'm inclined to step out of here and let you guys settle this amicably because this case, the way you've presented it in this indictment, ain't ever goin' to trial. Not in my courtroom, not like you blew this case up. You totally lied to the magistrate in order to get him to issue the warrant. Those files are your whole case, and you know they're now fruits of the poisonous vine. I'm gonna have to exclude everything in them, and then you ain't got no case or pretty close to it.'

"So then Rohl turns to me and says, 'Sam, my advice to you is to cut a deal for your young man, and let the doctor get this behind him and go on with his life. He's a bright kid, and he can rebuild. One thing I'm gonna give the prosecutors, Sam, is that I want a taste of incarceration,'"

Rohl was a real deal-maker. He gave each side something, so they walked away from the table feeling as if they didn't get beaten too badly.

My heart sank hearing this. Jail time? I had never even been sent to the principal's office. I was hoping that jail was a bullet I could avoid.

"At this point, Richard, the ADA is sweating because her case is evaporating," Sam told me. "So the ADA turns to me and says, 'Sam, I want your guy outta business. He tosses his license on the table voluntarily, or no deal. That's my bottom line. Sam, I don't give a hoot if this case gets dismissed. I'll hound your guy until I get him out of business. Let him do a few days out on the prison farm too. It'll be a nice change of scenery.' And then she chuckled."

I wasn't surprised, because that's what this was about all the time. They wanted to crush Personal Best from day one. I was told this was coming years before by many people. DA Patrick Henry's big campaign contributors wanted to squelch the competition we were giving the establishment, and they were salivating for years just for this opportunity.

Unfortunately, I had played right into their hands by aggressively marketing cosmetic surgery, stealing their patients, refusing to split fees with other physicians, and driving prices for facelifts and breast augmentations down as much as half off what they had been charging for years. And they knew where my Achilles' heel was. It was the same as theirs—the longstanding universal practice of filing insurance claims for nose jobs as "nasal reconstructive surgery" and all the other disingenuous games plastic surgeons play with insurance companies to maximize reimbursement. It was standard practice then, as it is now.

"Listen up, Richard," Sam Dawson continued. "This case against you is total garbage. It smells and so does that DA's office out in Suffolk. They've been an embarrassment to the Bar Association for years but they're the law out there. It's all about the bucks—your bucks, your beloved competitors' bucks, and all the dough they've funneled to the political machine over the years. Now they want payback. Bottom line: you come up short. If Rohl tosses the cases, which he will, all the files get excluded, and they ain't got much else, and they know it. But they'll come back at you in a few months with what they've got left. And what they do have is a few little fish—a few scared employees—who they'll criminally charge for giving out Band-Aids and Vaseline. And these little scared wimpy folks are gonna say whatever those creep ADAs tell them to say, so it ain't gonna be pretty. They'll turn your lights out. You're not going to take that chance, Richard. It ain't ever gonna be better'n this, boy-o."

"So what's the best we can do, Sam?" I asked.

"Okay, this is what I worked out. I just need you to pull the trigger, and you walk away from this God-awful mess, your hair a little mussed, a little battered and bruised, but you live to fight another day."

His words were meant to be encouraging, but they were also unfortunately darkly prophetic of events that played out two decades later in that exact same prosecutor's office. The prosecutors in that office had an elephantine memory, and they held on to grudges like grim death, particularly when they felt they'd been beaten.

I was quiet and nodded tentatively but approvingly. I had started having a recurrence of my seizure disorder a year before from the huge stress brought on as this began. I was no longer able to complete an operation without worrying about losing consciousness due to petit mal seizure. Disabled by it, I had retired from surgery. I was on Dilantin and Valium just to get through the day and even had to give up driving. I knew that I couldn't go on with this onslaught, and finally I was seeing a flicker at the end of a very dark tunnel. At that moment, I was depressed—but hopeful for the first time in years.

"So what's the deal, Pug?" I called him Pug with great affection and respect for his physiognomy as well as his pugnacious attitude. That is invaluable in a criminal defense attorney. After all, folks, we're talking about years of people's lives hanging in the balance. Sometimes decades. Sometimes life.

Sam was actually more of a bulldog. He got up slowly from behind his desk and came around to sit beside me and smiled. He was a full head shorter than me, and although he had a tough, nasty, US Marine-like aura about him, he put his hand on my arm and looked at me like a father.

"Richard, I told you when this started that they'd have to go through me to get to you. After the way I beat up old Judge O'Shea out there on that other case, Judge Rohl doesn't really want to go against me on this one, and neither does the DA. Judge Rohl wants cases like this dealt out fast so he can get back out on the Great South Bay in his clam boat.

"Most people would consider this a victory. The other side is peeved. They think they blew it. But you gotta know that the government always holds all the cards, even when they mess up. You never win, son. You never win. Not the way normal people define winning. Even when you rough them up and seem to beat them at their own game, nine times out of ten, there's a butcher's bill to pay.

"Here's the deal: forty-nine days in the honor farm out in Yaphank, nine months' community service over at the Red Cross. You toss your medical license on the table. You're not practicing now anyway. Case closed, and you go on with your life to do great things, older but wiser."

I was silent for a moment, pondering it in my heart. It was all over.

I was thinking about all the years at Hopkins. All the nights at Bellevue on the trauma service. I thought about one Christmas Eve in the trauma room. One stab wound after another. Gunshot wound after gunshot wound. My hands up to my elbows in the chest of some young New York City police detective lieutenant who got shot in a drug bust gone bad, with my finger finally finding and plugging the bullet hole in the right atrium of his heart, staunching the gushing blood so that he could live to fight another day. I was so soaked with that young cop's blood that I had to change my underwear after we saved his life. But that young guy went home alive a couple of weeks later. There were lots of others as well. I thought nothing of it—until I was about to lose it all.

I was still wandering in the darkness and had no clue at that time how my life had gone so badly off track. I wouldn't come to that revelation knowledge until many, many years later. But I knew in my heart, at that particular moment, that part of my life was over forever. No, that wasn't a part of my life; it was my whole life, as I saw it then, and it was gone. I was silent for a minute or two. Then I looked up at Dawson. We were silent for a minute. I spoke first.

"Done. Make the deal, Sam," I told him quietly.

Sam gave me a wink and joked, "Hey, Einstein, next time you get in trouble, make sure you do it in Manhattan 'cause at least the prosecutor here's got a half-a-brain. Ha-ha-ha!" Sam was beaming. Another day, another quarter-million-dollar fee earned.

With the die cast, I rose and left to go home to Tricia, who was waiting for me uptown. I walked out into a frozen January 1987 New York afternoon, making my way up Madison Avenue, past Brooks Brothers, oblivious to the crowds. I was trying to comprehend how things had become so ugly, how they had gone so horribly wrong, desperate to gain the bearings of my life, not knowing that although I would be back in our warm apartment with Tricia within an hour, it would be nearly two decades into the future before I would finally find my way "home."

I walked the cold city pavement alone, sensing once again a now-familiar aching emptiness inside me, broken by events and searching in the fog of my mind for an elusive goal. An anchor for my soul. It was a search that would chaotically consume the next twenty years of my life, as it had indelibly and horribly stained all the years of my life before that moment in the middle of that hopelessly broken Manhattan winter.

7

THE HOUND OF HEAVEN

I fled Him, down the nights and down the days;
I fled Him, down the arches of the years;
I fled Him, down the labyrinthine ways
Of my own mind; and in the midst of tears
I hid from Him, and under running laughter.
Up vistaed hopes I sped;
And shot, precipitated,
Adown Titanic glooms of chasmed fears,
From those strong Feet that followed, followed after.
But with unhurrying chase,
And unperturbèd pace,
Deliberate speed, majestic instancy,
They beat—and a Voice beat
More instant than the Feet—
"All things betray thee, who betrayest Me."

—Francis Thompson
"The Hound of Heaven"

Heading into Nut Country, July 2003

IN THE EARLY MORNING hours before Jack Kennedy had the right hemisphere of his brain splattered all over the pristine asphalt of Dealey Plaza in Dallas, while he and Jackie were dressing in the hotel in Fort Worth, the young president scanned the *Dallas Morning News*, read the vitriolic sentiments expressed against him, and prophetically muttered to his wife, referring to their trip into the Bible Belt, "Jackie, we're heading into nut country today."

On November 22, 1963, I was eleven years old and in Mr. Mohrman's sixth grade class. He was a former marine who had fought at Iwo Jima, a compactly built tough guy with a great gentleness about him. But by 2:30 in the afternoon, eastern standard time, this leatherneck was red-faced and in tears, and we were all wondering why.

We know how that day ended.

Almost exactly forty years later, I too arose early to catch my plane, headed for the Bible Belt—Dallas, Fort Worth, and beyond—on my own particular business. I was being reviled by many in certain quarters as well. In the gray darkness of the early morning hour, I snuggled close to Tricia. I was missing her already, and I hadn't even left. I have always been a childish homebody this way, and it was common for me to fly across the country to California or Arizona on business, decline dinner invitations, and return the same day, just to get home in time for Letterman. That morning, with my lips close to her warm ear, I ironically evoked JFK as I whispered softly to her, "Baby, gotta go. I'm headed into nut country today."

It was long before I got saved, and I had no idea what I was talking about. I was just idiotically emulating JFK, my childhood hero, with some throwaway lines. I was in a limbo existence, knowing well that soon it would be a very long time before I again—if ever—enjoyed those warm moments in our bedroom. All I saw was darkness and uncertainty, and I walked through those days, trying to ignore the fear that was working overtime to hold me in its grip. The seven-month trial was over, the legal battle fought and lost, the cushy plea deals spurned, all escape routes closed off, and all the opportunities and advantages of a very eminent lifetime wasted.

For the second time in fifteen years, the local DA had aimed its machinery and taken its shot at me. This time, not altogether unexpectedly, they won. I recalled the words of my old friend and attorney from years before, the fearsome Sam Dawson, who had previously beat them to a draw: "They always win, Richard, one way or another. They always win. Even when they lose, they win." On that day long ago he told me to "take the deal, a slap on the wrist, move on, and live to fight another day." Even Sam didn't recognize how prophetic his words were that day. This time, as far as "the deal" was concerned, I told them to forget it. It wasn't happenin'.

Big mistake. Big, fat, idealistic, principled mistake. Parenthetically, if you have trouble keeping track of the legal scrapes I got in, no worries, so do I.

After the guilty verdict, I was given a few weeks by Judge Arthur Pitts to get my affairs in order because the next time I stood in front of him, I would not be coming home for a very long time. So I was awaiting sentencing and was looking prospectively at decades in prison. To be sure, this was not the way I had planned for my seemingly charmed life to play out.

But it was a reality that I was stuck with, and I was going to have to deal with it in one way or another. I had absolutely no idea how that would work, so I shoved it to the back of my mind, as I had done countless times, and dressed. I kissed my wife softly. She hugged me, half asleep, and told me to call when I landed.

The limo was waiting in the long, winding, red-pea-gravel driveway, humming in the warm Long Island darkness before daybreak. I settled in for the ride to Kennedy Airport.

I turned my mind to the task at hand: attempting to bolster the infrastructure of the excellent business I had founded. I needed to support my family during the long prison sentence that I knew was coming. This was a huge longshot at best, but taking matters into my own hands was all that I had ever known how to do. This was not going to be a few days in the Suffolk County honor farm like round one, twenty years earlier.

This time around I was headed for the proverbial Big House upstate, about as far away in New York as you could get and still be in the United States. The north country of New York is the location of a vast gulag archipelago of prisons, reaching across New York State from Lake Erie all to way up the Saint Lawrence Valley to a stone's throw from Montreal. It is the American equivalent of Siberia.

I remember when I first got sentenced and was sent upstate. Tricia was so broken and alone, of course, and attempting to carry on. She is an amazing trooper. Totally self-dependent, substantively as well as spiritually. It is, sadly, a flaw that ultimately separates one from God.

She wrote me a letter my first week in imprisonment, the supermax reception center upstate in Dutchess County, saying that she dreamed that she and I had been in some terribly cataclysmic auto accident and that she was the sole survivor.

I was a bit taken aback, but I admired her authentic expression of grief. Tricia rarely expressed any kind of emotion, and she usually had a smile on her face, even when she was dying inside. I understood what she meant. I felt that way too. Honestly, I've never felt deader than I did in those early days, and as I sat silently in the back of the limo, I began to understand the term "dead man walking." I was still unsaved at that time and flying solo.

Only years later, lying in my prison cell way up by the Canadian border in Franklin County, listening to my radio, I heard the marvelous Christian defender Ravi Zacharias say, "Jesus Christ came not to make bad men good. Rather, He came to make dead men alive." I dimly understood what he meant at the time, but for some reason it continued to reverberate in my mind over the next decade.

It was years later before I fully began to comprehend the meaning of this metaphor in my life. In the darkness of that ride to the airport, I was dead and was only going through the motions of daily existence. Walking through our sprawling ranch house late at night, alone while my family slept, I had often taken to lying down on a couch in my study so as not to disturb Tricia and the kids with my restlessness. Indeed, she was hurting too during that limbo period, and there wasn't a whole lot of communication between us. I had always known, as a veteran family-type guy, that when Mom isn't happy, nobody's happy.

In reality, Tricia was gone. I know now she was just going through the polite motions of whatever was left of our marriage, with the seconds ticking down until I was gone as well.

Paraphrasing the words of James Taylor, my wife was already "gone to Carolina" in her mind, and once I was shipped upstate in shackles, our life together was done and gone as well.

During those nights that I dozed in my study, on two occasions I was awakened, still lying in the utter darkness with my eyes still closed. In my brokenness, drifting between wakefulness and slumber, I experienced a presence, a clear vision that consisted of a brilliantly luminescent figure.

At the time, I identified it, for lack of any better descriptive, as being a brightly glowing, white-hot "plus sign." It was curious to me but not the Ebenezer Scrooge-type epiphany that Dickens describes in *A Christmas Carol*. But make no mistake; it was real, and it was not a dream. I am a person who does not have visions, period. This was something that I had never experienced.

It appeared two times in nightly succession and was accompanied by a great tranquility that swept over me, allowing me to fall into a deep restful slumber until morning. After those two or three "encounters," the vision never returned again and at that moment, I had no idea at all what meaning it held, if any.

For two years I forgot about this vision until one night—shortly after I got born again in my prison cell upstate on December 27, 2004, at 8:30 in the evening—I heard the great Christian expositor Robert Schuller on the radio, expounding on the meaning of the cross.

"Jesus carried the crossbar," he said, "the patibulum on his shoulders all the way to Calvary, and before it was nailed to the upright, carrying the crossbar, this became the greatest sign of negative and evil. Jesus on the intact cross became the greatest, most miraculous plus sign in the history of the universe."

I was immediately struck by the significance of this statement and how it applied to my life, and I recalled immediately my vision of the luminescent plus sign, years before in the utter darkness of my library. I realized at that moment that before I was born again, lost in the darkness of sin and destruction, as He said in His word, I "was in prison and [He] came to me."

I had told a fellow Christian inmate a few months before about my visual encounter, and the next day, amazingly, having heard Dr. Schuller on the radio the night before as well, he sought me out in the big prison yard on the way to the weight shack.

"Rock, did you hear Dr. Schuller last night on the radio?" the chubby, jolly convicted Colombian drug dealer asked me excitedly. I said, equally excited, that I had, and we both understood in our hearts that in that lonely, dark study in the midst of my suffering, while I still despised Him, Jesus had revealed himself to me in a tangible material manifestation.

It was a blessing, but I don't talk about it much, even when I am in the pulpit or giving my testimony, simply because I think signs, while they may be real, are not really much to brag about, and they can easily lead to spiritual pride.

Our Lord does these little displays throughout the Bible, and even today, particularly with nonbelievers, as well as with baby Christians who are crying out so that they can comprehend his presence during a time of weak or little faith or no faith at all. Later, as we grow in "faith things," He will mostly withdraw these manifestations, which is why mature, strong-in-the-Lord believers rarely, if ever, experience tangible sensory Jesus encounters. Instead, they readily exercise their faith to apprehend Him, particularly in time of great human need.

The famous Christian spiritual director of the Anglican Church, R. Somerset Ward, in the 1920s, in his long forgotten masterpiece of Christian spirituality, *To Jerusalem*, wrote,

"It is axiomatic that the closer we approach to God, the more it is that we require faith in order to apprehend Him."

This is a profound understanding and is the underpinning of the Christian spiritual life. Jesus knows our hearts even long before we know Him, and once in awhile, when He thinks it is necessary, helpful, and not too ostentatious, He will throw us a bone—a sign, an encounter of some sort—and bridge the gap for our senses between the spiritual and the material. This kind of display is nice when it happens but, like shrouds in Turin or other so-called relics, it is *never* something on which we should base our faith. Our God is a faith God, and faith is the major currency of the kingdom of heaven. He taught us that lesson quite well with Thomas after the resurrection.

Alternatively, as an aside, the Lord has given us a sure-fire scriptural way to experience His presence in a wholly as well as a holy tangible manner. (Please excuse this irresistible double entendre!) It is through regular and faith-filled partaking of the Lord's Supper or Holy Communion. Those Christians who have relegated the Lord's table to nothing more than a memorial ritual rob themselves and/or their flocks of the profundity of this sacrament through which the Lord designed for His children to taste and feel His presence. In so doing, they strip the nourishment out of this spiritual meal designed by the Savior of the world to nourish our spirits until we are with Him again.

But in those early dark nights of my vision, I know what I know what I know, to employ common believer parlance. It did happen, and it was real. The best thing I can say about it is that it drives home to me now the certainty that, even when I thought I was alone, He was with me at all times. He has always been tugging at my sleeve. Ever the "Hound of Heaven," He sought me out even when I did not know Him. I do not long for signs, as I have now the main thing: a saving knowledge of Him. In spiritual affairs, it is thus always wise to remember this maxim: "The main thing is to keep the main thing the main thing." Of course, the main thing is our personal relationship with Jesus.

So as I rode in that limo to the airport so long ago in the dark early morning, I pondered the meaning of this vision but made no sense out of it and pushed it to the back of my mind with all the other stuff. In retrospect, the "eyes of my heart" were still closed at that point in my life, and, understandably, I was blind to spiritual things.

Little did I know that even then, the Hound of Heaven was on the chase, nipping at my heels.

My appointments in Dallas, Fort Worth, and Plano passed uneventfully, and I made the rounds of Waco and Midland and eventually headed for my last meeting near Lubbock, from which I was going to fly home. This was the Bible Belt all right, and as an Ivy-educated, Eastern elitist guy raised in the synagogue who, by then, had virtually no spiritual beliefs, other than a hunch that there was some all-powerful transcendent force driving the universe, I was indeed the proverbial "stranger in a strange land." The people were very nice and welcoming, but I was beginning to understand what Jack Kennedy, that poor lapsed cultural Catholic, meant when he said, "Jackie, we're heading into nut country today."

Even today among so-called Christians, practicing a close personal relationship with the God-Man Jesus Christ of Nazareth is considered nutty. Freakish. Of course, these are Christians in name only. Barack Obama, who keeps protesting that he indeed is a Christian, mocks the Bible Belt Christian when he sums them up them as being solely content in having "their religion and their guns." That is a hate-filled calculus, but it's the best one can expect from "performance Christians."

Of course, Jewish folks as well think real Christian evangelicals are tantamount to lunatics, which probably explains why no one in my family returns my calls anymore. Jesus said that would happen.

To the Jew, He's a stumbling block and to the world He is foolishness. But of course, the Bible says, "Our Lord takes the foolish things of the world [like me] and uses them to confound the [so-called] wise."

I can live with that. I have found that once the world thinks you're a fool, it takes a lot of pressure off you to be amazing and wonderful every day, and then you can really concentrate on Him.

With my meetings behind me and some moderate success at bolstering my failing empire achieved, I stood waiting for my plane in Lubbock airport, contemplating the fact that despite my being able to make the business work, it was all on my shoulders, and my time was running out. My broad shoulders would be gone from the scene in a couple of weeks, and nobody could do it like I could. Fear and anxiety began to set in, and it became a sense of hopelessness. I clung very tenuously to what was left of my life at that moment.

Standing in the airport in Lubbock, Texas, I was trying to get someone on my cell phone, because that had always been the remedy I sought when bad feelings came over me or life began to go sideways. Get on the phone and demon dial, pour my guts out to somebody, and that'll put a balm on it. Unfortunately, I was falling headlong into a dark pit where those former strategies were becoming useless, and I was aware of it. But I literally knew no other way than to save myself.

I was standing by a food court with my cell phone to my ear, absentmindedly looking at the people, and my gaze fixed on a couple of clean-looking young kids, a young man and girl, both probably in their late teens or twenties, probably college kids from Texas Tech. They were fresh-scrubbed and dressed neatly but modestly. I watched them with the phone to my ear as they carried their food trays, chose a table, and sat down. The periphery of the scene is a blur to me now, as it was at that moment, but my recall of what happened next is vivid, in laser-sharp focus, and it changed me deeply and profoundly forever.

I watched them as I still fiddled with my cell phone. Whether there was anyone on the line with me, I cannot recall, but I was transfixed inexplicably by the two kids about twenty feet away. As they sat facing each other across a small cafe table, they arranged their meals and put their trays aside.

Then they did something that I had never seen before in a public restaurant. They reached across the table to each other, clasped their hands securely, and bowed their heads in silent prayer. At that moment, I remembered I was in the "nut country" of which JFK joked. Somewhat taken aback by this raw display of simple everyday spirituality, I was engrossed.

Suddenly, in the next moment, I was struck by a force that I had never experienced, which held me in its powerful but peaceful grip. I was held back against the wall and experienced undulating waves of awe.

I was a lost, broken man, and at that moment, I did not know what it was that they had. I remember this clearly and little else. I remember saying to myself, "I don't know what those two plain kids have, but I know I want what they've got."

I didn't know it at the time, but what they had was the Holy Spirit of God, and its power was holding me motionless against that wall.

It was over in an instant, but my life was not the same after this little private moment I shared anonymously with these two during our brief journey into the realm of eternal life. The marvelous thing is that I know for a fact that these two kids were totally oblivious to me. Even today they know nothing of me or that I even exist. They certainly don't know how deeply and permanently I was changed by their prayer.

What I know now is that God pours out His grace through the silent prayers of faceless believers. Even when believers do not know for whom their prayers are intended, our Lord uses them as vessels to transmit the power of His Holy Spirit to heal, to change, to redeem, and ultimately to save whoever needs this dispensation, wherever in the world they may be, no matter how distant—or as near as a few feet away in that food court.

Looking back, even then I did not know Jesus of Nazareth, but it is clear, again, that He knew me and wanted me for His own. And He used the prayers of two ordinary humble believers to pour out His power to transform even a most lost and broken man. This is the way He works. Like the mighty Niagara—instead of pouring out dissipatively that huge amount of power in one huge waterfall, it is as if that boundless and endless power is poured into a zillion tiny, seemingly insignificant straws or channels and funneled precisely to where it can be used and put to greatest advantage. Nothing is wasted.

In a moment, it was over, and they opened their eyes, smiled sweetly and knowingly at each other, and ate their meal. It wasn't necessary for them to know exactly how the Creator of the universe had just used them to save a suffering and fearful Ivy League-educated Jewish doctor from New York. They knew His loving nature, and they trusted Him to use them as "jars of clay." That is the essence of our faith.

It was another year or so before I became acquainted with Jesus of Nazareth and made the decision to ask Him to take up residence in my heart and take over every aspect of my life. It had to take a while, because standing there in that airport food court in the Bible Belt, I did not know anything about Him. But no doubt, even then, the Hound of Heaven was both drawing near to me and drawing me close to Him. That is the way He works. It is His glorious *modus operandi*.

I boarded my plane and went back to my world of trouble and, to be sure, I experienced great days of sorrow and suffering after that. But since that day, I have never felt alone. But of course, that is not strange because He promises, "I will never leave you nor forsake you."

Supernatural manifestations can be great blessings when our Lord chooses to enhance our lives with them, but in and of themselves, the Lord does not ever mean for them to replace faith as the central spiritual force propelling us to seek His face.

Signs and supernatural manifestations are real and are very nice when they do occur, but they are a very low form of spirituality, as the saints are exhorted to "walk by faith, not by sight" (2 Corinthians 5:7).

The Bible tells us, "It is impossible to please God except by faith" (Hebrews 11:6–8).

Let's be honest: how much faith does it take to walk by sight? How much faith does it take to acknowledge the reality of a cross-shaped white light shining like a flashlight in the darkness of my study at 3:00 a.m., two or three nights in a row? How much faith does it require to know you've been body-slammed up against a wall in an airport food court in Lubbock, Texas, by an unseen external power? Really not that much. It happened. We all are attuned to sensory experiences, unless we're sick or intoxicated, and I was neither. So even now I am not impressed by the level of spirituality that these "theophanies" demonstrate, despite the fact that they are indeed divine manifestations of His grace.

Mature believers need to stand on the Word of God, not primarily divine manifestations, no matter how showy they may be, because they require no faith to believe that they were real. Sometimes when I am in the pulpit, I will take my big, thick, giant-typeface pulpit Bible and drop it on the floor beside me. That serves two purposes: first, it tends to wake the poor sleeping folks because when it hits the platform, it really makes a loud thump. That's real Bible thumpin', brother. But then, after I have their attention, I gingerly step up onto my Bible and stand flat on it.

"I'm standin' on the Bible," I tell them. "I don't care what the doctor's report reads. I'm standin' on the Bible. I don't care what the lawyer or the judge says, 'cause I'm standin' on the Bible. I don't care what the biopsy says, 'cause I'm standin' on the Word."

Try it. It's fun. Worshipping Jesus should be fun, just like a pep rally. If it's not fun worshipping the Lord, then we're missing it.

The risen Lord showed Thomas his nail-scarred hands simply because He knew his disciples' faith was weak. Before that, He stilled the wind and the waves on the Sea of Galilee after being awakened from His well-deserved nap in the back of the boat by His hysterical disciples, who cried in unbelief, "Lord, we perish!"

Saul of Tarsus was a "hard case," so He knocked him off his horse on the road to Damascus, shined a blinding white light, and spoke to him audibly. In each case, Jesus knew they were men of "little faith" who were still not saved but were lost in their sins. But He loved them and did what was needed to draw them close. Also, he had a mission for them, and He needed to "open their eyes."

After they matured in the faith, there was not a single instance recorded in the New Testament of showy supernatural signs and wonders in the lives of these men, with the exception of healings and the Pauline revelations, by which our Lord downloaded to the apostle Paul necessary information as to the Christian life.

My faith, thus, has never been based on that experience in the airport in "nut country," nor on the experience of the visions of the white luminescent cross. In fact, even after I asked Him into my life, for a long time I rather forgot about these supernatural manifestations. It is only relatively recently that these encounters have come back to the forefront of my mind, and I never spoke of them to anyone until I began discipling and preaching the Gospel to others in ministry. Even then, signs and wonders, when they have occurred, needed to be considered carefully in relation to the context in which they occurred. And that is not easy to do in street evangelism, when giving your testimony to a complete stranger in an elevator or even in the pulpit.

In the last few years, I have begun to cherish and understand the power and significance of the prayerfulness exhibited by "my two kids in the Lord" at that airport food court. Particularly when it comes to prayer, I think it is helpful to drive home to all believers the reality that they too can have a unique ministry of their very own, a prayer ministry for the world.

This is a ministry of vital importance for all believers, without ever leaving their seats or their homes or, in the case of nursing home and hospice patients, without their ever leaving their wheelchairs or hospital beds, for we know that God especially honors the prayers of His children who are on a bed of affliction.

"God hath chosen the weak things of the world to confound the mighty" (1 Corinthians 1:27).

Rarely does a opportunity go by that I do not preach the following to my nursing home and hospice congregants, exhorting them to use their restricted circumstances to serve the Lord in joy and victory:

"You hear, O Lord, the prayer of the afflicted" (Psalm 10:17).

These divine promises are great blessings from an extravagant God who is not impressed by worldly wealth, physical beauty, power, social standing, divinity degrees, or seminary certificates. Not a single one of Jesus's disciples was a seminary graduate.

Just as those great young kids in that food court at the airport in Lubbock, Texas, never knew me, the Lord of glory poured out His grace through their anonymous prayers over a lunch of burgers and fries. He used them as empty vessels, conduits, to channel hope into my life, a lost and broken sinner who at that moment in time had not even the faith the size of a mustard seed.

In the same way, any one of us, and most especially the afflicted, can open ourselves to the flow of the spirit of life in Christ Jesus and affect for the better even the lives of sick, suffering, or lost human beings on the other side of the room, across the country, or just as easily on the other side of the planet.

I have been walking into and ministering, in one way or another, in hundreds of hospitals, nursing homes, and hospice units all over the United States for the better part of the last forty years, initially as a physician, later as a financier, and for the last decade as a Christian chaplain, an ambassador for Christ, a role I am most extremely privileged to assume.

I am so versed in nursing homes and hospices by this unique life experience that my nose literally can smell the facility violations hidden in the dark corners. In years past, I was blessed to be ferried about by private jet and a limo that met me on the tarmac. In recent years I have trundled about by public transportation with my JanSport backpack strapped to my back. It is unimportant, because I have always been struck by the fact that in any kind of long-term care facility, such as a skilled nursing facility and most particularly hospice units for the terminally ill, the greatest challenge is hopelessness.

Moreover, this sense of hopelessness permeates not only the residents and patients but the staff and families as well. Thus, it has always been our task to minister to everyone within the four walls by bringing the good news of the gospel of hope.

In the thirteenth chapter of Paul's first letter to the fledgling church at Corinth, he made it clear that we are armed in this mission with three spiritual forces, weaponized to defeat the enemy—faith, hope, and love—and of course he makes it clear that the greatest of all three is love.

I have been blessed to know something personally about hopelessness. I can tell you that hopelessness is not a feeling. It, like its close cousin, fear, is a spiritual force. It is faith operating in the negative. I know how the enemy uses it to hold us in bondage. I think I first learned fear as a young child, during the long evolution of my father's illness, decline, and ultimate horrendous violent death in a VA hospital.

Later, during the darkest, most fearful days of my long imprisonment, I lapsed into hopeless depression. It affects a person's entire constitution, spirit, soul, and body.

It affects our health by altering our sleep and our appetite, as well as our metabolism and energy level. For example, many people experiencing clinical depression, including me, report that their personal hygiene begins to slip, and they cannot even muster the energy to groom themselves.

I suffered greatly from this, and in my darkest days in the pit of hopelessness, there were times when I bathed and brushed my teeth at least once a month, whether I needed it or not. I am not exaggerating about this. I was so emotionally weak that it was too much trouble to even pick up a toothbrush, and if I had not been in prison and told when to get up and when to go to sleep, in all likelihood I would not have gotten out of bed for weeks.

As it was, it was a caring, concerned Corrections Officer, the "regular officer" on our block, who took me aside one day, having quietly observed me from a distance for weeks, and said to me, "Dombroff, are you okay? I wanna see you taking better daily care of yourself. You know what I mean?" I totally knew what he was referencing, and, mortified, I got my act together. Shock treatment, interestingly, still works pretty well in depression.

The long-term care facility and the hospice unit is a form of a prison as well. Though there are no bars or guard towers, no barbed wire, and no walls, they are just as much a prison as the one in the Clinton hub where I served much of my time. Perhaps even more so, because in most instances, nursing homes and hospices are prisons from which there is no parole. For most, their only release is death.

But because of this, I am blessed to be qualified to consistently preach something that I know firsthand to be true. Just as those kids in the airport prayed for me without even knowing it, any prisoner—whether an inmate serving a sentence of conviction for a crime, or a terminally ill patient in a long-term care facility, or a man like me, gripped in fear, facing an uncertain, unpleasant future—can experience the inflowing of the power of the Holy Spirit by engaging every day or all day in his or her own personal prayer ministry.

The apostle Paul knew this when he wrote, "Pray without ceasing" (1 Thessalonians 5:17).

Paul wasn't assigning us a burdensome task or a chore. He was assigning each of us a prayer ministry. He was giving us a real purpose in life, even a life lived in a severely restricted environment. Paul knew this depression first hand as well, having lived much of his life, serving the Lord in prison. Even then, this odd, brilliant Jewish tentmaker managed to write almost half of the New Testament while imprisoned in jails of unimaginable brutality and discouragement.

He knew that through prayer, with the power of the Holy Ghost freely flowing through us and out into a dying world, the world can be changed, and we ourselves can be healed our darkest, most discouraging afflictions. Furthermore, it is the sick and the suffering, as was I for the dark years, who are best suited for this ministry.

For as Paul wrote, "In my weakness, His Power is made perfect" (2 Corinthians 12:9).

So it is a win-win situation. In our darkest hours, through the ministry of intercessory prayer, the world is changed for the better, and we ourselves, in the throes of our misery, discover that there is a purpose for our lives; that there is, despite all outward appearances, indeed something to live for. This applies to a terminally ill patient in a hospice as well as to a broken, defrocked, humiliated ex-physician convict locked away in a state prison.

This Balm of Gilead has not only seen me through years of suffering, but I also have seen it change the lives of other kinds of prisoners. Those in nursing homes and hospice care facilities discover a new and glorious use and purpose to their existence, no matter how brief it proves to be.

So through the lens of time, over the past ten or twelve years, I have been able to gradually discern more clearly the ultimate meaning of the supernatural events that early on led me to Christ. They had little to do with my faith development but much more to do with providing me with a testimony to help others.

For the Bible tells us two very important things:

"Faith cometh by hearing and hearing by the Word of God" (Romans 10:17), and "Now faith is the substance of things unseen, the evidence of things hoped for" (Hebrews 11:1).

Notice how God does not tell us that "faith comes by seeing signs" or "faith comes by feelings."

Moreover, faith is an actual substance; it is the "substance" of things unseen. Thus, my faith does not derive from these "miracles"; it derives from hearing and reading, speaking, and preaching the Gospel of Jesus Christ.

It is really very simple because the power comes not from ourselves but from the Gospel. Moreover, even in those early days, Paul revealed that Christian believers inhabited a first-century "nut country" and were mocked and ridiculed, just as we are today, for they were "a peculiar people," just as we are today:

"I am not ashamed of the Gospel of Christ for it is the Power of God unto salvation" (Romans 1:16).

It is clear to me now that God intended these supernatural manifestations in my life to be teachable moments for me and for others whose paths I would cross in the years to come. Furthermore, He had planned this since before the foundation of the universe, because He knew He had plans for me that far transcended anything that I had ever planned out for myself.

In my brokenness, the Great Physician began to let me know that His ultimate plan for me was not to do facelifts or to broker multimillion-dollar deals or even perform heart surgery. No, there is nothing wrong with those things, but it was not necessarily His plan for my whole life. He had bigger plans for me, and they are summed up in Jesus's words in the Gospel of Luke:

"The Spirit of the Lord is upon me because he hath anointed me to preach the Gospel to the poor; He hath sent me to heal the brokenhearted, to preach deliverance to the captives, and recovering of sight to the blind, to set at liberty that are bruised" (Luke 4:18).

In fact, this is His plan, in one form or another, for all believers—to preach, to heal, to deliver, and to set free from bondage. It is a beautiful calling and far exceeds the magnificence of anything that I have ever done before, and of course, it is for all believers as well, our highest and best use as human beings.

And like our Lord, for He exhorts us to be like Him, after all the darkness and loss of our lives, we too can declare,

"This day, this Scripture has been fulfilled in your hearing" (Luke 4:21).

So indeed we realize that this is His plan for us all; that is, to fulfill the prophecy of Luke 4 in our lives and in our own unique way.

Over time and through His grace, I learned something I never expected during those cold, hard days of my sojourn into "nut country." When we allow Him to execute His plan for our lives and are willing to walk according to His purposes, according to His will, the Hound of Heaven, who pursues us tirelessly and lovingly, will surely "restore the years the locusts ate" (Joel 2:25) in wonderful and miraculous ways for which we could never ask or imagine.

8

Beauty from Ashes
Discovering the
Sacrament of Suffering

> To give unto them beauty for ashes.
> —Isaiah 61:3

AFTER DOING ABOUT FOUR years in prison way upstate, most of it up by Canada in the Clinton hub, the faceless Albany bureaucrats sitting behind computer screens at the central office monolith decided, in their wisdom, that I was ready to be sent to work release, which meant I still was a prisoner in the custody of the commissioner, but I would get to go home—if I had a home. I didn't, until my buddy Marc said, "You're staying with us."

Go to work during the day, sleep at home, and report back a couple of times a week. I had always been recommended for work release by the superintendent of the facility where I was imprisoned, but despite excellent programming and a flawless behavior record, the central office in Albany denied me five times over a two-year period, offering no rationale. The bottom line was that despite my eligibility for early merit release, I wasn't going home until they were good and ready to drop-kick me out. And they would do that when they felt like it.

After four years, I left Franklin Correctional Facility (CF) and took the long bus ride, shackled at the wrists and with my legs shackled to the fellow next to me. The ride seemed to take forever, but I didn't care. I was headed to a minimum security facility in Manhattan, so when I looked out the bus window and saw Yankee Stadium, I knew I was delivered at last. The long nightmare was behind me.

Not exactly.

It was just another chapter in the long journey.

Still, it was amazing. I got my life back. Actually, a new life. I was in the world again, and everything having to do with being "behind the wall" was in the past. It was a great blessing but not an easy program to navigate because I could be pulled back instantly, without doing anything other than looking cross-eyed at someone in authority. They play a Sylvester-and-Tweety game and play with your freedom. Why? As a Corrections counselor once told me, only half jokingly, "Because we can."

Power corrupts, and absolute power ... well, you know the rest.

But I had done pretty well upstate in the thick of it, and I figured I could negotiate work release without a hitch. I just made sure to obey all the rules. Report back on schedule, adhere to curfew, report all my wages so New York State could appropriate 20 percent. No driving, no drinking, no drugs, and so forth.

No problem.

And everything went pretty much fine for the next four years. I became the longest-running act at Lincoln Correctional Facility in Harlem. Lincoln was a dreadful building, about a zillion years old, but I was glad to be there, considering the alternative.

The only other inmates who were there longer than I was had "bodies"—prison-speak for inmates who were serving their sentences for a homicide, from manslaughter to murder. One of them was the chap who had assassinated Malcolm X back in the 1960s. Decent guy. After doing about thirty-plus years upstate, Mario Cuomo gave this guy and a whole bunch of other violent convicts work release.

The program was an amazing success because the vast majority of the formerly violent offenders had been able to transition in society and become productive members of the community. Amazing success.

Then George Pataki came along and ended work release for violent felons and tried to yank back the guys already in the program. Fortunately, the courts interceded and slapped the governor's wrist, ruling, "They stay right where they are." So Pataki had to swallow it, and he and his successors just kind of let work release, an excellent and enlightened alternative to incarceration for nonviolent offenders, just dwindle down to almost nothing

I had a few bumps along the way, but that's "all part of the bid," in prison parlance. In regular English, that translates to "It's all part of serving a sentence."

Corrections is a reverse universe. In most settings in real life, when you do everything right and obey the rules, you are rewarded and then advance to the next level. In the Corrections universe, when you do everything right, you're told, "You've become institutionalized." Then, if you get a disciplinary violation or a misbehavior report, you're adjudged to be "regressing." Talk about double-binds and psychobabble.

This happens all the time. It is literally the land of "no," particularly after Michael Dukakis was accused of letting a dangerous convict, one Willie Horton, out of prison prematurely in Massachusetts about a thousand years ago and lost the presidential election. Parole, work release, and all the other programs that actually helped offenders' recovery and reentry have been shelved or vastly curtailed.

For example, when Mario Cuomo, a thoroughly decent guy and an old-school progressive who loved this country, was governor of New York, there were as many as fourteen thousand inmates in work release at facilities all over New York. That was about one in four New York

State inmates, with a total prisoner population of about sixty thousand. By 2005 after twelve years of George Pataki's unenlightened reactionary policies, the number dropped by more than 90 percent to about one in fifty or about a thousand inmates total. Sadly, this had been one of the most progressive and successful programs from a rehabilitative standpoint. It's been largely scrapped while politicians stand around, scratching their heads and wondering why the United States has the highest incarceration rate on the planet.

The fact is they're effectively phasing out early-release programs and abandoning anything other than a meaningless milquetoast pretense of commitment to rehabilitation. When I first arrived at Lincoln in July 2007, for instance, there were three work-release facilities in New York City. By 2011, just before I got kicked back upstate for more "schooling," they had closed every work-release facility other than Lincoln. So much for enlightened criminal justice theory.

Fully 70 to 80 percent of all the inmates incarcerated upstate are extremely low risk to the community, if they were to live at liberty, particularly if they were released to more intensive, professional community supervision and given real employment assistance. Probably 75 percent of the upstate prison beds could be shut down and more than fifty thousand dollars per year per bed could be put to better use.

That ain't gonna happen, though, because the upstate communities' economies are totally dependent on the prison-industrial complex. The annual budget for the New York State Department of Corrections and Community Supervision (DOCCS) is approximately three billion dollars, and much of this goes to facilities and operations that are located far away from the major metropolitan areas, as the state prisons are almost exclusively located in rural areas. This is for security concerns, to be sure, but even more important, it is a perpetual "Marshall Plan" of economic assistance to depressed communities upstate and in central and western New York.

Because of the reversal in the DOCCS's commitment to work-release programs, there is virtually no real, meaningful employment assistance in work release, other than being handed the Yellow Pages.

I did pretty well in work release for several years and was coming up on my fourth "anniversary." On Friday, July 15, 2011, I was working in my office on Long Island, looking forward to a nice summer weekend and savoring freedom.

At that point I was out of the facility every day and only had to sleep there two nights a week. I was looking forward to going "seven and zero" in a few days. This meant that I would never have to sleep in a correctional facility again and would be allowed to take up full-time residence in my apartment like a normal person, reporting in during the day once a week for about twenty minutes.

During the time I was in work release, I had a perfect employment record, and for several years I was a professor at a local medical college. There were haters at the facility who really could not quite stomach the fact that they were supervising a convicted felon who held such a respectable, prestigious position. But for the most part, there were many really decent Corrections professionals with whom I came into contact over my ten-year imprisonment, and my observation is that they tend to hold the bad apples and the haters in check.

But sometimes the balance of power changes.

My counselor, Ms. Harrison, was a gem, but she was no pushover. The first time she saw me she reamed me out pretty good, drill-sergeant-style for heavens knows what, but over time, she demonstrated that she really cared about helping me getting my life back.

Albany's overall mission was to cut the budget, so next on the chopping block was Lincoln, and when Ms. Harrison was transferred, I knew I was in for rough sledding. In every meat-grinder type of organization, everyone needs a guardian angel, and Ms. Harrison was mine. When she was leaving, I stopped in her office.

"Ms. Harrison, I just came by to say goodbye and to wish you well in your next position," I told her.

She smiled a big grin, and we shook hands.

"I just want to let you know how much you've helped me over the last four years," I said. "I didn't always get the answer from you that maybe at the time I was looking for, but you've been a blessing in my life."

She knew I was trying to do the right thing, and she also knew I was a target of the hater contingent, who resented the success I had in the past and that I was experiencing again. I was the Great White Defendant. Actually, now the Great White Offender.

So on that particularly hot Friday mid-afternoon in July, I had come back into the office, and Marc said to me curiously, "I just got a call from someone at Lincoln. They asked for you. They want you to call them back."

My heart sank, and I got a cold chill. I could not imagine remotely what the problem was, but I knew that there was a serious problem. These people don't call you up on a summer Friday afternoon to wish you a nice weekend. No, this was serious.

Marc told me to relax. "Don't worry so much. You're being paranoid. You're doing everything right. Glowing reports. Just call 'em, and you'll put your mind at ease."

I love Marc. He is totally naive about these things because he's always my biggest booster, and he was effectively my "sponsor" in the community for the entire four years I had been in the work-release program. He too had known Ms. Harrison and had kept in close touch with her over my progress. Unfortunately, she was long gone from the scene at this time.

Marc was my main guy, BFF since childhood, but he didn't know what these people were capable of doing. He was a respected businessman who thought most people were straight-shooters and that you could pretty well spot those who weren't. The thing he never got was that this was a system a normal person could never figure out. At least, I never could.

I was living in a chaotic reverse universe with Corrections. It was a game of cat-and-mouse gotcha, twenty-four/seven. And the situation at Lincoln had grown particularly nasty over the recent months as the population swelled with inmates imported from the other facilities that had been closed, and the staff had shrunk due to budget cuts. Then Albany added new meaning to their budgetary doctrine of "do more with less." For the staff that remained at Lincoln, including the new superintendent, that meant "less inmates."

They were on a mission to kick inmates back upstate in order to balance the population. You can't kick 'em out. Only the parole board could do that, and they were holding on tight to me. So the only alternative was to kick me up north.

For months, every one of my fellow inmates would share with each other how nasty the atmosphere was getting and how we literally dreaded coming back on report days. We all knew that when that gate closed behind us, we could never be sure that we were ever going to see the street again. And a lot didn't, for seemingly trivial missteps.

But kicking an inmate out of work release and shooting him back upstate is a tricky situation, and Corrections had to do it with finesse. Of course, they were experts at making the paperwork look good. Frankly, nobody cares about right or wrong as long as the paperwork is filled out okay.

I was faced with a dilemma: either call back the parole supervisor immediately at Lincoln and deal with it, or tell them on Monday night when I was scheduled to report that I never got the telephone message from Marc.

Little did I know at the time that if I had not returned their call and had avoided them, they would have showed up at my doorstep on

Schoolhouse Lane in fancy Lido Beach, Long Island, with a SWAT team and transported me to a special fugitive unit at Sing Sing. I learned this a few weeks later from other inmates who had been part of the big population-reduction sweep at Lincoln.

As usual, I elected to continue to play it straight, buckled myself in, and called them right back. Besides, as Marc reminded me, I hadn't done a thing off the straight-and-narrow, so what was I worried about anyway? But I was still petrified because I knew this system. It was never, ever a level playing field, despite the fact that for all the years I was in the system, there was never a single time that I hadn't played it straight.

So I dialed the facility with a sinking feeling in my stomach.

"Hi, this is Richard Dombroff," I said to the operator. "Could you please transfer me to the Parole Office?" Parenthetically, the Department of Correctional Services utilized field parole officers to supervise work-release inmates while they were in the community.

"Community Supervision. Mrs. Williams speaking." She was my parole officer. I had had a perfect track record with her. She had met Marc and had come to where I was living every month. She visited me at the college where I had been an assistant professor. I figured so far, so good. She knew I was not a problem, but make no mistake about this: there is no such thing as being "juiced in" in Corrections. The staff is very nice. Until they're not. And then it's as if they never knew you.

"Oh, great, hi, ma'am, this is Richard Dombroff. Someone called my office when I was out for lunch."

By that time it was about three o'clock on a super-hot July afternoon—103 degrees. I was still mystified and apprehensive but trying not to panic.

Then she uttered the words every one of us in the system dreads: "Mr. Dombroff, you need to come back to the facility immediately."

"Well, my report day is not 'til Monday."

She repeated herself. "Mr. Dombroff, you need to come in immediately."

"Can you tell me what the problem is, Mrs. Williams?" I barely got the words out because my worst nightmare was beginning to play out before me.

It's important to understand that there is no meaningful rehabilitative therapy operating in Corrections. The system thrives by perpetuating a consciousness of guilt, which inevitably wears down the soul and views actual redemption as impossible—or at least with cynicism and derision. While I was upstate, some geniuses who thought they knew something about criminology decided that the term "inmate," which has been used universally for hundreds of years without repercussion, was politically incorrect, and the entire department began referring to inmates as "offenders." Nice, huh?

It seems like a small thing, but it's not. It reveals that the entire system is a fixture in a "culture of condemnation." I know something about criminal justice, and I also know something about condemnation and the soul. It makes redemption impossible and leads to recidivism because the condemned individual can never visualize himself as receiving anything other than ongoing condemnation, and he shapes his behavior to not disappoint such low societal expectations.

So by this time, after eleven years of being beat up by this system, I always was fighting a worst-case-scenario consciousness anyway. Indeed, I was living out, at that moment, my worst case scenario. The phone conversation on that hot Friday afternoon was a realization of my worst fears. Somebody once said, "If you always expect the worst to happen, eventually you won't be disappointed because that's the way life is." Eventually, something bad happens. Just ask Job. He spent the first part of his life praying endlessly in doubt and unbelief, always in fear that his crazy kids would curse God. Eventually, his worst fear happened. His is both an inspiring life for us and a cautionary tale about the dangers to believers who walk through life in fear and a sense of condemnation.

"No, Mr. Dombroff, I can't discuss this over the phone. You need to come back to the facility immediately."

I was silent for a moment. My mouth went dry, and I could barely form the words in my mouth. I felt powerless.

"No problem. I'll take the next train. I'll be back by six."

I must have been as white as a sheet. Marc was pretty shaken too because he was listening to my end. I told him what Mrs. Williams had said, and I said this was pretty bad.

This kind of thing never had happened in all the years that I had been there, but it was the realization of rumblings that were going on for months at the facility.

We all agreed that when we went back into the facility, there was a 90 percent chance we were coming back out on schedule to go back home or to work after an hour or so, or the next morning if it was an overnight.

This time, I didn't think it was even fifty/fifty. Something was very wrong, and the worst part was that I had no idea what the issue was. One thing I always knew, however: "It's all part of the bid." No matter how weird things became, it was all part of the bid. So suck it up, put on your big-girl panties, and take it.

I went to the room I was renting in a nice home in Lido Beach, right across the street from Marc, to get some things into my backpack that I wanted with me. My assumption was always that I wasn't coming back, and this time was Code Red, big time.

I always left in my locker at the facility a good supply of texts, Bibles, and devotionals in case I was put on hold and not allowed to go back out. They were constantly putting people on hold for inane administrative reasons and then letting them back out.

It just really served the purpose of terrorizing people and constantly reminding them, "We can yank you back any time we want for no reason at all." Of course, there are statutory due-process regulations, but they never pay any meaningful attention to them. The courts, virtually without exception, tend to rubber-stamp the department's behavior, no matter how egregious, so the net result is to foster a sense of lawlessness on the mentality of the system that says, "We're gonna do anything we want." And they've been doing anything they want for a hundred years. At its most extreme, inmates are beaten to death by staff in the system, and no one is held the least bit responsible, no one is disciplined, no one is charged, and life goes on as usual. So running roughshod over the constitutional-liberty interest of an old, broken-down discredited "offender" like me meant less than nothing to them. And it meant even less to the judiciary. The public couldn't have cared less because as far as they were concerned, all convicts were trash anyway. Nice.

Later on, in my appeal, a justice of the New York State Supreme Court thought differently. But that was after literally years of my being wrongfully imprisoned. Justice prevails, but it is very, very slow.

So this time I loaded into my backpack three or four Bibles and a couple of devotionals that I used every day and did not want to be without. I turned out the lights, closed the doors, and steeled myself for that late-afternoon trip back to Manhattan. My last.

As I walked back across the street to meet Marc, who was driving me to the Long Island Railroad station, I started quietly praying in tongues, my heavenly language, because I couldn't even begin to formulate coherent prayers in English. At the risk of sounding melodramatic, I comprehended at that moment how Jesus felt in the garden of Gethsemane before going to the cross. He knew it was going to be bad; He just didn't know how bad. I felt the same way. I have no proof for this, but something in my gut tells me that our Lord was praying in tongues in the garden that night as well. A human being just cannot formulate words and sentences in times of immobilizing distress, and our Lord was sweating bullets of blood. We know He was all man and all God, not some cosmic superman with a divine cape.

I realize now, although I don't remember being conscious of it at the time, that Jesus was with me at that moment, even as I was befuddled by fear and dread.

As He spoke in the eighth chapter of the Gospel of John:

"I am the light of the world. Whoever follows me will never walk in darkness, but will have the light of life" (John 8:12).

This is the interesting metaphysical aspect of our walk with the Lord. He exists outside of time. Often, we look back at a terribly painful moment of our lives that may last minutes, days, or even years. We are conscious of remembering in a temporal sense, of feeling alone, but when we have made Jesus the Lord of our lives and have asked Him into our hearts, He bridges a space-time continuum for us in our eternal spirits, and even years after the event, we are often able to know His presence with us at the event. It is palpable, and because He is alive inside of us, we are able to bridge the intersection between the material and the spiritual, and chronology, a created thing, becomes meaningless. It is a miracle that all believers experience.

Because we walk by faith and not by sight or feeling, He stands with us, and together we look back at a terrible time. That is where we are able to sense His healing in our souls. That revelation may come even years later, but Christ, who is literally residing in our spirits, knows no time boundaries, and thus we are not bounded by time either.

"With the Lord a day is like a thousand years and a thousand years is like a day" (2 Peter 3:8).

We drove to the railroad station in complete silence, both of us heartsick, and Marc in disbelief. I, however, knew exactly what was transpiring and just how bad things were going to get.

"Marc, I don't think I can deal with getting locked up again, and I've got a real bad feeling about this."

"Richard, you're overreacting. You didn't do anything. All you've been doing is coming to work, ministering at the nursing home, and being in bed by ten," he countered in an exasperated tone.

He had been my most excellent cornerman for eight years as this whole mess played out. He was familiar with this system, but he could be naive about how dark the human heart can be and how nasty systems like this can treat people. I had to keep reminding him that these people were the same ones who carried out human executions by lethal injection because it was part of their job description. This was a different universe from the one in which nice, normal people in the world existed. Interestingly, I had one foot in the system and one foot in the world. That's what made it a blessing but also a terrible challenge at times.

When you're upstate, that's it. You're there, and you hunker down and buckle in for the duration, and you turn your eyes away from the world. When the world impinges on you from time to time, such as when you get a visit, it is a blessing that is intoxicating for a couple of hours, and then, as they leave, the whole thing tears your heart out again. When I would get back to my cell after a visit with Tricia and the kids in the early days, I was so low that I could barely take my face out of my pillow.

We all were issued one small green towel upstate. One fellow, another long-time inmate who looked out for me, used to ask me, "How's Mr. Green today?" He knew periodically, on the darkest days, I would soak my green towel in tears of anguish, particularly in the early years when there was no tunnel, let alone a light at the end of it. Even hardened convicts can be tender and caring to people in need.

The psalmist said it best when he wrote,

"I am weary with my sighing; Every night I make my bed to swim, I dissolve my couch with tears" (Psalm 6:6).

I had been through that trip on many, many days and nights upstate. I'd thought that part of my life was over, but now, I made way back uptown to enter the facility for what turned out to be the last time.

In my journey over the years, I have become intimately acquainted with suffering—but I'm not complaining. When suffering is the result of random misfortune or sickness or even persecution, it is difficult, of course, but when we suffer as a direct result of our own folly or ineptitude, it is even more painful and fracturing.

When we get over blaming everyone else for our reduced circumstances and finally move past the finger-pointing stage, we are confronted with the proverbial "man in the mirror" or, worse yet, the "jerk in the mirror," and we can't stand the sight.

Our pain is intensified because not only are our circumstances painful, but we also are forced to acknowledge that life has somehow bridled us simply because we failed to bridle ourselves. Only after accepting responsibility for our situations, even when we are treated unfairly—and to be sure, there's plenty of persecution in the Christian life—can we begin to move past the paralyzing self-pity and utilize the suffering as a sacrament. This seems counterintuitive; it's not. Christians should never seek suffering of any kind. It's not necessary because life generates more than enough unpleasantness to go around.

But one of the many beautiful and miraculous things about Christian life is that nothing is wasted, not even the ample suffering that life doles out.

As Christians, we are not to seek suffering. The self-mutilation and extreme self-abnegation of various cults in past centuries is absolutely ungodly. It is not part of real Christianity but rather is a perverted, devilish counterfeit. Our Lord made this admonition clear when He said,

"I came so that ye shall have life and have it abundantly" (John 10:10).

Jesus was an ascetic man, but He did not seek suffering. In the garden of Gethsemane on that Thursday night, He knew that suffering and the cross lay ahead, and He passionately asked His Father if there was some other way.

"And He went a little farther and fell on his face and prayed saying O my Father if it be possible let this cup pass from me: nevertheless, not as I will but as thou wilt" (Matthew 26:39).

This poignant human moment experienced by Jesus, the second person of the Trinity, in the flesh, breaks my heart and has, for years now, made me love Him all the more. Moreover, the fact that this "tough guy" God-Man went to the cross totally and completely separated from the Father, without the Holy Spirit, and smashed the gates of hell makes me want to love Him even more.

Pilate got it right when he said, "Behold, the Man" (John 19:5).

And we bow our knee to Him gladly, for we remember His words from the cross as He cried in anguish, dying a criminal's death.

"Eloi, Eloi, lama sabachthani? My God, my God, why hast thou forsaken me?" (Matthew 27:46).

So in my suffering, I made my way back to the facility with the only possessions that I knew I could take with me if I was not to come home again. My books were strapped to my back. I walked up the few steps and was buzzed into Lincoln, leaving the street behind for what turned out to be years.

The officer at the desk swiped my ID card and, as I feared and expected, turned to me and said, "You're on hold. Go sit over there."

Ultimately, they took the money from my pockets and stripped-searched me, shackled me, and, without explanation, led me to the Special Housing Unit, or "the Box," where I spent the next three days in the

100-degree heat, having no idea why this was happening after my consistently excellent performance evaluations.

I was never given a misbehavior report or a disciplinary violation. I was shocked and broken but, in a vague sense, not surprised because I had come to know that this was the only system that I could never figure out. I could master everything else, but this universe kept me guessing and off balance always. Frankly, it's designed very carefully to be that way. These folks have been doing this for over a hundred years, and they've got it refined to an art form.

After a few days of being kept incommunicado in the withering July heat, I was led one morning into a small room off the Box for what passed as a hearing; in actuality, it was nothing of the kind. I would call it a kangaroo court, but it didn't even rise to that level. No due process; no lawyer; no ability to present evidence, call, or examine witnesses; no impartial judge or hearing officer. It was obvious they were on a mission to simply cut the number of inmates at Lincoln, and my number was up.

I know this for a fact, because as I submitted to the New York State Supreme Court in an appellate brief later, my rights were totally trampled. When I finally got back upstate about a week later, I met with my new Corrections counselor, who told me frankly, "We've seen more work-release kickbacks from Lincoln in the last two weeks than in the last twenty years. I don't know what's going on at Lincoln, but there's something that's not right down there."

Although what this very nice woman candidly told me was not consolation, in a strange way it was confirmation that I had not done anything to deserve this. To be sure, they had made some veiled references that they were uneasy with, of all things, my volunteer activities as a member of the Christian Chaplain's Association and other related work. Despite the fact that they knew this outside program had been approved by my former counselor, Ms. Harrison, once they had their minds made up in advance, which is the case in 99 percent of these attacks, they are resistant to any change in the outcome. I knew this going in, from my experience, and I simply had to suck it up.

The next day I got the written decision—a formality, really. A confirmation of what I'd seen in their cold stares: "Removal from the Program."

Game, set, match. Nice knowin' ya. See ya; wouldn't wanna be ya. Sayonara.

For me, that meant another two and a half years back upstate as a prisoner again. There were eligibility dates, of course, for early release, but that is false hope, as we used to call it, 99 percent of the time. When I was called back into Lincoln, it was July 15, 2011. I didn't see Long Island again until August 2013. This was not part of the plan.

In a very real sense, this was the lowest point of my life. Although I never questioned my faith, this setback knocked all the blocks out from under me, and I questioned who, in fact, I was as a human being. Whatever was left of my fleshly strength was gone. "How could I fumble the ball so badly and so lose control of the events of my life?" I asked myself, sitting in the scorchingly hot Box upstairs at Lincoln.

What I really didn't appreciate fully in my grief was that we are never in control of things. I sat in my cell after I received the removal notice and cried silently—deep, broken, sorrowful sobs. The kind I hadn't wept for years. I could not forgive myself, and I felt worthless and weak beyond description. Much more so than in the beginning of my incarceration, just after I was sentenced eight years before. Then, it was all part of a process that I, to some extent, mentally had prepared for. I knew there was a beginning, and I would just have to go with the flow until the end, whenever that might be.

But with this, I'd been home and rebuilding my life in a good way when this came out of the blue, as tragedy often does, whether business reversal, sickness and disease, or some other horrible aspect of life. But this wasn't supposed to happen.

I really started to beat myself up. I recall telling myself, "I have to change," although I didn't know what that meant. I began to hate and condemn myself bitterly. Then, in my heart—and I recall this vividly— the Lord spoke to me and said, "Rock, stop that. Hush that. I made you, and I love you just the way you are. Just give this to Me. Let me fight this battle."

"For you created my inmost being, you knit me together in my mother's womb" (Psalm 139:13 NIV).

"The Lord will fight for you while you keep silent" (Exodus 14:14 NASB).

At that moment, I gained peace and clarity, and I stopped trying to control events. I poured my heart out to Him and lapsed into a deep, restful sleep on my bunk. I was relieved, because I could not fight this battle. I had nothing left. I was finally an empty vessel—just the way He wants us.

In the morning, I was gone. Packed up. History.

For a long time after this, until my ultimate release years later, my soul—that is, my emotions, my thought life, my personality—was broken and weak. But it was as a result of staying close to Him that I learned the meaning of Paul's words, probably from prison as well, that "in our weakness His power is made perfect." I had lost everything, even my personal possessions, which had been put into a basement on the South Shore of Long Island and were totally destroyed by superstorm Sandy in October 2012.

But during this time again behind the wall, I learned to allow the Lord to take me out into deep water. I learned to keep my eyes on Him, lest I begin to sink into the deep, as Peter did when he was walking on water. He took his eyes off the Lord and sank like a stone. Although the suffering never abated very much, I learned again and again that we walk by faith and not by sight. So for Christians, then, it's not about our feelings or our circumstances but wholly about His promises.

God is not the author of disasters in our lives. He does not ever visit sickness and disease on His children to teach them a lesson. That's what His Holy Spirit is for.

But we know that when we walk according to His purposes, He can make all things in our lives, even the evil, synergize to come together for the good of those who love Him. Ultimately, we can gain victory in even the worst circumstances, and, of course, He gets all the glory.

So indeed, in the life spent in Christ, suffering can be a sacrament. There are two ways that Christian suffering can be a blessing, albeit a painful one. First, our earthly suffering allows us the opportunity to emulate our Lord's suffering throughout His life and of course at Calvary.

"That I may know Him, and the Power of His resurrection, and the fellowship of His sufferings" (Philippians 3:10).

While we should never seek suffering, life always cooperates with this end, one way or another. Of course, everyone always wants His resurrection power, but let's be honest; how many of us really want the fellowship of His suffering? No matter; life itself here on earth creates the imperative, whether we want it or not. But in His presence we can put our suffering to noble use.

Second, and perhaps more profoundly, this scripture establishes that we can indeed fellowship with Him through our earthly suffering. Every human need, every sickness and disease, every perverted act, every evil thought was owned by our Lord on the cross at Calvary, and He took our sin upon Him. So in a very real sense, Christian suffering—today, yesterday, and tomorrow—facilitates His perfect, finished work on the cross. This is not simply a metaphysical analysis. It is a reality. A fact. Every single act of suffering we bear fuels His passion. Thus, despite its pain, it is a blessing by which we may be empowered if we submit our lives to the cross.

This defies the so-called wisdom of the world and sets us apart as a "peculiar people." Given the amount of suffering that is shed abroad in the world, it may be one of the most profound concepts in all of Christendom.

We would do well to remember that our Lord, the Man of Sorrows, won the great victory of all time and space on that little hillock on the outskirts of Jerusalem. Here's the best part: we don't have to do it ourselves anymore because He did it all.

By bringing our heartbreak, our failings, our setbacks to the cross; by lifting up our sorrows as a sacrifice to the Man of Sorrows who made the one-time all-sufficient sacrifice for us; and by joining our suffering circumstances to His suffering by the power of His shed blood, we too, in a very literal way, can live life in joy. His joy. We can appropriate His victory on the cross as our triumph over tragedy as well. Then our lives in Christ truly become a great adventure. We can lift up our sorrows and make them a sacramental sacrifice to Him, simply because He wants them. The songwriter Michael Card speaks of it as lifting up our sorrows and shame and offering as a sacrifice to our Lord. Worshipping Him with our wounds because He's wounded too.

It is a miracle—I tell you from personal knowledge—that is available to every believer. As we know, "Weeping may endure for a night, but Joy cometh in the morning" (Psalm 30:5).

Because of His love, after a very long, dark night of the soul, against all odds, I am in the morning of my life.

Truly, it is beauty from ashes.

9

COMING HOME

THE TEN YEARS OF being an all-expenses-paid guest of the state of New York was over when I awoke at 6:00 a.m. on Friday, August 28, 2013, virtually ten years to the day from when I had started on this journey. I crammed the few remaining things I hadn't given away into a transparent vinyl bag that I had stored under my bunk for years in anticipation for just this day

In prison, for security purpose, lots of things have to be in transparent plastic, like radios and headphones, storage bags, and, in certain facilities, televisions (where they were allowed in cells at all). It made it easier for the officers to search for contraband like weapons or drugs when they "tossed" your cell, which they did on a routine basis. People hide contraband—drugs, blades, whatever—in places where the cops won't easily find them when they are tossing a cell or a cube, which is a cell without bars. These searches are the most stressful part of prison life for many reasons. Even when you know you've hidden nothing purposefully, there are still things to worry about.

Most dangerous is the possibility that someone has planted a shank, or a homemade weapon, in your personal property, under your bunk, or under your locker, simply to create problems for you. I was searched relentlessly because cops knew that straight-shooters like me often were used by inmates to store drugs or other contraband for others because they thought I would not be a likely suspect. Generally, they were correct in this assumption, but over a decade, there were plenty of cops who were contrarian enough in their thinking to make me a target.

Searches ruin your whole day. They can occur literally any time during a twenty-four-hour period, but mostly they occur early in the morning, just after chow. Suddenly, a team of ten or twenty officers come plowing onto the block, put everyone up against a wall, search your person, and then put you in a holding area with everyone else while the cells or cubes are searched. Everything you have neatly and meticulously stowed away is gone through, examined, and then tossed onto your mattress in a big messy pile.

As I said, it really ruins your day. Thus, the need for transparent plastic things like radios, tape players, headphones, and so forth.

But today, that was all behind me. No more being roused from sleep to have everything I own thrown into a big pile on my bunk.

All I was taking with me was pretty much everything I owned in the world, as everything I had left behind was gone. I mean, literally everything was lost in superstorm Sandy in October the year before. So talking about starting with a clean slate, this was about as fresh a start as anything.

Zero, except the clothes I was wearing; my cheap, clear-plastic, obsolete Walkman; and a few books. I also brought my fourteen-dollar headphones, which were actually pretty good. (I use them to this day, years later.) It's considered by some old-timers to be bad luck to bring any possessions with you that you had in prison, but as a Christian, I don't believe in luck. Frankly, I thought the headphones were just fine for me.

I left tons of books behind for others and actually donated a favorite set of twenty-one Patrick O'Brian novels, the Aubrey Maturin Series, to the facility library. They were paperbacks, and I've been making a little project of reaccumulating them from Amazon. Plus, I knew thousands of inmates coming in after me would enjoy them over the years, so I felt it was a good investment and was pretty good "seed" to plant going forward. Christian radio, NPR, my Bibles, my devotional books, and the O'Brian series pretty much kept me sane for ten years, and I can truly say that I was never bored.

I walked with two other inmates who were also being released that morning, and we were led by an officer through the big prison yard along the running track, where I had jogged thousands of miles to dull the pain over the years, to the visiting room, which was connected to the gate, and beyond that, to the outside. Now the residue of that pain seemed to be concentrated solely in my right knee, which effectively ended my brief career as a runner.

Today, the pain of the ordeal is pretty much a fading memory. I take care of the pain in my right knee with 800 milligrams of Advil.

I changed into regular clothes that my son, Richard Jr., had sent in for me and felt odd in real threads for the first time in years. The fabric felt strange against my skin.

To say it was surreal is not doing the term justice.

It's a funny but sort of cruel thing that happens to your mind when you've been locked away for years. Although you have a definite, bulletproof, specific release date marked on the calendar, in your mind, and eventually on your release papers, you labor under the delusion that your release is not real; it's never going to come, and even if it does, something's going to happen. They are never gonna let you go home. I suffered greatly for years under this FEAR, an acronym for False Expectations Appearing Real.

It's a consequence of a broken heart. Fear can become a free-floating long-term side effect if you don't address it. It can ruin your life.

Prisoners talk a lot about going home, but that's a very imprecise word, as many prisoners have no home to go to. I was one of them.

Is that being homeless? Sure, it is, but we prefer to call it "undomiciled." My release plan instructed me to report to the Department of Social

Services in Nassau County, where I was being paroled to, but when I finished the eight-hour bus ride from Watertown to the Port Authority Terminal in New York City and then the train ride to Long Island, it was already late in the evening on the Friday night before the Labor Day weekend . The Social Services offices in Hempstead, of course, was long closed, but at about nine o'clock, I got the social worker on call to call me back on the cheap throwaway cell phone I had purchased while waiting between buses.

"Don't you have somewhere to go?" she inquired, incredulous that she was being bothered at this hour. "Don't you have anyone you can call and stay with? Family … friends?"

"No, ma'am. I was released from prison this morning after ten years, and I've been on buses and trains for more than twelve hours. I have no family or friends to go to. They told me to report to you when I got back. Now, I'm understanding that you're closed until Tuesday morning."

I wasn't mad or anything. Frankly, I was ebullient at being free and was kind of amused at the whole situation. Typical government boondoggle.

For years, every single movement and activity of mine was prescribed, observed, and regulated. When to sleep, when to eat, when to go to work in the mess hall or scrubbing toilets, when to stop and come back to the dorm, when to shower, and when to use the phone. No detail of my life went unnoticed. Then, by virtue of a certain day on the calendar, they drop-kicked me back into the world to fend for myself. And this was after months of so-called "discharge planning."

The nice lady from DSS told me there was a men's shelter where I could sleep that night in Roosevelt, a largely depressed area in Nassau County. Sounded sketchy to me, and I was wary of what I would find. I was accustomed to state prisons, which are meticulously clean and orderly—you could literally eat off the floors. Secure and almost sterile. But I suspected the shelter was going to be different.

But having no family that I could turn to and no friends who were near, I had little choice. I headed over to the address she gave me as the hot night deepened its intensity.

The taxi from the Hempstead station let me off in front of a dreary, ramshackle single-family home in Roosevelt on Front Street. I was sweating profusely, even in the darkness of the late-August heat, as I heaved my shoulder bag over my back and rang the bell a few times.

Walking in, it felt about ninety degrees, and some black fellows were sitting in the dark, staring semi consciously at a flat screen. I had noticed a shiny new Mercedes outside the house at the curb, and I asked, "Nice car outside. Whose is it?" I was not thinking for a moment that it was any one of the residents. But I was starting to get a nasty vibe about the place. I knew from the moment I walked in that I wasn't staying, but I didn't want to cause a commotion by being impolite. I was on parole, after all, and I didn't need any police contact my first night back. Or ever again, for that matter.

"Oh, that car belongs to the lady who owns this place." That figured.

"Is she here?" I asked.

"Yeah, she in da office," answered one of the residents, without lifting his eyes from the television screen he was peering at in the dark.

As I was waiting for Mrs. Mercedes Slumlord, I walked into the dining area and saw the longest line of huge insects—thick black lines marching up the walls of the kitchen in all directions. I called the nice DSS lady and told her politely that this place was unfit for human habitation and that I was leaving to go to a motel.

She answered, "Do whatever you want. This is one of the better places we have. See you Tuesday morning. Oh, by the way, don't call this number anymore."

"Yes, ma'am. Have a good night. Thanks for your help."

Very sweet, I thought, but nothing could ruin the good mood I was in, so I called a cab and went over to the Yankee Clipper, a motel nearby in Freeport near the water, which the driver said was nearest. Decent place, especially from where I had come. It looked like a palace in comparison, and for the first time in years, I slept in a real bed with real linens and not on a thin, two-inch pad on top of the welded iron pallet that the state calls a bunk bed.

It was about midnight when I pulled down the typical motel bed cover to reveal the clean white sheets, nicely tucked in, as chambermaids customarily do. I slid my legs in against the cool, crisp linens, listened to the hum of the room air conditioner, and lay in the utter darkness and quiet for the first time in years.

There is one experience that is universal for virtually every prisoner that normal people on the outside rarely hear. There is never real darkness in prison. A light is always on in one manner or another. When the big, bright fluorescents go out at 11:00 p.m., the officer turns on bright halogen "night lights" that illuminate the dorm for security purposes, so you're never in real darkness unless you cover your eyes with homemade eyeshades, which prisoners fashion out of sweat socks or old underwear. My personal choice was just to tie a long black sock around my head. But it's not like experiencing the joy of sleeping in a dark room. In that motel, the first night back in the world, I was savoring the darkness for a few moments. I began to feel vaguely uncomfortable, not used to being in extreme darkness, and I turned on the bathroom light.

To this day, I sleep with a light on in my room.

The brutality of being in a human cage is mostly subtle and subthreshold torture, taking place over very long periods of time and not the kind that makes for good TV or movies.

I experienced panic attacks once or twice in my life, primarily as a very young man, and I've noticed that it seems to run in the males in my family, as both my sons experienced them for a while in their late teens. Like me, they mostly outgrew them. In all the years away, I was blessed to never go through a panic attack behind the wall, although once or twice I was on the cusp of one.

But that first night in the utter cool and quiet darkness, I felt one just about to come on, and automatically, I rose, switched on the light in the bathroom, turned the television back on to heaven knows what, lowered the volume, and fell fast asleep thinking about Jesus. He was my Savior, and I ran to Him.

I remember thinking, *All in good time. It'll all fall into place. Don't expect too much too soon.*

Upon reflection, I began to understand why so many fellows released from prison lapse quickly back into alcohol and drug addiction, bad behaviors, and ultimately into criminal thinking. Recidivism runs high. Yes, my brothers in chains were largely tough guys, but the human organism can only take so much pain, and beyond that point, something's gotta give. And it usually does. I still am impressed by how many of my "brothers"—often decent gentlemen with difficult and hard life experiences, with limited personal resources and adaptive skills—are actually able to reintegrate into society as well as they do.

Often, they can't. Four billion dollars a year is devoted to the prison-industrial complex in the state of New York, yet so little meaningful effort, attention, or funding is directed to reentry. A lot of lip service goes down, as well as meaningless bureaucratic paper-shuffling, but very little substantive resources are devoted to taking care of humans at perhaps their loneliest and most vulnerable time: coming home. Most sadly, aftercare is virtually nonexistent.

Well, in the morning light, I took my first shower without underwear on; in prison, it is *de rigueur* to shower in boxer trunks only—never, ever totally naked. I packed up and left, headed for the Full Gospel Church in my hometown of Island Park. Maybe they could help me. Either way, it was important to me to actually make it back to my hometown, a dream I had envisioned for years.

I had many friends there—good Christian people, a great pastor, and people who cared about me. My best friend, Marc, who had backed me up for years, had contacted them several times to let them know that I was being released at the end of August, but we never heard anything, other than how they were faring from the water damage after Sandy a year before, how nice the new granite countertops in the church kitchen looked, the color of the new carpeting installed after the flood, and how they had to replace the beautiful hardwood pews with padded upholstered seats.

I knew they had a lot on their plate.

Undaunted, bright and early on "morning one," I took the bus to Island Park to check into the Long Beach Motor Inn, only to find it shuttered, now nearly a full year after the flood.

Surprised and somewhat disconcerted because this was not an area rife with quality hospitality establishments, to say the least, I was beginning to feel adrift but headed over to the Plantation Motor Inn, a total welfare dive I had passed for years while thinking, *When are they gonna tear down that dump?*

Well, that dump was where I set up base camp and then trooped over to the church, which was just down the block.

"Hi," I said to Lourdes, the church secretary, who was busy working in the office upstairs. "Remember me?"

Lourdes looked up and was puzzled for a moment, searching her mind. Then she recognized my face and jumped up and gave me a big hug.

"Where have you been?" she exclaimed.

I wasn't sure whether she was just being polite and really knew that I had disappeared into the gulag of state prisons up in the north country of upstate New York, or if she actually had not been clued into the inevitable gossip that swirled around church congregations. But it was nice to know I was missed. She was genuine and sweet .

"I just got home from upstate," I said sheepishly, without getting into the whole nine yards of the past ten years.

We exchanged pleasantries, and I got the lowdown on how the church was consumed by the flood of superstorm Sandy. She told me Pastor Pete was not in.

At that point, I explained that I had no place to live, was staying just down the block at the roach motel, and quizzed her on any way they could help me. She drew a blank but reassured me that she would talk with Pastor and the others, and they would come up with something. Immediately upon hearing that, I felt encouraged.

We chatted a bit more and then she recommended that I go downstairs to talk with the representative from Rev. Franklin Graham's multimillion-dollar international disaster relief organization, Samaritan's Purse, which had used the church as a regional staging area from which their staff could coordinate the recovery from the Sandy's destruction, including assisting the local residents who had been left homeless by the worst storm in more than a century. I had heard that Sandy had cut a huge swath of destruction in low-lying coastal areas of New York, New Jersey, and especially the South Shore of Long Island.

"Well, that sounds promising," I told her hopefully, and I trotted joyfully downstairs to Samaritan's Purse.

I knocked on the door of what I remembered was the church library before I was sent back upstate. A young blonde woman looked up from her desk and, smiling, waved me in.

"Hi, my name is Richard, and I'm a member of the church. I've been away for a few years and came back to town yesterday. Uh, actually I was just released from prison yesterday, and I lost all my possessions in

Sandy. Bottom line is … uh … I've got no place to live, and I need your help. Uh … don't worry. I'm not a sex offender or anything … just a white collar … ya know, like millions-of-dollars type stuff."

"Congratulations," she exclaimed in a charming Southern drawl. "It must be nice to be home."

I smiled. "Well, it is, but it would sure be nice if I had a home. I guess you could say I'm kinda homeless. Could you guys help me in some way?"

"We'd love to, but … er … we just provide building and construction assistance to disaster-relief victims."

I swallowed hard and was crestfallen. I turned my head, disappointed. "It's okay. I understand," I said.

I shook her hand and blessed her and asked her if she could call me if she heard of anything that came up. She said that she surely would.

By the end of the day, I had called the Red Cross, the Salvation Army, a few pastors I knew, and some friends. The next day was Sunday, so I mentioned my plight to ten or twenty folks after the service who had known me from the old days. I figured for sure that in a congregation of 1,500 families or so, somebody had a cot in a garage or attic.

Always the same thing. Some said they'd put the word out. They all told me, "No worries; we'll find something"—or trite, meaningless variations of that.

I never heard a single thing more from anyone. And I didn't have the heart to ask again. I guess I understood how they felt, not wanting to get involved in something so sketchy. I told everyone how nice the new carpeting was, how beautiful the rich chestnut granite countertops looked in the new church kitchen, and how much more comfortable the new upholstered chairs were in place of the hardwood pews. Everyone was so excited about the renovations after the terrible flood, and they all looked forward to the dedication ceremony that would be held the following week. Big, exciting anticipation.

Wallowing in ridiculous self-pity, chapped about it, and soured, I heaved up my bag of possessions and trudged back to the Plantation Motor Inn. It was the prototypical roach motel that was the eyesore of the entire village, but at least there was room at the inn for those early nights, and it was better than the animal trough where the Savior of the world had slept in His first night.

It was the best I could do at that moment after so many years away, and I smiled reflexively as I lay down in the cool room decorated in odd oranges and browns.

I switched on my radio that I'd brought from prison and tuned it to the Christian music from which I had received so much solace for ten or twenty thousand hours over the past years. Matthew West was singing yet again about forgiveness.

Stupidly, I was feeling resentful and angry. I wasn't in the mood to hear it. But before the pity party started, strangely, as if I was hearing it for the very first time, poisonous self-love began to lose its grip on me, and the Lord spoke into my heart through the words of the song. I was reminded that forgiveness was free, but it was the hardest thing to give away. It always goes to those who don't deserve. Like me, of course.

A couple of lines from Matthew West's song *Forgiveness* floated through my mind:

> *So let it go and be amazed*
> *By what you see through eyes of Grace*
> *The prisoner that it really frees is you.*

And God spoke to me in my heart the word of knowledge.

"Forgiveness isn't a feeling or a thing, Rock. He's a person."

I remembered His Son's words that I had hidden in my heart.

"I make all things new" (Revelation 21:5).

That night, I learned a lesson about forgiveness. The divine forgiveness He had given to me, I could shed abroad to others. Moreover, I could forgive myself.

I knew that night that it was the only way I would be able to put the shattered pieces of a curious life back together and go forward. That night, I apprehended in a new way what the old-time Quakers called "peace at the center."

Even alone in that bare, sleazy, hot-sheet, welfare motel, I was no longer a prisoner, and I knew I would be able to put the past where it belonged.

I drifted off to sound sleep, His word lodged deep and dissolving into my bitter root, healing my brokenness and finally knowing.

Knowing that my release was real. It was over. I was indeed home.

10

....

THE GREAT PHYSICIAN, PART 1

TO FULLY COMPREHEND THE spiritual foundation of Christ-centered healing, it is vital to establish for yourself two controversial assertions c as givens:

1. It is always God's will for us to be healed.
2. God's will is rarely done on earth.

If you doubt number one, simply look deeply into the scriptures, or better yet, perform a Google search on "healing scriptures." Remember that God does not lie, and you will be encouragingly convinced.

If you doubt the second assertion, simply scan the news on TV or, old-economy as it may be, pick up a newspaper, and you will be convinced quickly. Depressed, yes, but deeply convinced, nevertheless.

So endeth the lesson.

There is in the entry foyer of the old Johns Hopkins Hospital on East Broadway in East Baltimore a huge, towering statue of Jesus Christ of Nazareth, executed in flawless, white Carrara marble. I passed it every morning for five years on my way to class or to the wards, as have generations of young medical students and physicians, as well as untold thousands of the sick and suffering who travel from all over the world to come to "mecca," the popular nickname for the Johns Hopkins Hospital, known the world over.

For young students, it is a prototypical Hopkins rite of passage. In my memory, this quite extraordinary statue, standing under the equally quite extraordinary Queen Anne-style dome of the old hospital building, towered thirty feet high. I have since researched it and found that the Great Physician stands ten and a half feet high.

Like other Hopkins people, including men like Doctors Osler, Halsted, Kelly, and Welch—the original Hopkins "Big Four"—I touched His toe as I passed Him, but, having been raised in the synagogue, I never actually understood why He was placed there. Of course, I did not know Jesus personally until almost four decades later, so, like the pagan world, I treated him as a touchstone instead of the cornerstone in my life that He came to be. Quaintly curious, at best.

Interestingly, most "Baltimoron" secularists at the time of its placement, in 1896, felt similarly disaffected or worse. Today, it would be terribly politically incorrect. It would never happen in a secular institution, and this is a sad commentary on our "politically correct" secular humanist society.

The wealthy Baltimore merchant and trader Johns Hopkins, a philanthropic visionary who founded the hospital and medical school, was a Christian. Hopkins is a secular institution and always has been. The world has changed radically for the worse over the past one hundred years, with respect to God in the marketplace. But Mr. Hopkins, the old Quaker, got it right. As Christians, we're not too crazy about statues either. Too "Romish," as the Anglicans say. We tolerate the occasional religious sculpture but feel that if you absolutely must build them, then make them of Jesus, and leave it at that.

That stuff is just way too reminiscent of pagan idol worship, and that's a slippery slope we don't want to approach. As evangelical fundamentalists, we "worship in spirit and in truth."

"God is a Spirit and they who worship Him must worship Him in spirit and in truth" (John 4:24).

There is a very humorous true-life anecdote about the actual name, Johns Hopkins, which through the years is commonly mispronounced, leaving off the unusual but mandatory "s" in the founder's first name.

It seems that the president of the Johns Hopkins University in the late 1960s, Milton Eisenhower, the brilliant brother of Dwight, was being introduced one evening to a large banquet gathering at the University of Pittsburgh. The president of the host university introduced President Milton Eisenhower as the esteemed president of the "John" Hopkins University, and he left off the S of the founder's first name over and over again throughout the long and flowery introduction. It got embarrassing, according to Eisenhower.

Having heard enough, when it was Eisenhower's turn to speak, he graciously thanked his host, politely corrected his host's repeated mispronunciation, and then turned to his rapt audience, saying, "Well, it is certainly a privilege to be here in 'Pittburgh' this evening." Obviously, this priceless impromptu witticism turned the tables on the "Pittburgh" official, and Ike's brainy brother brought the proverbial house down.

Hopkins in the 1970's was a paradigm of old-school Southern graciousness, far more than any of the most prestigious medical centers in New York City where I later trained.

Crossing East Broadway and watching the horse-drawn fruit wagons go by in the Baltimore of an earlier age, as a medical student for five years in both the basic science years and then my clinical clerkships, I was greeted by the wonderfully gracious white-gloved doorman, an African American gentleman who stood as a genteel sentry, a watchman on the wall of sorts, guarding the Broadway entry to the hospital dome, under which the statue of the Great Physician stood.

This was a long time ago, but the memories are still warm. I might add that Baltimore of the 1970s was not more than a decade from Jim Crow, segregated train stations and lunch counters, and the rest of that whole stinking mess.

Whenever I think of that statue, I always remember this kind and elegant gentleman who made everyone who crossed that august threshold feel welcome and special. I must admit that my fellow students and the teachers that I trained under were indeed special people. The best of the best. Top guns, everyone of them. The 1970's was not a particularly genteel time in America, but Baltimore was still lost in time, and the whole thing was a beautiful "set piece" of genteel, uncompromising excellence that I have never experienced anywhere else.

Having fallen in love with Jesus since then, something that is rather unthinkable for a nice Jewish boy from the South Shore of Long Island, I absolutely adore the fact that the Great Physician stands right there today, in this era of political correctness and inclusiveness, smack dab inside the entrance to the greatest, most revered medical and scientific institution on the planet.

But of course Jesus has always been for the whole world, and He always seems to show up in the most unlikely places.

He stands there today, a hundred years later, silent as the stone from which he was perfectly sculpted. Quaint and curious, even now. With outstretched arms, loving the sick, the suffering, and the fearful who pass through its doors, as well as the men and women who study and toil to heal the sick. He loves even those who don't know Him or, at worst, even those who despise Him, as most of us did before we ran out of options, woke up from our long, dark dream state, and asked Him to take over our lives and be our Lord and Savior.

But that's His nature because His essence is love, and Love, Himself, lives inside of us.

Wow, how could the world not want some of that?

Interestingly, in looking back, this is just one of the many ways that I see that the great "Hound of Heaven" was tugging at my sleeve, even as I fled from Him.

I fled Him, down the nights and down the days;
I fled Him, down the arches of the years;
I fled Him, down the labyrinthine ways
Of my own mind; and in the midst of tears
                                    —Francis Thompson
          excerpted from "The Hound of Heaven," 1893

Despite the bitter and humiliating trials and tribulations I have endured, I have spent the better part of my professional life as a surgeon. At least the better part until I entered the ministry as a hospice chaplain, ministering the Gospel of Jesus Christ to the sick, suffering, and twisted. Even though the surgical life is now a train that has left the station, it was definitely the better part, compared with the things I've needed to do to pay the rent since I fumbled the ball so early on out of selfish aims.

But nothing is wasted in the Christian life. As a Hopkins graduate, a published surgical researcher, and a fully trained reconstructive surgeon, I am blessed to know something about the art and science of healing. For years, my operating room was frequented by visiting medical pilgrims from all over the world who came to see and watch and learn from someone who many thought was uncommonly good at what he did.

For a time, I was, for better or for worse, perhaps the most prominent plastic surgeon in the world. At least editors and producers at places like *Newsweek* and the *Today* show, as well as people such as Regis and Kathie Lee, Bryant Gumbel, Danny Thomas, and Bob Hope thought so, as well as thousands of other happy people.

Interestingly, so did the US intelligence community, who asked me to help them out with refugee Afghan freedom fighters who had been tortured by Soviet interrogators. It seems as if the Soviets, in the early 1980s, had a penchant for forms of enhanced interrogations involving jumper cables hooked to military truck batteries. Genitals were involved, and scarring required many reconstructive procedures, skin grafts, and so forth.

No charge.

I'm sorry that this doesn't fit the narratives of the many detractors out there who want to rewrite history, but these are facts. Despite everything else, they're stuck with the facts. Truth has a way of not always fitting a preconceived prosecutor's narrative. The bottom line is that over the course of time, (1) I did a few things; (2) I crashed and burned; and (3) I then gave my life to the prototypical Man of Sorrows:

Jesus, who took His share of body blows, admonished us not to be people-pleasers:

"Woe unto you when all men speak well of you for so did their fathers to the false prophets" (Luke 6:26).

Because of the arcane twists and turns my life has taken, I have been blessed to be armed with a unique world-class education and training, resulting in an intimate knowledge of the human organism. Ironically, I have also been blessed by prison confinement, as it has permitted me to devote the better part of the last twelve years to a monastery-like lifestyle, permitting intensive around-the-clock, seven-days-a-week immersion in the Word of God.

Literally tens of thousands of hours of my life have been devoted to analyzing and absorbing the writings of the finest thinkers, teachers, Bible expositors, and preachers in Christendom. As a prisoner, I could have spent ten years in the gym, the weight shack, or playing poker, but like the Magdalene, I was blessed to develop a thirst for Jesus, the Word of God. Unlike chocolate cake, ice cream, lusts of the flesh, and all the other amusements of the created world, the Word is something that you never get filled up on. Sitting on the couch in the house of Mary and Martha, the Savior of the world gently rebuked Martha, whom He dearly loved.

"But one thing is needful, and Mary hath chosen the good part" (Luke 10:42).,

There are many prisoners in many cells around the world. There are also many physicians as well. There are exceedingly few prisoners, I think it safe to say, who are medical scientific experts with a world-class education spanning nearly twenty years, resulting in a theoretical and working knowledge of human biology, biochemistry, physical chemistry, quantum physics, calculus, and other studies, who have had the blessed opportunity to combine this with total decade-long immersion in the Gospel of Jesus Christ. It is, by any analysis, a very uncommon blend.

One medical doctor I think about a lot is the exceptional Dr. Francis Collins, the chief of the National Institutes of Health, who is also an evangelical Christian and a brilliant medical scientist. It was Dr. Collins who oversaw the mapping of the entire human genome.

I have conducted and authored groundbreaking cardiac surgical research that has saved millions of human lives, but I do not put myself in Collins's league as a career scientist. As Christians, I assume we both love the Lord. We have similar academic pedigrees. I must be candid when I say that when I regard a guy like Francis Collins, admiration as well as waves of regret overwhelm me sometimes because I am inundated with the self-consciousness of what could have been in my own life, had I done things differently.

Of course, I look at guys like Billy Graham the same way. They are monumental human figures, but in the mind of Christ, so is every believer. My life experiences are certainly not their life experiences, but neither do they have the unique life experiences that have shaped me and brought me to this moment and opportunity to glorify the Lord, in a way that is unique to how God handcrafted me, according to His plan for me, which He conceived before the foundation of the universe.

However, without the totality of all the circumstances of my life, even the intensely painful ones, I would not be the person I am today in Christ. After so many twists and turns, I believe that God has me positioned precisely where He wants me. That is, in His service. Of course, He had to chase me around for decades, tugging at my sleeve while I was totally oblivious to Him. Once I managed to push the envelope so far that I wound up behind bars, it was obvious to even me that the Lord had me now just where He needed me—painted into a real hot corner where I could no longer depend on anything else. I discovered there that when Jesus is all you have, Jesus is all you need.

It is interesting to note that the Bible is filled with highly flawed men and women who have had deeply checkered pasts, who God has especially selected to use in mighty ways.

Rahab the harlot helped save the Jewish nation. Abraham, the "heel," constantly told cowardly lies about his wife being his sister to save his skin. Jacob, the "schemer," defrauded both his father and his brother Esau shamelessly. Noah, at his pinnacle of greatness, got sloshed on cheap wine and ran around the tent, flaunting his nakedness. There are many, many more examples. Joseph, the big-mouth, show-off dreamer, was raised in a desert and served in a palace. Moses, the murderer, was raised in a palace and served in a desert. Instead of standing trial for manslaughter, he fled to the backside of the desert, where he spent the next forty years up to his ears in sheep poop. Compared to these folks, I'm shootin' par.

The Bible has to be true. You couldn't make this stuff up!

The point is that to the world, this combination of top-flight science education and fundamentalist believer—or rather, Jesus Freak—just doesn't compute. They just can't comprehend how anybody with a brain can believe all this Jesus stuff. "Isn't it all a fairy tale?" they ask, or worse, they tell you to keep this religious stuff to yourself and make believe you don't exist. The thing they don't understand is that I didn't choose God first. He chose me. For that, I am forever thankful.

It is not an accident that I have been led on this path. It is a divine appointment. In the life of a Christian, there are no accidents or coincidences, although even those of us who love the Lord can, at times, lapse back into ruinous self-love, work our way out of His will and purpose, and fight Him tooth and nail. When we get out of His will and drift into that "sin bin," that's where all the accidents of sickness, disease, loss, and heartache come falling down on our heads.

"The Law of the Spirit of Life in Christ Jesus hath made me free from the Law of Sin and Death" (Romans 8:2).

A great, contemporary Christian teacher with an active prison ministry has asserted his belief that many—perhaps a majority of—strong-in-the-Lord Christian men and women in prison have a calling on their lives, from the beginning, to the ministry, which is why they have been particular targets of the enemy, who seeks to take them out through demonic attacks. I cannot prove this, as it would be a hard study to do, but I do believe it to be so and have plenty of anecdotal evidence and personal experience to support this thesis.

At least I know that this has been His calling in my life, and although I do not believe that God is the author of sickness, disease, addiction, strife, or chaos in our lives, if we yield to His will for us, He will synergize every experience in our earthly existence for good, even the terribly nasty times.

Paul articulated this in his epistle to the fledgling first-century church at Rome, just a few decades after the Crucifixion.

"And we know that all things work together for the good of those who love God, those who are called according to His purpose" (Romans 8:28).

There is a well-worn aphorism I have heard and heeded many times throughout my journey, applicable to everyone but custom-tailored for those who are looking at long imprisonment: "You do the time, or the time will do you."

From the time I went behind the wall, I was faced with this imperative. I am thankful I was never interested in crossword puzzles or Sudoku, but realized early on, in my brokenness, that I was blessed to be armed with a lifetime of worldly knowledge that, in all likelihood, I would never be able to use again. I was greatly pained by this, seeing it as waste, and out of utter desperation I sought a Savior who "makes all things new."

I turn my attention now to the things for which I am best-suited by the gifts with which the Lord has blessed me, as well as the "burden" He has put on my heart. To be sure, it is His burden.

"Come unto me, all ye that labor and are heavy laden and I will give you rest. Take my yoke upon you, and learn of me; for I am meek and lowly of heart: and ye shall find rest unto your souls. For my yoke is easy and my burden is light" (Matthew 11:28–30).

Parenthetically, the Aramaic word that Jesus used, *halakhah*, which was translated as "yoke," means the teaching or doctrine of a particular rabbi. Each rabbi in ancient Israel had a somewhat distinct *halakhah*, or yoke, that his students were versed in and were expected to follow in their lives. Jesus tells us that his *halakhah* is easy. Good deal! At this point in my life, I really welcomed something easy for a change, where I didn't have to do all the heavy lifting. Honestly, I was spent, empty, and out of options.

When Jesus spoke of his "burden," he was speaking of the same burden he talked about years earlier when he enumerated, in that ancient synagogue in Palestine, when it was His turn as a young man to read the *Haftorah*, the scroll of Isaiah, in ancient Nazareth two millennia ago.

"The Spirit of the Lord is upon me, because He hath anointed me to preach the Gospel to the poor; He hath sent me to heal the brokenhearted, to preach deliverance to the captives, and recovering of sight to the blind, to set free the oppressed" (Luke 4:18).

Later, he told His disciples something that blew their minds and is as applicable to all us today, if we are believers, as it was to His first-century disciples.

"Verily, verily I say unto you, he that believeth on me, the works that I do shall he do also; and greater works than these shall he do; because I go unto my Father" (John 14:12).

This is some amazing promise from the God-Man who healed the sick; made the dumb to speak, the deaf to hear, and the lame to walk; and raised the dead. This is a man who literally changed the molecular structure of water into wine in an instant and fed five thousand men and their families by performing a *de novo* act of creative multiplication on a few loaves of bread and some fishes. The implications of John 14:12 in our lives today are enormous, in terms of opportunity. The challenge to those of us who love the Lord is inescapable.

"If you love me you will keep my commandments" (John 14:15).

Actually, for believers, in John 14:12 Jesus makes it clear that He expects us to do even greater things than He did when He walked this earth for thirty-three years. He never went to seminary and only the last three years were spent in ministry. Not only does He expect us to do all the wonders and marvels that He did, but even more important, we, as believers, have been empowered to do something Jesus never did while He was alive on earth in the flesh.

It might surprise you to realize that in all of His life on earth, Jesus never got anyone saved. "Wait a minute, Chaplain Rock, whaddya mean He never got anybody saved? He was Je-e-e-sus!"

Yes, He surely was. But no one could be saved or redeemed until the God-Man went to the cross, bore our sins, died a criminal's death, smashed the gates of hell, took "captivity captive," and rose on the third day. That's just a fact. I always enjoy the thought that the first person Jesus redeemed was probably that thief on the cross who said to Him, "Lord, remember me when you come into your Kingdom" (Luke 23:42 NASB).

Of course, just before Jesus died, he answered the malefactor.

"Truly I say to you, today, you will be with me in paradise" (Luke 23:43 NASB).

The implication is that we are being expected and equipped to "do greater things than these." Jesus has given us the Comforter, through the indwelling of the Holy Spirit, and He has given us the authority to use His name. Above all else, He exhorts us to get people saved, something that is very much "greater" than the things He did while He walked among us. It's not just a promise. It's our imperative and our spiritual marching orders.

In terms of my own life, the deal was sealed when I put this scripture together with the sixteenth chapter of Mark. Just before He ascends to the Father, our Lord speaks His final words to the disciples: "Go ye into all the world and preach the Gospel to every creature ... And these signs shall follow them that believe: In my name shall they cast out devils; they shall speak with new tongues. ... [They] shall lay hands on the sick and they shall recover" (Mark 16:15, 17, 18).

Thus, we have a calling on our lives, and we, as believers, need to discern how and when we are going to answer His exhortation. Meditating on His call was both exciting and perplexing to me as I went through the daily routine of prison life.

In my studies during the long prison years, I came across the writings of perhaps the most famous American evangelist of the nineteenth century, Dwight L. Moody. His preaching to a long, unbroken chain of believers who were led to the Lord over decades was traceable, years later, to the ultimate Christian conversion of a lanky, sandy-haired country boy from Charlotte, North Carolina. That country boy's name was Will Graham, and, because decades earlier a chain of believers, including Billy Sunday, Mordecai Ham, and others heeded the call, this kid from the back hills came to Jesus.

That young country boy from North Carolina grew up to become Billy Graham, the world's most famous preacher, evangelizing the Word to millions around the globe.

Dwight L. Moody, the great evangelist, quoted in 1873 the words of his friend, the famous British revivalist Henry Varley, and he made these words so famous that they are frequently attributed to Moody, who added the last line on his own, personalizing it as well:

"The world has yet to see what God can do with the man who is fully consecrated to Him. I aim to be that man."

Reading this in my prison cell, nursing my brokenness and despair, years ago, God's purpose for me in bringing me through this travail became clear.

I spoke, with faith, the words Varley handed down to Dwight L. Moody over a hundred years earlier. Kneeling in my cell late one night, I made those words mine. It was the night before I was to be released in the morning after ten years.

At midnight in my cell, on my last night behind bars and barbed wire, in my worn, faded prison greens for the last time, I kneeled in the darkness in prayer. I thanked Him for bringing me through. I uttered this promise to God, surrounded by "so great a cloud of witnesses" as I made this vow mine. I invite you to make it your own.

"I aim to be that man."

11

THE GREAT PHYSICIAN, PART 2
THE ENIGMA OF CHRIST-
CENTERED HEALING

Water saw its Creator and blushed.
—Lord Byron

Jesus said unto him, if thou canst believe,
all things are possible to him that believeth.
—Mark 9:23

AS SERIOUS CHRISTIAN DISCIPLES we must accept the literal truth and infallibility of the ninth chapter of Mark, as well as accepting all of its daunting implications, no matter how they challenge us, and no matter how uncomfortable that challenge may make us.

Jesus did not exaggerate. When He was speaking in parables, which by nature are hyperbolic, He made it clear He was speaking symbolically and in metaphors. When He was speaking literally, it was unmistakable, and we do Him disservice to discount the truth of His literal pronouncements.

As an aside, I see absolutely nothing in Jesus's discourses regarding the Lord's Supper to even remotely suggest or indicate that He is speaking symbolically. His words in the sixth chapter of John's Gospel are articulated and offered literally, and he who fails to take the Lord at His word is foolhardy and does so at his own peril. Jesus was God come in the flesh, and it is a heresy, Docetism, discredited long ago, that He was solely a spirit who never died and who was never resurrected. Accordingly, to overly spiritualize everything He said and did is the logical extension of that heresy.

If we are constantly "walking back" statements, such as Mark 9:23, then we embark on a slippery slope of faith, and we put the entire body of His work in doubt.

Here's the risk: if Jesus was lying—or at least exaggerating—in Mark 9:23, then we would need to consider that perhaps He was lying or exaggerating in John 3:16.

Then, as Paul wrote, "Our faith is in vain and we are still lost in our sins" (1 Corinthians 15:14).

Lost in our sins like those in the world, who know no absolute truth, the unredeemed who never find the way but their own way, and former family or friends who make it up as they go along, as it seems right to them in their own eyes. People who never find real life or experience it abundantly as the real Christian does. One thing is for certain: once we develop a taste for it, we can never go back to living life at that base level of mere existence in the natural. Once we taste the supernatural, we can never settle for less.

As a physician and fully trained, experienced reconstructive surgeon, I have been blessed to develop an expert grasp of the care, healing, and handling of human tissues, as well as their molecular and submolecular structure and function. Further, as any medical scientist who is candid will agree, while we can describe down to a certain level of detail the sequence of events that takes place in the healing process, science knows next to nothing about the most fundamental substrate of healing or even life itself.

As a fundamentalist Christian who also happens to be blessed to hold an M.D. degree, I firmly believe in and adhere to the controversial doctrine that physical healing is part of the atonement. Having Jesus literally alive inside of us, unencumbered by sins that "so easily beset us," and disturb that power flow, healing is most definitely for us today. Simply put, that means that healing of all our sicknesses and all our diseases was purchased by Jesus' shed blood two thousand years ago, as part of His finished work on the cross at Calvary.

I have seen enough of cold, dead, ceremonial religion, a passive form of godliness that denies the power. I want nothing of this weak religion that calls itself Christianity but never takes a chance, where empty religious ritual so often tries to pass for true faith. It's religion that is "always learning but never able to come to the knowledge of Truth" (2 Timothy 3:7 NASB).

Understandably, as a Christian physician, I am not only intrigued but rather enraptured by the challenge to discern the substrate of the Christ-centered healing of human tissues bound up in a disease process. It is insufficient for us to write it off with the throw-away line, "God works in mysterious ways." As a country preacher used to say, "That ain't in the Bible."

But God's statement—"[We] have the Mind of Christ [and know] all things" (1 Corinthians 2:16; 1 John 2:20)—most definitely is in the Bible. It is incumbent upon us to keep pushing back the shroud of spiritual ignorance and cowardice gone to seed that holds us back from "doing greater works than these."

Let us embark on an exciting adventure of discovery that uses as our vehicle the Word of God and the anointing, which we as believers possess. Christianity is not a religion, but religions, unfortunately, have been made out of it, usually by a watering down of the Word and overly spiritualizing everything in an attempt to get it to say something it does not mean.

Christianity is about God and His family. It is reality in the highest. Christianity is a great adventure by which we can know the Creator intimately, and by knowing Him, by coming into deep communion with

Jesus, we can come to know intimately all the mysteries of His creative handiwork and of creation as well. "All things were made by Him and for Him" (Colossians 1:16).

Earth is just a rehearsal for heaven, and just like loving parents who put a little child on the bus for the first day of school and whose hearts break with joy, love, and expectation for their child, the Lord of Glory is crazy about you!

"For the Lord God is a sun and shield; no good thing would He withhold from them who walk uprightly" (Psalm 84:11).

Not only did our Lord pay our sin debt at Calvary, but the scriptures are replete with direct references to physical healing as well.

"Who forgiveth all thine iniquities; who healeth all thy diseases" (Psalm 103:3).

"Who His own self bare all our sins in His own body on the tree that we, being dead to sins, should live unto righteousness: by whose stripes ye were healed" (1 Peter 2:24).

Here's the good news: Christian healing is not a "promise."

It is a fact.

We got our healing two thousand years ago at Mount Calvary, and most Christians are just finding out about it. The controversy regarding healing stems from doubt and unbelief that pervades the body of Christ, making the heavens seem to turn to brass and causing the prayers of God's people to often seem as if they don't rise above the ceiling.

I am very sympathetic with so many of God's children who feel this way. It is understandable that even good, strong Christians truly seeking His face cannot get their hands or their hearts around the concept that Christ-centered healing is real and is available today.

The world and the church itself are so pervaded with negativity that it is often just as challenging for the contemporary believer to step out in faith as it was during the persecution of the first century. Today, in many parts of the world, professing Christians are beheaded. Here in the United States, they are being arrested or otherwise hassled by a totally and absolutely godless government and media, which purposely confuses the "freedom of religion," on which this nation was founded, with "freedom from religion."

It is a world where God has been banned from the public square and the marketplace by popular acclamation in favor of kings of other sorts: political, sports, and entertainment. God's people are marginalized and written off as quaint crazies, at best, or, at worst, as self-righteous haters. It's an old story, though. As old as the Bible. Listen to the word of the Lord when the prophet Samuel grieves that the people have rejected him in favor of having a secular king, like all the other nations.

"And the Lord said unto Samuel, Hearken unto the voice of the people in all that they say unto thee for they have not rejected thee they have rejected me, that I should not reign over them" (1 Samuel 8:7).

In the face of this kind of rejection by the world, it is important for contemporary believers to remember that they have not rejected you; they have rejected God. But in the most encouraging scriptural promise for believers who lose their families and friends for His sake, Jesus tells Peter that anyone who has lost house, or friends, brothers or sister, children or properties for His sake, "but he shall receive an hundredfold now in this time, houses, and brethren, and sisters, and mothers, and children, and lands *with persecutions*, and in the world to come, eternal life" (Mark 10:29–31, emphasis mine).

This is where the believer's strength comes from, not from the world.

It is ironic to note that even in our contemporary world, it is in primitive and underdeveloped societies where those involved in Christian healing are witnessing regular healings today. This is so because in less developed areas, people often have little or no access to medical alternatives, and those who love the Lord and are afflicted, find themselves out of options very quickly. Thus, in underdeveloped areas, believers are more amenable to release their faith and receive the dispensation of healing bought and paid for with the precious blood of the Lamb at Calvary.

This is exactly the situation relating to the woman with the twelve-year issue of blood in the New Testament, who had "spent all her substance" seeking worldly cures and saw a scruffy itinerant rabbi coming down the street one day "in the press," surrounded by thousands of people.

Jesus never laid His eyes on her and did not know anything about her until after she received her healing. He then felt "virtue," or power, go out of Him and asked, in the midst of the press, "Who touched me?" She saw Him first at a distance and said in faith, "If I but touch the hem of His garment I shall be made whole."

Indeed, she was. It is critical to note that it was solely her faith that was operating here, not some magical power present in Jesus, the God-Man who had divested Himself of His divine prerogatives as a man, or a charm present in the knots in His tsitsis, His prayer shawl. This prayer shawl is rendered by the Gentile Christian King James translators as "the hem of His garment."

But it is indeed a fulfillment of Old Testament prophecy: "But for you who fear my Name, the Sun of righteousness shall rise with healing in His wings" (Malachi 4:2).

The word rendered as "wings" is a translation of the Hebrew word *kanaph*, which refers to the border, edge, or hem of something such as a garment, which in Jesus's case was His sacred prayer shawl.

What is critically important here is that Jesus never knew she was there, and her healing was initiated and fully facilitated by her faith, not by any action He might have taken, such as the laying on of hands, which He does often elsewhere in the Gospel accounts.

Add to this the biblical fact that in Nazareth, because of unbelief, "He could do no great works," save a few minor healings. This is eye-opening because we rightly ascribe to Jesus as God the quality of omnipotence. But here, even the Savior of the world's spiritual hands are tied, so to speak, by rampant doubt and unbelief. In his hometown He is discounted as nothing more than another local yokel—and a *mamzer*, or illegitimate child, at that.

We see Jesus, then, in the eyes of Nazareth, as an outcast, unfit by his suspect birth to take part in the religious life of this insular community. Thus, from the very beginning, this little Jewish boy's heart was broken by the Jewish community He loved with every fiber in Him. Sadly, this little boy was rejected even before He was born.

Jesus fit the prophetic descriptions of the coming anointed Messiah, the Christ of God, but his people were blinded to that. The New Living Translation renders it quite eloquently when Jesus told them,

"A prophet is honored everywhere except in his hometown and among his relatives and his own family" (Mark 6:4).

As we embark on this adventure into Christ-centered healing, we know that faith in Jesus and the ability to receive is absolutely the essential currency of Christian healing. We live in a faithless age, which helps to explain why God's people, constantly surrounded by doubt and unbelief, find it difficult to believe and even harder to receive healing and all the other facets of salvation.

More than once on Christian radio, I have heard otherwise highly respected evangelical preachers discount all Christ-centered healing ministries as misguided, at best, and outright frauds, at worst. No wonder these famous preachers never see healings in themselves or in their congregations. The minute they walk in the room, they squelch the fire of the Holy Spirit and short-circuit the whole process. They make the whole thing seem improbable, and their poor congregants wonder why their prayers don't work. Talk about self-fulfilling prophecy! It all just seems improbable to them.

RICHARD LAWRENCE DOMBROFF

Moving on in our journey, we have to ask ourselves, "Do we have the courage to believe and receive this improbability?"

The great Anglican spiritual director of the last century, R. Somerset Ward, posed the challenge in one of the most compelling treatises of Christian spirituality written since the New Testament, *To Jerusalem*. In it, Reverend Ward explores the mystery that is the essence of the Christian life and declares that it requires "reckless courage" to be a real Christian; otherwise, the world would be full of them, and we know, sadly, we are not going to heaven in a crowd.

He speaks of the weak, nominal kind of faith that appears to be so common and discovers that more often than not, it is a thin veil over fear and cowardice. So often we are fearful to commit ourselves, spirit, soul, and body. But we soon learn that ultimately we need to make a decision. No, not a single decision; rather, Christianity is a never-ending series of daily moment-to-moment decisions. And the essence of decisions is that, in the final analysis, we have to take a chance and plunge headlong into wherever our faith guides us.

Decision-making requires courage. This is the essence of the life in Christ. Why courage? Are we not assured of the certitude of our faith? In theory we are, but nary a day goes by in the life of a real Christian that we do not face, even in a passing way, the question, "Have I pledged my life to what would be viewed as a distant probability in the natural world? But the essence of faith and the substrate for our Christian courage lies in the Christian saying so sweetly, "I know what I know what I know."

It is the courage to be wrong, combined with the faith to know in our hearts that we are not.

To believe in Him—to really believe and to fully consecrate ourselves to Him—requires courage every day, yet no more so than to receive the healing purchased for us on a faraway hilltop two thousand years ago by a bloodied, dying itinerant rabbi nailed to a Roman cross.

I speak in richly woven images only because mere sentences on pages cannot suffice to describe the gift He gave us on that sixth day of the week, the day God created man in Genesis and the day that God died on a Roman cross. But we know that the world turned upside down between that Friday afternoon and Sunday morning, and the life of man on earth was never the same after that.

Do we have the courage to receive this deliverance from sin, sickness, disease, poverty, and every other form of bondage? Do we have the Christian courage to believe this reality and receive His gift of healing?

Why courage?

I have found that often we are afraid to believe for our healing or some other thing clearly purchased for us at Calvary because we are secretly afraid that if it does not come to pass, we're going to ruin God's reputation and that in the fear of failure, our delicate tissue of faith is going to be undermined.

The answer to that, pilgrim, is simple: God can take care of His own reputation.

Further, to be a real Christian will always put you at odds with the world that is so lost in its sin that it does not have ears to hear the Gospel. But we are exhorted by Jesus to be the "salt of the earth" and the "light of the world." Jesus said Himself that they are going to throw us out of the councils, and we are going to be betrayed by our closest and dearest friends and family, who may grow to despise and hate us for our preaching of the Gospel. However, He gave us hope as well when He reassuringly told us that this would be our common experience with Him.

> Think not that I am come to send peace on earth: I came not to send peace, but a sword. For I am come to set a man at variance against his father, and the daughter against her mother, and the daughter-in-law against her mother-in-law. And a man's foes shall be of

his own household … And he that taketh not his cross and followeth after me, is not worthy of me. He that findeth his life shall lose it: and he that loseth his life for my sake shall find it. (Matthew 10:34–36, 38–39)

Yes, you will have family repudiate you for your faith; you will have friends and those close to you turn their backs on you and ridicule you because they despise Him and everything He came for. Frankly, this is the baseline position of a fallen world.

Walking the road to Calvary is not an easy journey. It is long and painful and solitary. It is a journey, Christian, that you will have to take every day of your life and fear, which is a faith disconnector, is often a feature of the landscape of our walk.

But He exhorts us, "Fear not; believe only" (Luke 8:50).

We know, "There is no fear in Love and perfect Love casteth out fear" (1 John 4:18).

How do we access "perfect love"? This is all-important because perfect love seems to be the key to everything. Where is it, and how do we get it?

We do so by first remembering that love is not a feeling. Love is a person, and His name is Jesus.

"In the world ye shall have tribulation: but be of good cheer; I have overcome the world" (John 17:33).

"Draw nigh to God and He will draw nigh to you" (James 4:8).

So we access "perfect love" by drawing closer to the presence of Jesus, and His overcoming becomes our victory over fear and persecution. We turn daily to prayer, meditation, devotions, and ridding ourselves of those sins that "so easily beset us." (Hebrews 12:1).

"For I determined to know nothing else among you than Jesus Christ and Him crucified" (1 Corinthians 2:2).

Compared to knowing Jesus in an intimate, moment-to-moment communion, Paul considered the approval of men as "dung."

Parenthetically, I want to emphasize that everything Jesus gave us was a gift. You don't owe Jesus a thing—and I really mean this. Otherwise, it wouldn't be a gift. He did this for us before we even knew Him or even while we despised Him. He did this for the most humble believer, and He did this for Osama bin Laden, Adolf Hitler, and the worst child molester in history, whoever that may be. God loves even the worst, unregenerated, unredeemed sinner, but He has no covenant with these people. Not by His choice but by theirs, for love is His nature, and His desire is that no one should perish. That's why He seems to have been doing back-flips to get our attention while we were still lost.

Ultimately, after all the pain, we come to realize that He has been a giver, not a taker, since before the beginning of time, and all He ever wanted was our hearts.

12

THE GREAT PHYSICIAN, PART 3
MODERN SCIENCE, THE BIBLE,
AND HEARING THE
VOICE OF CREATION

WE ENTER THE KINGDOM of Heaven by our hearts, but we are not required to check our heads at the door. Scripture can and does always hold up to any kind of scientific advance. Not uncommonly, we find that scripture predicted fundamental scientific discoveries about the Creation and the nature of the universe long before these discoveries were made.

For instance, for most of human history, up until about the last hundred years, the entire universe was thought by the most revered astronomers to be static. Much more recently, the atheist pop astronomer Carl Sagan spoke of the "cosmos," as we see it, as "all that is, all there ever was, and all there ever will be." That was merely thirty-five years ago—Sagan should have known better. He's dead now, and unless he grabbed hold of Jesus on the way out—and I pray he did—the only measure of Sagan's life that "is, was, or ever will be" was his brief, insignificant vapor of a meaningless existence on earth.

The real physicists know there is a God, or a "First Cause." They even have a name for Him—the Singularity. They use this name because they know that an intelligent designer exists—this all didn't get here by itself—but they need to protect their university professorships and government grants and win their Nobel Prizes. They don't want to be ridiculed by guys like Sagan who go on television and spew their atheistic ramblings. Ironically, in his lifetime Carl Sagan never made a single significant discovery in cosmology or astronomy. He was a science commentator posing as a first-rate scientist. The closest Sagan ever got to a Nobel Prize in physics was a cocktail hour he shared with Nobel Laureate Arno Penzias, discoverer (with Robert Wilson) of the cosmic microwave background radiation echo of the big bang, in 1978. This electromagnetic radiation, viewed everywhere our radio telescopes look, is the cosmic echo of Genesis 1.

On the other hand, there is the case of the great contemporary astrophysicist Professor George Smoot, the Nobel Laureate and legendary cosmologist at the University of California, Berkeley. Dr. Smoot is an exception because his groundbreaking work on elucidating the origins of the universe is so monumental that he is rendered untouchable.

I do not know whether or not Dr. Smoot is a Christian, but his discoveries are an example of the great Dr. Louis Pasteur's quote: "Discovery favors the prepared mind." While Dr. Smoot may or may not know the Lord personally, the Bible tells us that the Holy Spirit, like the wind, "bloweth where it listeth" and God can confer his anointing and download His revelation wherever He chooses. The Great One of ancient days certainly chose Dr. Smoot, whose peerless work in cosmology is surely anointed.

While Smoot may not be a student of the written word of God, ironically, he is intimately familiar with the literal voice of God. He and his team at the Lawrence Livermore National Laboratory have discovered, through highly sensitive astrophysical means, the literal echoes of God's spoken words at the moment of the Creation. Through excruciatingly meticulous measurement and analysis of satellite observation of the cosmic microwave background radiation all over the universe, which are the remnants of the big bang at the moment of the Creation (described in Genesis as "Let there be light"), Dr. Smoot and his team have discovered what they term "baryon acoustic peaks." This refers to the discernible evidence of matter before it was matter and light energies from the microseconds after the Creation.

Below is what they look like; they are exact measurements and exact graphical representations of the sound energy oscillations of the voice of God at the moment of the Creation as He spoke the universe into existence. Dr. Smoot, in his Nobel address in Stockholm, got it just about right when he referred to them as the "fingerprints of God." What is amazing is that he discovered that these primordial energy oscillations were sound waves generated by acoustics, or sound, spoken into the fluid, formless plasma of creation, from which the heavens and the earth took shape.

Proving the accuracy of Genesis 1:1 has never been so elegantly described outside of the Bible. The five peaks in the graph, generated by the NASA/Wilkinson Microwave Anisotropy Probe Science Team, represent the sound energy distribution of the voice of the Creator, or as Dr. Smoot termed it, "the Maker."

This is a voice graph of the actual voice of God as it sounded during the moment of the Creation as He literally spoke the universe into existence:

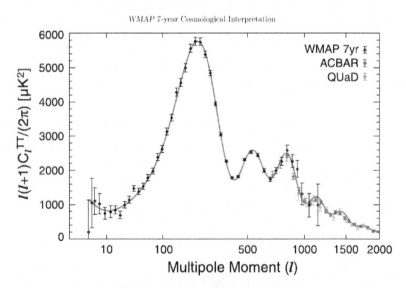

Baryon AcousticOscillations
The Sound of the Voice of God at the Moment of Creation

"In the beginning God created the heaven and the earth ..." (Genesis 1:1)

This is arguably the most profound and momentous discovery in the history of humankind and was rightly recognized by the Nobel committee, which, as politically correct as they may like to be, knows scientific truth when they see it—at least the Nobel Committee on Physics knows. To be sure, the spiritual implications are not something you're going to hear about on network television. Thanks to Dr. Smoot, the world, which generally hates God, is stuck with it because this brilliant astrophysicist shoved it down the throats of an unbelieving world that thinks the Bible is just a nice collection of myths.

Despite its theological implications, it could not be ignored by the secular scientific world that describes God, the First Cause, as the Intelligent Designer or the Singularity, beyond which their instruments and equations cannot apprehend.

It is a law of spirituality that the closer one approaches to reality in "religion" or spiritual matters, the more one needs faith to apprehend it. I am intimately familiar with the way great scientific researchers think as a whole, and it is extremely distressing to most of the godless scientific community to even use the term *intelligent design*, which they choke on as it come from their mouths.

Another physicist, Albert Einstein, speaking expansively on his lifetime of monumental discoveries regarding the space-time continuum, said, "I want to know the thoughts of God; the rest is all details." Einstein was the real deal, not a Carl Sagan-styled wannabe.

So Einstein wanted to know the "thoughts" of God? It was a pity that this brilliant professor never went over to the corner drugstore and spent $5.99 for a Bible. Or perhaps he should have spent more time in Hebrew school, studying the word of God. It's all there.

Only in the last sixty years have cosmologists learned that the universe had an abrupt beginning, commonly called the big bang. Yet God-inspired Bible writers thousands of years ago, who knew nothing of a big bang, or cosmic microwave background radiation, or acoustic baryon oscillations, wrote, "And God said let there be light and there was light."

This is so arcane that the only way they could have known that light (or electromagnetic radiation) was the physical underpinning of all creation was by divine revelation from God Himself. This is because there is nothing in visible light that leads one to intuitively know that it is the foundation of all creation or that matter and energy are two forms of the same thing. Thousands of years after Moses brought the books down from Sinai, Albert Einstein wrote on a blackboard that energy is equal to mass multiplied by the speed of light squared. For that matter, how did John know that God is light.

So the Bible can be relied upon to explain things in the physical realm, and when the word of God seems to be at a variance with what we observe or think we observe, it's usually because science, astrophysics, cosmology, mathematics, quantum physics, or even the biological medical sciences haven't "caught up" with what we as Christians know to be true from His word.

Kenneth Copeland, the great Bible teacher, controversial word of faith proponent, and heir to the great teacher, Kenneth Hagin Sr., tells the true story of a world-famous Russian-Jewish mathematician, who called one of Brother Copeland's ministry partners, a world-famous scientist in his own right, who resided near Copeland's ministry in Fort Worth, Texas.

This Russian mathematician was the most revered mathematical scientist in the world at the time and was breaking scientific frontiers that others could barely even grasp. He called Brother Copeland's close friend, the American scientist, who was also a well-known Christian minister, and told him, in a thick Russian accent, the reason for his unexpected international call.

"I have gotten to a place in mathematics where I have proven the existence of God. Through our equations and formulae we have come face-to-face with Him. I have closely examined and analyzed every 'religion,' so to speak, in the world, and there is only one person who can stand the test of our mathematical models, and that is Jesus Christ of Nazareth."

The American listened quietly, stunned at what he was hearing.

The Russian professor continued. "I've made inquiries, and I understand that you know this Man personally."

"Yes, I certainly do," answered the American scientist.

"Then, sir, if I were to fly to the United States tonight, would you be good enough to introduce me to Him?"

The American agreed. They met a few days later, and the Russian scientist received Jesus and made Him his personal Lord and Savior.

This is a true story, but you're not going to hear it on *60 Minutes* or on CNN.

What we see here is a coming together of the material and the spiritual. It rarely happens like this. Commonly, as God's people, steeped in the word of God and kingdom affairs, we see clearly how the spirit realm is the highest reality, underlying the natural, material world. Rarely, however, do scientists come along with us like Professor George Smoot, the NIH's Dr. Francis Collins, or our born-again Russian-Jewish mathematician. These are men so brilliant and so anointed that they are able to go further in the physical realm, almost to the verge of punching through into the spiritual. Of course, they come to realize that they cannot fully apprehend the Creator God without faith. But what is so gratifying is the fact that they have gotten so close that they know He's really there. Like Moses in the cleft of the rock, they never see His face, but, seeing his "aftereffects," have gotten close enough to sense with certitude the divine reality.

Of course, what we're alluding to is the coming together of the spiritual and the material. We, as Christians, endowed with the mind of Christ, have long known things that these great scientists are just learning. That is, we know that the ultimate expression of this intersection of the spiritual and the material is the God-Man, Jesus Christ of Nazareth.

"And the Word was made flesh, and dwelt among us" (John 1:14).

Not only scientists but also artists recognize the impossibility of apprehending God, short of faith. Bruce Springsteen wrote a song in 1995, "Secret Garden," and there is a line that evokes this exact concept. Of course, he is writing about human love as a metaphor for a larger spiritual search, but that's not unbiblical because we know Solomon in Song of Songs wrote of some of the most erotic and expressive passages on human romantic love as a shadow of our love for Jesus and our eventual betrothal to Him.

In "Secret Garden," Springsteen writes of two human beings who are able to come so close and who are immersed in one another but only up to a certain point, beyond which they cannot go. Close enough to sense their spiritual presence but unable to enter because of the natural world. So it is with even the most enlightened astrophysicists who are able to deconstruct the heavens that declare the glory of God. But as talented and as brilliant as their methods are, even with all the integrity of science, they cannot, through purely physical means, come to know him and enter into His presence. They can come close enough to know that He is real, and that is not a small thing, particularly in a world of atheistic science and naturalism. Moreover, these scientists are blessed because of their dedication and courage that has allowed them to catch even a glimpse of His presence and provide for the rest of us a confirmation that we are indeed on the right path and have chosen wisely "the needful thing," like the Magdalene at the foot of the Savior.

As believers, we need not be terribly surprised at this, for did not the Lord tell us in His word that "the heavens declare the glory of God"? He certainly did.

Yet it is only through faith that we come to Him, and that is by faith in His Son, Jesus. The very best scientific minds and the most talented artists can get to a point where they "know He's really there," but without "believin' on Jesus," they ain't gettin' into the secret garden. And in God's secret garden is "everything you want, everything you need," to paraphrase

the poet.

The best thing is, not only did He bring us back into the garden after Adam's debacle, but better yet He put the garden in us, and as well His Holy Spirit tabernacles with our born-again human spirit, now endued with power from on high.

These lyrics are anointed, but then God can use the most unlikely characters to serve His purpose, and we know He is "the God of all flesh," so why not use a middle-aged rock star from New Jersey? We know that the Lord "hath chosen the foolish things of the world to confound the wise" (1 Corinthians 1:27).

Remember John 3:8—"The Wind bloweth where it listeth."

Armed with these truths, let's move forward in our attempt to discover the substrate of the Great Physician's healing. In other words, how does it work, and what are the laws that govern it? Can we know it?

From a spiritual standpoint, which we know is the higher, controlling reality because everything in the created universe comes from the Spirit dimension, it is clear that our Creator God is both as infinitely small as He is infinitely large.

Below are critical scriptures that, taken together, form a holy grail of sorts for the application of spiritual healing power by believers.

"If I go up to the heavens, You are there. If I make my bed in the depths, you are there" (Psalm 139:8 NIV).

"Through faith we understand that the [universe was] framed by the Word of God, so that things which are seen were not made from things which do appear" (Hebrews 11:3).

"Now faith is the substance of things hoped for, the evidence of things unseen" (Hebrews 11:1).

"Faith worketh by love" (Galatians 5:6).

"And now these three remain faith, hope, and love. But the greatest of these is love" (1 Corinthians 13:13 NIV).

"Love never fails" (1 Corinthians 13:8).

"The Law of the Spirit of Life in Christ Jesus hath made me free from the Law of Sin and Death" (Romans 8:2).

The above verses operate as "spiritual laws" and govern the underlying spiritual mechanism for physical healing, as well as the rest of the material creation.

These spiritual laws are just as dependable as the physical laws with which we are much more familiar on an everyday basis. We know that the controlling power in the universe is the spirit because all material creation is derived from the "unseen," or the spirit. Spiritual power is available to every born-again Spirit-filled believer if he or she is willing to get in line with the above spiritual laws, especially the Law of Love.

Every born-again Spirit-filled believer has the spirit of life in Christ Jesus living inside him. This is not a feeling. The Holy Spirit is a person and His name is Love. This power of the Holy Spirit living inside of us is not a theoretical force; it is the force that hovered over the waters at the Creation. It is the power that got you born again, and it is the power that overshadowed or hovered over the waters of the dark, warm, wet womb of a Jewish virgin named Miriam and conceived a God-Man in an act of *de novo* creation.

It may be applied on a vast scale, or it may be focused through faith, which worketh by love, on the most infinitesimally minute subatomic particle whizzing around a nucleus in a cloud of uncertainty—so infinitely small that even the attention of a regenerated human spirit arrests it, gets its attention, and brings this dot of a particle under its control.

Four hundred years before Christ, the Greeks ruled the known world. The Greek philosopher Democritus theorized that the smallest indivisible unit of matter was something he called *atomos,* or what we called the atom. The word derives from the Greek prefix *a,* which means "not," and the Greek word *tomos,* which means "cut" or "divided." Thus, *atomos,* or atom, meant the smallest unit of material that cannot be further subdivided into smaller subunits.

For the better part of the next twenty-five hundred years, this was believed to be the ultimate nature of matter. Of course, we know this is not true, and over the past one hundred years, through the use of larger and more powerful particle accelerators, we are constantly smashing subatomic particles to smithereens, into their component sub-sub-atomic particles, until we have reached the understanding that there is probably not a smallest particle but only smaller and smaller, carried to an infinite degree.

Yes, God the Holy Spirit, living inside you, is just as infinitely small as He is infinitely massive, and through prayer and meditation, under the right conditions, we can contemplate that is it possible that the attention of a born-again human spirit can arrest subatomic particles. They are so infinitely small that the focus of the power from a human regenerated spirit can manipulate one particle after the other after the other and get them to do what a believer operating in the power of the indwelling Holy Spirit wants them to do. This is not mere fanciful speculation; rather, it is a hypothesis based on factual knowledge of both material and spiritual laws.

It is also a possible substrate for Christ-centered healing. For instance, once the believer gets one particle after the other lined up, and this is repeated on an astronomical number of particles, he then has an organ system under control. Or a tumor. Or a blocked artery. Or perhaps a missing limb. Indeed, Christ-centered healing puts the believing Christian right out onto the frontier between the spiritual and the material, the twilight zone between the natural and the supernatural. But this kind of believing requires boldness.

Some might call this mind over matter. Insofar as we have the mind of Christ, and all physical or material systems are subordinate to the spiritual—because the physical comes into being from the spiritual—then we, as believers, should indeed have the courage to put this power to use to do the things Jesus did and "greater things than these."

Let's hop back to Colossians, which is by far the most intriguing and exciting metaphysical treatise in the Bible.

"He is before all things, and in Him all things hold together" (Colossians 1:17 NASB).

Here, Jesus is telling Paul that His power controls, on an ongoing basis, all the matter and energy in the universe, and because He lives inside each believer, we have the power to "do greater things than these." This verse surely supports our hypothesis on the mechanism of physical healing. In all frankness, compared to the new birth, physical healing, albeit dramatic, is a comparatively low form of spirituality.

This is a great challenge and a great adventure as well. He beckons us to come along with Him in Ephesians, where Paul writes,

"Now Glory be to God, who by His mighty Power at work within us is able to do far more than we would ever dare to ask or even dream of—infinitely beyond our highest prayers, desires, thoughts, or hopes" (Ephesians 3:20).

Paul wasn't writing idle, flowery, Shakespearean-type lyrical poetry to tickle our ears. This was either direct revelation from the Lord, or it wasn't. I pose the question to you: do you really want to do things beyond your hopes or imaginations, or are you content just to read about it? Do you really want to live the anointed life, the Christian life, to the fullest, or do you just want to go to Bible study on Wednesday nights?

Paul was being real, and he was direct. To write Ephesians 3:20 off as having some kind of flowery, symbolic insignificance does the Lord a great disservice, and it robs the body of Christ of its uniqueness in all the world and saps its power. No wonder the body is weak and anemic and, crying like the heathen, speaking words of doubt and unbelief, of sickness instead of health. We see God's people saying what they've got, instead of getting what they say. Christianity has been rightly called the Great Confession, but for the last two thousand years, our confession, on the whole, has been pretty miserable.

The Christian life has always been a series of decisions, beginning with the decision to receive Him and all the gifts He bestows upon us by His immeasurable grace—healing, prosperity, renewal, and redemption of spirit, soul, and body.

His gifts are freely given to those who ask. There are conditions in our lives, however, that are within our power to control that can optimize or hinder our ability to effectively exercise this flow of power.

Somerset Ward, in his devotional studies in Christian spirituality, lays out some guidelines for us to walk in strength, power, and victory, in his masterful analysis of the relationship between discipline and power. It is required reading for all disciples because in it he explains the rationale for discipline in the Christian life, apart from forced, blind adherence to a self-serving regimen doomed to end in false spiritual pride. The last two thousand years have seen enough of that hypocrisy.

We come to understand that it is only through living the life of a true disciple—that is, through discipline—that we can harness the limitless power of the Holy Spirit and the love that He "sheds abroad in our hearts." In his seminal work, *The Cost of Discipleship*, Dietrich Bonhoeffer makes clear repeatedly that the cost of living a fruitful and joyful abundant life in Christ includes obedience, discipline, repentance, restraint, and the denial of oneself. In the end, even though offered other easier paths, Bonhoeffer, in an act of faith, denies himself to the death at the hands of a Nazi concentration camp execution squad. A. W. Tozer, Oswald Chambers, Andrew Murray and two thousand years of other Christian expositors testify expansively on obedience and humility as being fundamental to the useful and fruitful life in Christ.

For fun, however, let's take a different approach to analyzing the need for constraint in the life of a Christian. Let's take a mechanistic look at power in general, and we'll find that the thermodynamics of all kinds of power, including the most fundamental source of all power, Holy Ghost power, are similar and analogous.

First of all, from the point of view of physics, power in the material universe is defined as the amount of energy consumed per unit of time. Power itself is a scalar quantity. That is, it has no direction. Electrical power has no direction and consequently performs no useful function unless it is directed along a conductor and confined within that conductor by a heavy insulation. When it is constrained properly, it can energize a civilization. Steam power will dissipate uselessly until it is confined in a rigid piston or a turbine, and then it can run anything from a riverboat to a nuclear submarine. The power liberated from gasoline, when it is ignited and not restrained in a rigid container, becomes a Molotov cocktail, but when that same gasoline is ignited by a sparkplug in a steel automotive cylinder, it produces power that wins the Indy 500.

In the natural, material world, power needs to be contained and carefully directed to achieve great work. In the spiritual realm, which is the greater underlying reality, spiritual power—and most particularly, the power poured out to us by the Holy Ghost—must be poured into a vessel where it is restrained and directed. Otherwise, we allow it to be dissipated uselessly. God is simply not going to allow His infinite power to be poured into an unsanctified vessel and become the spiritual equivalent of a Molotov cocktail, destroying everything around it. This is why many fine Christians lead lives devoid of power and then moan and groan about how their prayers are not answered or why the Word-of-Faith system doesn't work. And that is a sin that we might not have yet considered because we become powerless in every area of our own lives, as well as powerless to help others.

When we, "who love God and are called according to His purposes," count the cost of discipleship and walk along those purposes with discipline, our lives will flourish with abundance and fruitfulness for ourselves and for others.

In other words, "Strait is the gate and narrow is the way, which leadeth unto life." This verse is not merely an exclusionary signpost for the elect; it points out that the disciplined life is required if the Holy Ghost power within us is to be effectively utilized and directed.

Thus, we arrive at the greatest of these admonitions, and that is that we must walk in the Law of Love, or the Law of the Spirit of Life in Christ Jesus, which has set us free from the Law of Sin and Death. When we get serious about "laying aside every sin that so easily besets us" and get ourselves out of that "sin bin," where disease, sickness, poverty, lack, and defeat run rampant, and we walk in love, where they can't touch us, then we can realize in our life His words, "Faith worketh by Love."

Then—and only then—can we win the victory over every bondage the enemy seeks to put on us. We abstain from sin not merely to be a Goody Two-shoes but to allow God to turn up the volume in our lives.

In my own life, I wind up apologizing to people I despise in the natural. Why do we forgive people who don't deserve it? Simply because real Godly forgiveness is only given to those who don't deserve it. When people hear that I am a chaplain at nursing homes and hospices, they usually say to me, "Oh, it's so nice that you have a heart for old people."

Frankly, this makes me cringe because it's not about me; they totally miss the point. Bottom line: I don't know whether I have a heart for the old and twisted or the sick and suffering. Perhaps I do. But I do know that I have a heart for Jesus.

I also know one thing: like most people, I've been through so much unpleasantness in life that I do not want to go backward. I absolutely, positively cannot afford to *not* get my prayers answered. So I need to stay right smack dab in the love walk, because "strait is the gate and narrow is the way."

One other thing: "Love never fails." I've had way too much failure in my life to walk any other way. Perhaps you have as well.

We walk the victory walk with discipline and love. It never fails. It works every time.

Our Lord is the supreme gentleman as well and will never force anything upon us. But you are His body here on earth. The body of Christ. His boots on the ground. He paid an infinite price to endow you with great and wonderful gifts. On the cross at Calvary, the Savior of the world paid a debt that He did not owe because we had a debt we could not pay.

Every single day, Calvary calls us. Whether or not you heed the call by receiving and utilizing His marvelous gifts in your everyday life and make these Scriptures your own is a decision crucial to abundant life.

"I am come so that they should have Life and have it more abundantly" (John 10:10).

Again, Christianity is a series of personal decisions, not a series of personal moods or feelings. We walk by faith, not by sight, not by feelings. Finally, the Great Physician calls us to be as He is.

Whether or not to heed this call is my decision alone as I recall the image of the Great Physician, long before He was represented in Baltimore by a white marble statue that towers triumphantly in the domed foyer of a great medical center, located in a grimy corner of the New World.

The vision to which we dedicate our lives is one of a different sort. A vision of ultimate reality in the highest, one of promise, of triumph.

It's the vision of a Savior King in the flesh, not of marble but one who hangs—bloodied, rejected and alone, betrayed and abandoned— suspended by spikes and splintered wood atop an ancient, faraway hill on the other side of space and time.

He hangs there, loving you.

In His triumphant reverie, His work finished, He hangs there, dreaming about you. Waiting on you to pick up your cross and follow Him.

He hangs there, waiting patiently and tenderly, for you to "do greater things than these," having given you all the power to do them.

C'mon, pilgrim; it's your turn to turn the world upside down.

13

BY THE RENEWING OF OUR MINDS

Be ye transformed by the renewing of your mind.
—Romans 12:2

"**THERE HATH NO TEMPTATION** taken you but such as is common to man: but God is faithful, who will not suffer you to be tempted above that ye are able; but will with the temptation also make a way to escape, that ye may be able to bear it" (1 Corinthians 10:13).

It is the common condition of man on earth to go through varyingly long periods of suffering of all kinds. Suffering often affects our bodies, but just as often it leaves an even more destructive toxic residue in our minds. Sadly, this often begins in early childhood and remains all the way through adolescence, while our minds and neurological architecture are still being laid down in development.

We also know from scientific research that these environmental insults can impress themselves permanently in our synaptic neural architecture, shaping our behaviors, our thought content, and our personalities and affecting every aspect of our future lives. A person often seems to sail through a terribly painful period of his or her life, showing no obvious physical aftereffects, but scratch a bit deeper and the neuropsychiatric damage is dramatic and lasting.

Family dysfunction and rancor, bullying, defective body image, physical and emotional abuse, and all other diverse kinds of insults from a broken, fallen world are cumulative. Worse still, we are too often taught to grin and bear it as big boys and girls. Unfortunately, we struggle and learn to obey this command by an unredeemed world, and we learn this lesson all too well, carrying resentments, bitterness, fear, and anxiety forever. We are taught wrongly to view this as being adaptive, strong, and mature, but, in fact, this is all too much a part of the agenda of secrecy spun by the enemy to keep us isolated and suffering in silence. Remember, the enemy comes solely to steal, kill, and destroy you. He doesn't primarily aim to make you suffer except to further his ultimate goal which is to kill you.

Isolation was a weapon the enemy used in the Garden in the early days after the Creation, when the serpent peeled Eve from her husband and deceived her. It is also part of the rebellious spirit that the Devourer sought to stir up in the garden, and this spirit of rebellion, born of self-love, seeks to hamstring us today as well.

This condition is as old as humankind being drop-kicked out of the Garden into the arid desert east of Eden. It is exactly the condition that we experience today. Broken relationships, broken dreams, broken hearts, broken minds, broken promises, all ending in broken lives. The question that we all struggle with throughout the earth is, "How do I get past the past?"

The simple answer is that it's all about forgiveness. Taken to its spiritual ultimate, that invariably leads us to an odd fellow traveler, an itinerant rabbi who walked the lanes and byways of ancient Palestine on his way to a barren hilltop where three Roman crosses stood on a Friday morning, two thousand years ago.

Yes, it is about finding the power and ability to exercise the all-releasing forgiveness that He gave to us. Remember that forgiveness is not a thing, and it is not a feeling. Forgiveness is a Person: the second Person of the Trinity.

But the tricky part is that this kind of true forgiveness, His forgiveness, always goes to those who don't deserve it. And that rankles our worldly, selfish sense of justice. We continue to default to our old, carnal, worthless strategies and rely on philosophies containing bankrupt worldly values. We surf through hundreds of mindless channels on the vast wasteland called television and the internet, which has become a mirror image of our broken and godless world, a world where anything goes.

The truth is that this kind of divine forgiveness is not a feeling; the essence of true forgiveness is a Person and His name is Jesus. And this amazing God-Man wants to come to live inside you. What's more, He knows just exactly what you are, in every dark detail, and, amazingly, He still wants to move in and take up residence. He knows your worst, darkest thoughts and deeds, and He is still crazy about you. He's not shocked or surprised by anything you do, no matter how filthy or perverted, simply because he experienced your worst on the cross on that Friday afternoon at Calvary hill. What's more, He paid for it with His blood. He experienced your worst so that you can experience His best, and He comes to us when we're at our worst. Just as you are.

Not only does He yearn to tabernacle with you, but He literally wants to remake you in His perfect image, just the way He intended you to be when He envisioned you before the foundation of the universe. He has those blueprints for your renewal in His mind. He does not want to just rearrange the furniture of your inner house. He wants to totally make you into a new person. And He has the power and the wisdom to do it perfectly, if we let Him. Just like it happened to someone else.

Unfortunately for us, that entails something on our part that runs against the grain of our biology: complete and total surrender, which is difficult and feels unnatural for men and women like us, who live in a broken, hostile world conditioned by fear; a world in which, too often, we must walk in alone, cold and with little love.

Jesus wants to come and inhabit your spirit, but He needs nothing from you. He doesn't need your money or your good works. All He ever wanted was your heart. And when we fulfill His one pure, selfless desire to come to Him in faith, we put ourselves in line to receive His redemption and healing.

I learned this behind the wall as a prisoner for ten years. As a free man, I have learned it more each day over the years, since the day I walked out of the New York State prison in Watertown, with all my possessions in the world crammed into a transparent vinyl state-issue storage bag, purchased at the prison commissary for five dollars.

I returned to a world where billions of dollars of self-help programs, books, and publications are peddled constantly—"Recovery for Dummies" and the rest of the reading list of publications devoted to false hope and false promises. All are vain philosophies of man that might work for a while but then become bankrupt and leave us more broken than before.

Unfortunately, "self-help" is a lie from the depths of hell, because it plays directly into the hand of the enemy, the satanic presence who seeks to further his demonic agenda of secret silence, to isolate us, much as the wolf peels off an errant sheep and isolates him from the flock. Then he can devour the target at will in deadly silence. And make no mistake about it; generally speaking, most of us suffer in isolation and silence because we are so ashamed and fearful of being found out.

Studies of highly successful individuals who excelled in highly responsible positions in business, industry, and the professions revealed that the vast majority of these highly accomplished individuals felt, deep inside, that they were frauds and that someday the world would find out just how bad they were. Clearly, that reflects our fallen nature and the inner subconscious recognition, even by the unsaved, of the utter futility of a salvation by works. It also demonstrates how much even outwardly successful people suffer in secret silence. Edwin Arlington Robinson wrote of this in his poem "Richard Cory":

> Whenever Richard Cory went down town,
> We people on the pavement looked at him:
> He was a gentleman from sole to crown,

Clean favored, and imperially slim.
And he was always quietly arrayed,
And he was always human when he talked;
But still he fluttered pulses when he said,
"Good-morning," and he glittered when he walked.
And he was rich—yes, richer than a king—
And admirably schooled in every grace:
In fine, we thought that he was everything
To make us wish that we were in his place.
So on we worked, and waited for the light,
And went without the meat, and cursed the bread;
And Richard Cory, one calm summer night,
Went home and put a bullet through his head.

Sadly, this is not an uncommon end for so many high-achievers in the world.

Our purpose of here, with an autobiographical backdrop, is to lay out gently a proven path for our renewal, leading to our ability to enjoy a better life. A life that perhaps, in the midst of our darkest hours and anguish, we could not even ask for, hope for, think of, or imagine.

After many years in an unimaginable pit of my own making, I have found this proven path to healing, and I want you to be able to heal all the broken places in your life too. All the broken places of which Ernest Hemingway wrote but, unfortunately, was so unable to heal himself that his brokenness ended in a shotgun blast to the head in his vacation home in Ketchum, Idaho, in the summer of 1961. Sadly, we have no evidence that this monumental talent ever knew the Lord, so his efforts at self-help ended, like Richard Cory, predictably, in just another form of solitary self-destruction. Most, like Hemingway, know suffering, but few know healing, renewal, and real transformation.

Suspend your sophistry and skepticism for a moment and come along with me. You have nothing to lose but your misery. I don't know you, but the good news is that I know a Man who does know you perfectly and He lives inside me. He is the Hound of Heaven, and He is never through seeking you. He will use anything to win your trust and your heart, even the over-the-top life and times of a weather-beaten convict with an MD from Johns Hopkins and a trail of heartbreak, redemption, and renewal.

I have learned that despite our scintillating brilliance and our irresistible charm, our education and our street-smarts, our common sense and our insight, our rationality and our spontaneity, our diplomas, licenses, and certificates, we cannot renew our minds by our own steam.

I have discovered in my own life that this is possible only through a process that occurs miraculously by the power and intelligence of the indwelling Holy Spirit. Accordingly, the scientist in me is ever eager to explore the conditions that most favorably facilitate this miraculous process. Don't misunderstand, however: There is literally nothing we can do in our own power to help. Jesus doesn't need our help.

However there is much that we can do to thwart Him, because He will never compel us to change, despite how much He loves us. Christianity has always been about freedom, even the freedom to remain dead in our sins and misery.

As an aside, it is the essence of the Christian life that we can witness the plenitude of miracles that take place within the interior of our existence each day, if we remain sensitive to the work of the indwelling Spirit that operates upon and within our regenerated human spirit. These miracles are solidly evidenced by the changes that inevitably overflow into our souls—that is, our personality, our emotions, our thought life—and eventually into our behaviors as we yield control incrementally to His will.

In other words, it is exciting when we can see real, amazing changes in ourselves. Changes we never thought were possible. Changes we never imagined or even sought. And these changes result in our becoming transformed into people who, on one hand, we barely recognize but on the other hand, we come to finally recognize ourselves as the men and women who, as we seem to intuitively know in our hearts, are the men and women we were always intended to be. For the first time in our lives, we often feel comfortable in our own skin, and finally, we get to the point where we realize we can stop trying so hard because He is walking with us, doing the heavy lifting. We do not have to put on a show for Him because He is intimately familiar with what the "backstage" looks like.

If we are honest with ourselves, it becomes apparent, as we grow in the way of the Lord, that the vast majority of the problems and brokenness in our lives stems wholly or partially from strongholds in which we have become imprisoned. More often than not, these are the direct result of toxic self-love. And to be sure, self-love is always deadly, even in small doses.

Self-love is the absolute antithesis of godliness. As love of money is the "root" of all evil, self-love is the common denominator of all evil.

In the history of the world, there rarely has been a noble, well-intentioned human project gone awry—a marriage, a career, our physical health and well-being—whose corruption and ultimate demise cannot be traced to the virus of self-love in one or more of the participants. Usually, even in believers, there is more than enough fault and selfishness to go around, accounting for the disastrous results of even what we foolishly believe are our noble best efforts. And more often than not, this is because we have refused to yield and surrender control to God, thinking we have everything "under control." Self-confidence is a lie.

Particularly with the broken areas of our lives, we become heavy-laden with burdens. Burdens we have become so accustomed to bearing, day in and day out, that we literally cling zealously to them. In a perverse way, they become our comfort zone. We bear them alone, fearing that no one will understand. We are embarrassed and fearful of being found out, or we have the notion that no one else is as qualified as we are to manage them, even the Savior of the world, to whom we have sincerely pledged our hearts.

But the problem is that we renege on these pledges, and we stumble from pain to pain and finally wonder despairingly, "Why is all this happening to me ?" Duh!

The simple answer is this: everyone of us wants a Savior. But how many of us are truly comfortable with having a Lord? It usually is only when we hit rock bottom that we give it all up to Him.

I originally came to Jesus after a long and excruciating period of chaos, contention, and abject humiliations. No longer sporting three-thousand-dollar custom suits but ultimately sitting in prison, clad in my state "greens," I recognized I was out of options and realized that all my worldly strategies were worthless. I was in a final downward death spiral in state prison, having lost a three-year legal battle to prove my innocence in a complicated corporate financial case.

I needed a savior, plain and simple. At that time I was not thinking about needing or wanting a Lord. It was only after nearly a decade in prison, during which time I came to know Jesus more intimately, that I came to love Him. And in loving Him, I gladly became willing, at last, to give over every department, committee, and subcommittee of my existence to Him. In fact, I learned that giving Him my hurts became an act of worship. I worshipped Him with my wounds.

We make Him our Savior in an instant of confession, out of desperate, last-ditch need.

We make Him our Lord progressively but ultimately out of a mature, tender, and pure God-kind-of-love. It was a heart full of this same kind of pure love that created the universe.

14

The Natural Heart of Man

The heart is deceitful above all things and
desperately wicked. Who can know it.
—Jeremiah 17:9

IF YOU THINK THAT man is basically good at his most fundamental
level, think again.

Let me illustrate this. Let's take a look at a most instructive and disturbing
real-life case study, that of a young prep-school student named Owen
Labrie. Eighteen years old, with tousled hair. Rosy-cheeked, wearing
tortoise-shell spectacles. Baby-boy handsome. Graduated from the
most prestigious prep school in the nation, St. Paul's, and accepted to
Harvard. A choir boy. Blue blazer, gray slacks, Topsiders—everything
correct. "What a nice boy," all the neighbors said.

Yet now he stands convicted of a sex offense, of criminally luring and
sexually abusing a pretty, trusting fifteen-year-old girl, also a student, in
a prep-school tradition, where a senior boy finds a willing younger coed
hook-up partner. Generations of students at the elite academy called this
abomination, "Senior Salute."

Unfortunately, from the young man's point of view, the young, very
underage girl felt manipulated and went to her parents, who brought
in the authorities. The young prince, Owen Labrie, was charged with
rape and a host of other heinous offenses. It appeared incomprehensible,

and the media accused the local prosecutor of blowing up a case of two youngsters who just got "carried away" with heavy petting. It certainly seemed that way—that is, until the prosecution issued a search warrant, and the nice young man's e-mails were examined, revealing the dark criminal malevolence of his real intent.

Seemingly, it was consensual; on the face of it, two young kids went a little too far in good-natured physical affection and heavy petting. That is, until the prosecution discovered an e-mail in young Owen's computer, bragging to a friend exactly how he entrapped his underage female prey, a modus operandi he laughingly called "the Labrie-zy Sleazy."

"First I feign affection ... then I stab them in the back ... then I throw them in the Dumpster," the young man wrote of this and other co-ed sexual encounters. The nice young man was seventeen years old when he wrote this, and the world was left speechless and shocked, wondering, "From where does such utter depravity come in such a nice boy?"

It did not take long for a jury to convict Owen Labrie, and the court sentenced him to state prison, When he is released, he will be required to register for the rest of his life as a sex offender. Nice way to start out one's job search.

Obviously, Harvard withdrew its acceptance of the tweedy youngster. He'll be lucky if he gets to go to the local community college. Frankly, I'm more concerned about one's eternal destination than I am about their resume'.

This illustrates a much deeper problem than the ugly indiscretion of an immature young man. The mystery is multifaceted. How in the world does this happen to such a "nice" young fellow from an ostensibly privileged, loving family? Where does this unregenerated evil and depravity come from?

Let's replay Jeremiah's admonition; it is part of the crucial foundation upon which we can build a new life:

"The human heart is the most deceitful of all things, and desperately wicked. Who really knows how bad it is?" (Jeremiah 17:9 NLT).

Yes, the answer comes from Jeremiah 17:9 . It comes from the heart of the inner man in his natural state, so twisted and dark that it is unknowable and incurable by anything we can do in this world to fix it ourselves.

That is precisely why we need a Savior. We absolutely cannot fix things ourselves. We need a Savior to first regenerate our human spirits and then to transform us by the renewing of our minds.

Even though our spirits are redeemed by His work on the cross at Calvary, death has been woven into our broken DNA over the millennia following the Fall. This results in our contemporary human organism, conceived in His image but progressively, over the eons, becoming a broken creature with a soul of darkness that is characterized by aggression, self-aggrandizement, pride, ego, and all the other attributes that we attribute to the very horrible, real nature we possess. Of course, we are conditioned to aggression and self-seeking in a broken world, which is governed by the very real and very sad doctrine of "survival of the fittest."

Charles Darwin, the father of the theory of evolution, did not invent this attribute of biological systems on our planet. He merely described his observations and erroneously extended it to supplant the true creation program described in Genesis 1, when, in fact, it simply describes man's march forward after the Fall. Darwin incorrectly described "survival of the fittest" as the biological motive force of man's fictitious rise out of the amoeboid muck, when, in fact, it was the biological result of man's fall from the most idyllic of starting points, the Garden of Eden.

"Survival of the fittest" was not present in the garden until it slithered in on its belly. It was never part of God's plan for the way man was supposed to live then, and it's not part of His plan for how we're supposed to live now. But make no mistake about this: it is operational today, even in the lives of the redeemed, and it fairly dominates the behavior of the rest of lost, unredeemed mankind, as well as the rest of life on earth.

But it was not God's intention that the doctrine of survival of the fittest be the motive biological force for the multiplicity of life that He created. Our natural tendency to exhibit self-love is the direct result of our forebear bowing his knee to Satan in the garden in past millennia, and the fact that at that exact moment in time, death lodged in our human spirit. Sadly, and in a very literal sense, spiritual death is still wedged in there at a ninety-degree angle, and that is why we needed a Savior to come to get it out. However, even for the saved, whose spirits are born from above and in whom the life of God now is lodged securely in their spirits, the damage has been done to our natural souls, our minds, and our bodies. In other words, our spirits are regenerated, but our minds and our bodies—that is, our "biology"—is still broken.

But there is hope because we know that it is not God's will for life on earth to stay mired in this depravity and aggression.

"The wolf also shall dwell with the lamb, and the leopard shall lie down with the kid; and the calf and the young lion and the fatling together; and a little child shall lead them" (Isaiah 11:6).

This Old Testament prophecy describing the New Earth reveals the Lord's original blueprint for life on earth. Had not Adam sinned in the Garden in the early innings of man's existence, this would describe a universe of love that would have existed today. Of course, had Adam not so badly fumbled the ball in the Garden, the Bible would be about three pages long, as the rest of all the scripture tells of our heavenly Father's unfolding plan to bring us back into the Garden by sending His Son to pay our debt, redeem us from the hand of Satan, put the garden in our hearts, and dispatch His Spirit to tabernacle within us.

It worked out fine, but as living organisms, we're still left with a broken protoplasm dominated by self-love, self-aggrandizement, and all the other residue flowing from the imperatives of survival; having to toil on earth to scratch out a living is still ingrained in our mortal flesh and carnal nature. The good news is that He's given us His power to overcome the past and rewrite our futures, according to His purposes, His thoughts, and His plans, which are higher than ours.

"For as the heavens are higher than the earth, so are my ways higher than your ways, and my thoughts than your thoughts" (Isaiah 55:9).

"For I know the thoughts that I think toward you, saith the LORD, thoughts of peace, and not of evil, to give you an expected end" (Jeremiah 29:11).

In addition, no longer is primary authority rested in man, as it was in the early days in the Garden before the Fall. The Lord God blessed Adam and crowned with His glory and gave man dominion over creation and everything in it. In that blessing was all the power and authority bestowed by God unto Adam to be His under-boss, as it were, and run the universe.

"And God blessed them, and God said unto them, Be fruitful, and multiply, and replenish the earth, and subdue it: and have dominion over the fish of the sea, and over the fowl of the air, and over every living thing that moveth upon the earth" (Genesis 1:28).

But after the Fall, man was stripped of his authority and, in the fullness of time, "the Word became flesh and dwelt among us," and the Lord's plan of eternal salvation, formulated before the foundation of the universe, was revealed.

"And Jesus came up and spoke to them, saying, 'All authority has been given to Me in heaven and on earth'" (Matthew 28:18).

Never again would man's finger be on the "cosmic switch," a term coined by the great expositor of scripture, Professor Werner Wolff, of Bard College, in his classic treatise, *Changing Concepts of the Bible*, published in 1951.

So with Jesus as our Lord and Savior, we are no longer in charge, because all Power (Authority) is given to Him. Thus, certainly, mankind is exhorted to come to Him "just as you are." However, although He wants us to come to Him just as we are, it is absolutely not His purpose that we stay fixed in that wretched condition. A major goal of His work at Calvary is to supply us with the wherewithal to fulfill His admonition not to stay conformed to the way this broken world has misshaped us but rather to be not of this world.

"Be ye transformed by the renewing of your mind" (Romans 12:2).

Let's analyze Romans 12:2 to be clear. Paul never said, "Renew yourself."

That's the bankrupt wisdom of the world. Don't even try to renew yourself or try to make the changes. We can't. We've tried, and we've come up empty every time. No, we are to let Him renew our minds, just as He has regenerated our spirits.

The only question left is, what are the free-will decisions that we can make that will foster this process and allow Him a free hand in transforming us?

A word about what we call "strongholds." Traditionally, Christian believers come to regard strongholds as some bondage placed on them by a demonic personality from the outside, over which they can execute little or no control. This misstates and mis-characterizes the exact nature of the stronghold, in that it shifts blame and responsibility away from the individual, which is never healthy or constructive, and indeed will tend to create and foster a more intense feeling of helplessness and powerlessness that intensifies the state of bondage. Further, it is in correcting our mistaken view of the exact nature of strongholds that lies our ability to break them and enjoy abundant life as the Lord intended.

In reality, the stronghold is more often exercised by our old carnal nature, which insists on holding on to sin expression. It is rank rebelliousness on our part, in that we mouth platitudes about surrender, Savior, and Lordship, but we only are willing to give up a part—perhaps 90 percent—of control to our Lord, if that.

That remaining 10 percent (or even only that 1 percent or less that we insist on holding on to) control constitutes the stronghold. In point of fact, the stronghold is literally *our* stronghold because we are the ones holding on strongly. Certainly, this kind of toxic self-love and rebelliousness opens a portal for all other kinds of demonic activity, but make no mistake; we are the ones exercising the stronghold. This becomes a stranglehold on our very existence, and everything else follows from rebellion against His will. God is a freedom God, and this is a freedom universe. Freedom, however, cuts both ways, for good as well as for evil. He gives us freedom to go our own way.

"For that which I do I allow not: for what I would, that do I not; but what I hate, that do I" (Romans 7:16–19).

It is critically important to recognize the true nature and origin of the strongholds of which we speak and teach, in order for us to ultimately be able to be delivered from them. Until each individual takes personal responsibility for sin, we cannot begin to hope that we can move past it and live a healed, sanctified existence.

Additionally, taking responsibility demands much more than uttering the words, "I take responsibility." More often than not, those declarations are little more than empty cop-outs. Mental and verbal affirmations or assents at best. Nothing more than wishful thinking. And while that may fly on *Oprah*, in front of the Lord Himself—or perhaps before a parole board or a Senate subcommittee—it's really meaningless. Taking real responsibility in a spiritual sense is a form of spiritual confession.

Truth be told, it rarely flies before the parole board. They've heard it all before, so even when you do take sincere responsibility, they ain't buying that brand, so don't even waste your breath. I know. I was before the parole board five times, and it's not a level playing field. It is generally known that the deck is stacked against you before you walk in the room/ The decision's already been made, and the rest is just a nice "meet-'n'-greet." Currently, the dirty little secret is that less than 10 percent of all inmates in New York State prisons who are fully eligible for parole release are granted it after parole-board hearings, even those offenders convicted of nonviolent offenses. Any statistics that are published for public consumption are unreliable. I saw the miserable monthly parole results from the inside over a period of ten years. I saw it every month in the dejected eyes of decent men who had worked hard inside to do the right thing in getting their lives together as they opened the envelope from the parole board, looked downward, and crumpled the denial in their fists, time after time.

We live in a culture of condemnation that defeats any attempt at rehabilitation because without redemption, there can be no meaningful rehabilitation, and without forgiveness, there can be no true redemption.

Taking personal responsibility for and coming to grips with our sinful natures and behaviors and extinguishing denial is critical to our healing. Let us look at a particularly common sin that is sadly epidemic within the body of Christ: addiction to internet pornography. This is a besetting sin that many struggle with in silence, shame, and secrecy for many years.

Like every other besetting sin, it is often stated among us, "Satan has no power over us to make us do anything that we do not want to do." This is a true statement, and it begins to help the Christian who is seeking transformation from this addiction or any other domination by the lusts of the flesh, because it is the first step toward taking full and real responsibility for one's actions, as opposed to sloughing it off on someone else and saying, "The devil made me do it." That is never a defense in court, whether earthly courts or those in the Kingdom of Heaven.

What is worse is that this kind of blame-shifting, while it may assuage our consciences for a time, anesthetizes our consciences. This results in a spiraling upward in the level of sinful stimulation that we need to get the same level of response. Our conscience becomes seared by this kind of destructive rationalizing, and we actually entertain a "victim consciousness" that paves the road to self-pity, a close cousin of self-love. As we have previously noted, it is self-love that destroys and dooms to failure most human endeavors that started out with the best of intentions but that end badly.

The Word tells us that "we are more than conquerors," and adopting a victim consciousness is antithetical to this. Condemnation chokes off our attempts to access His healing, simply because we have moved ourselves out of a position where we are able to receive. It is an axiom of our Christian life that wherever self-love is, He is not. And with Him goes our peace and our victory. This is because self-love, like its close cousin, fear, is a faith-disconnector, for we know that "faith worketh by love."

Ted Turner, the famous industrialist, was quoted as a young man as saying, "Christianity is a religion for losers."

Raised as a "cultural Christian" in mainline churches, an all-too-common environment promoting a "form of godliness but denying the power," Turner, scarred as a young man by his father's suicide, became further embittered and disillusioned when his younger sister died, despite his attempt at prayers. Ultimately, he divorced himself from any belief.

On the face of it, his statement is false, sadly misguided, and grown out of a bitter root. In a worldly sense alone, one need only look at the thousands of universities, hospitals, and other pillars of civilization springing forth from Christendom to know the falsity of his statement. This clearly was a declaration made in anger, doubt, and unbelief, flowing directly from an early victim mentality that he sadly allowed to take root in his mind.

Now nearing the end of his life, he has begun to walk back to his earlier characterization as he faces the limitations of his existence and contemplates the real meaning of his life, much like another wealthy, self-indulgent mogul, Solomon, a real king (not just a wannabe), who wrote,

> Vanity of vanities, saith the preacher; all is vanity.
>
> And moreover, because the preacher was wise, he still taught the people knowledge; yea, he gave good heed, and sought out, and set in order many proverbs.
>
> The preacher sought to find out acceptable words: and that which was written was upright, even words of truth.
>
> The words of the wise are as goads, and as nails fastened by the masters of assemblies, which are given from one shepherd.
>
> And further, by these, my son, be admonished: of making many books there is no end; and much study is a weariness of the flesh.
>
> Let us hear the conclusion of the whole matter: Fear God, and keep his commandments: for this is the whole duty of man.
>
> For God shall bring every work into judgment, with every secret thing, whether it be good, or whether it be evil.
>
> —Ecclesiastes 12:8–14

"Train up a child in the way that he should go and in the end he will not depart" (Proverbs 22:6).

Solomon certainly got it right, finally, after so much of his life was wasted. Better late than never. Our focus, therefore, should never, ever be on the enemy but always and exclusively on the source of all life and light, Jesus. In releasing our strongholds, we do not dwell on Satan, and we certainly should not fear him. Satan is no match for a born-again child of God who is in Christ and who stays under His blood. No, we do not fear him; we resist him:

"Resist the [enemy] and he will flee" (James 4:7).

One of the most destructive elements present in individuals in recovery or seeking recovery from addictions of all kinds is fear. For most, the thought of giving up their drug of choice strikes fear in their hearts. Paradoxically, it is this fear reaction, which comes from the author of fear, that usually sinks their efforts at breaking their stronghold. It is not weakness of character or even physiological dependence that extinguishes during the detoxification period after only a few days.

Fear is not just a feeling. It is a spiritual force. It is a kind of twisted faith acting in the negative. Fear invariably flows directly from the person's self-love, which rules his or her complete existence, and any regimen that is not aimed at obliterating this toxic self-love is doomed to fail. The only way to destroy self-love, which is idolatry in its most rank form, is a saving relationship and true fellowship with Jesus of Nazareth.

We do not dwell on the enemy because he has no power to make us do anything that we, in our natural state ruled by self-love, do not want to do.

This does not mean that we allow ourselves to lapse into error, as we see in Christian Science and other cults that deny the reality of Satan. Not at all. We do not deny his existence; we simply deny his authority. Again, the inability or unwillingness to recognize the existence of evil and name it accurately will doom us to failure in overcoming it. We see this tragic phenomenon even on the world political stage today, where we have a president of the United States who is incapable of uttering the words "radical Islamic terrorism," rendering him impotent to do anything about it. I submit that this is a voluntary stronghold of his. The enemy is incapable of forcing him to do anything he does not already want to do—and this reveals where his inner desires and hidden agendas lie.

Let's look at this through the lens of the rebellion. What I'm proposing is that strongholds of sin are simply the tip of the iceberg of rebellion. Rebellion flows from the culture of death and self-love in which we exist in our natural, unregenerated state. It becomes clear that the big sin is not adultery. The big sin is not theft. The big sin is not lust. The big sin is not doubt or unbelief or even apostasy.

It is clear that the big sin is self-love.

Put another way, the big, overriding sin is failure to obey the biblical Law of Love, as articulated by Paul in Romans 8:2.

"For the Law of the Spirit of Life in Christ Jesus hath made me free from the Law of Sin and Death" (Romans 8:2).

Let's continue with sin that many view not as sin at all: "shacking up" with mates to whom we are not married, viewing pornography in the privacy of one's own home, or a host of other behaviors that are increasingly common to the world.

"What's the big deal?" says the world. It's free, so it does not involve the misallocation of finances. It's done in the privacy of one's own home, so it restricts any reverberatory effects outside of one's private life. It's consensual, and we love each other; divorce takes such a long time, and we're getting on with our lives. Nobody gets hurt. It makes people feel good.

So if it makes us feel good, then it must be good. So where is the path to destruction? How are such private indulgences a violation of the Law of Love, and how do they run counter to the Law of the Spirit of Life in Christ Jesus, which Paul articulates in Romans 8?

The answer is that they are spiritual strongholds. Make no mistake about it; we hold on to them strongly. Why is this?

Simply because we want to. We are endowed by our Creator with free will, and we are free to act out anyway we want to. We are creatures who, through the Fall, come to want what we want. And we want it now, completely indifferent to the fact that there is a butcher's bill to be paid down the road.

Unfortunately, this is the oldest story in the book and has characterized human history from the Fall in the garden through antiquity, all the way to the present day, where it characterizes contemporary society, which has fallen to a new low with a total absence of morality, something that was unimagined even a few decades ago. Even recreational drug use is not only countenanced today but increasingly and broadly becoming legalized. The breakdown of morality in our contemporary culture is unprecedented over the last two thousand years. Indeed, it is of biblical proportions, and many Christians believe a new flood is coming.

"In those days there was no king in Israel: every man did that which was right in his own eyes" (Judges 21:25).

"There is a way which seemeth right unto a man, but the end thereof are the ways of death" (Proverbs 14:12).

Lifestyles and private conduct of this nature, despite how benign it may appear to the individual, is spiritually destructive, plain and simple. Often, it destroys our souls—that is, our minds—and ultimately our bodies. But why is this seemingly private behavior destructive?

Let's take pornography. It's private. It doesn't involve another person against his or her will. It hurts no one. How does it violate the most important, most fundamental law of Christianity, the Law of Love?

Frankly, in every way. Simply put, it is ungodly. The proscription against lust and concupiscence is all over the place. There's no need to quote chapter and verse; that's obvious. For most, this is just a theoretical or perhaps a theological hazard. But what is not so obvious is the deeply spiritual, metaphysical dangers and damage that is wrought by the secret, ultra-private sins that seem to not involve anyone but ourselves.

"For we wrestle not against flesh and blood, but against principalities, against powers, against the rulers of the darkness of this world, against spiritual wickedness in high places" (Ephesians 6:12 KJV).

When an individual lives outside of marriage with another, views pornography, engages in any kind of gambling (from church Bingo or lotto cards, all the way to wagering), tarot cards, Ouija boards, or any other secret stimulative behavior—behavior that the unredeemed world thinks is just fine—it puts that individual in direct contact with demonic hosts, powers, and principalities that control those activities and that are attached to the other human individuals engaged in them.

Particularly, in fornication with people outside of marriage, we unite ourselves with each and every spiritual demonic personality that has attached itself to that other person without the cleansing benefit of the sacrament of marriage. It opens a portal for Satan to take us at his will. Make no mistake about it; he does. Indeed, he does. Once we put ourselves outside the Law of the Spirit of Life in Christ Jesus, we put ourselves smack dab into the sin bin. Then comes sickness; then comes disease and everything else. Next thing, we're running from doctor to doctor, from one specialist to the other, muttering to ourselves, "Why is all this happening to me?"

Like any other sin we practice, when people view pornographic videos, they put themselves in union with each and every one of the legions of demons attached to the cast and production crew of the film.

"No," you say, "that can't be. It's only a video, and it is ten or fifteen or twenty years old. It's just an image. It's just a shadow on some film or digital data. It's not real or tangible."

No matter. If we consider ourselves "spiritual" people, which is so popular these days, judging by the sales of New Age books, publications, and other media, we need to realize that this entails comprehending the concept that the spiritual dimension is the ultimate reality underlying the tangible material dimension.

Thus, the pornographic image, whether it's a photograph, a video, a digital image, or even a mental image, directly connects the viewer to the real thing, as well as to the host of demonic spirits behind it. And we know that demonic hosts don't care a whit for time or space, and in the spiritual realm, chronology and locus in time or space have no meaning. Neither does the lack of materiality of a digital or a mental image mean anything to the demonic host. It's all a pathway connected and controlled by powers and principalities and demonic personalities in high places in just the same manner as if we were engaged in the illicit behavior ourselves in "real" time.

Moreover, I submit that it is the viewer's connection with and the resulting connection with the host demonic evil behind the pornography itself, or behind any addiction, that provides the stimulation. This is so because in the final analysis, sin is about rebellion. The literal activity itself is little more than a seemingly innocuous hook that establishes the connection to the kingdom of darkness. And make no mistake, the kingdom of demonic darkness is real and exists outside of time or space limitations.

"But I say unto you, That whosoever looketh on a woman to lust after her hath committed adultery with her already in his heart" (Matthew 5:28).

Jesus wasn't speaking figuratively here. The God-Man understood the spiritual reality underlying the tangible material reality when He said this.

The legendary United States Supreme Court justice Potter Stewart wrote in an opinion involving an obscenity case, "I don't necessarily know how to define 'obscenity,' but I know it when I see it."

Each believer needs to exercise the power of godly discernment when navigating the lanes and byways of this very broken world.

How about the saturation of music and other forms of modern media with rhythm and imagery of death, lust, and destruction? It might be said as well that we don't know how to define the "devil's music, but we know it when I hear it. That's true, because it is not necessarily the rhythm or the melody or instrumental elements that define the evil connection; rather, it is the entire composition for which careful and mature Christians must exercise their powers of discernment.

I also submit that different kinds of music may affect or stimulate imagery different in different individuals, depending on their past history and environmental conditioning. While there are obvious examples of certain types of music that should be avoided by all Christians, there are great variables from one individual to the next, and these reactions are necessarily subjective. Because of this, it is even more important in this area of music and the arts that each person take responsibility for himself or herself in discerning the truth, according to the word of God through prayer and godly meditation.

To reiterate, because this is a vital understanding, the demonic host is not controlling an individual against his or her natural will; rather, they are providing a facility for each of us, in our own way, to act on the things we really do want to do in the flesh. These desires flow from the wellspring of carnal rebelliousness and self-love that flows forth from the incurably sick and twisted "heart of man," described in Jeremiah 17:9.

The purpose of coming to grips with these things lies in the fact that if we are going to see our minds renewed and be transformed, it is critically important that we parse out the threads of our depravity. We can actively engage in this activity by turning to the Word as the controlling factor in every aspect of our lives.

"For the word of God is quick, and powerful, and sharper than any two-edged sword, piercing even to the dividing asunder of soul and spirit, and of the joints and marrow, and is a discerner of the thoughts and intents of the heart" (Hebrews 4:12 KJV).

This is the way that the Lord effectuates the transformation of our lives, which yields our healing. Only therein lies the remission of our sick state. Through the Word, He communicates with us, and it is a two-way open, clear channel for us to commune with Him as well. Jesus knows all of our depravity, and when He hears it from us by our confession directly to Him, He cleanses us from all unrighteousness.

The Word of God is much more than merely inanimate words or even lofty ideas printed on pages in a book. It is a living organism. It is a person. The Second Person of the Trinity, God the Son, and His name is Jesus. Through His word, sharper than any two-edged sword, the Great Physician, the Ancient of Days, can surgically remake our souls.

Indeed, therein lies the power of confession as well. Being honest with ourselves and with Him. Knowing full well that He cannot love us less or more than He already does. But when we confess our sins, we can literally, through the power of the tongue, push them away from us because "He is faithful and just to forgive us our sins and cast them into a sea of forgetfulness." The Bible says He actually puts them away from us, as far away from us as the East is from the West.

Ponder this amazingly profound statement for a moment. Thousands of years ago, how could the Bible writers know—except by direct divine revelation—that, conceptually, there was nothing in geography more distant than the East from the West? We can travel west infinitely and keep going west. We never transition into going east. However, if we were to start at the South Pole and travel north, we eventually would travel all the way north to the equator and keep traveling, still going north, all the way up to the North Pole.

Then an interesting phenomenon occurs. When we hit the North Pole and go past it, we start going south. Imagine—the Bible writers wrote "as far away as the East is from the West" and not "as far away as the North is from the South."

Three or four thousand years ago there was no such thing as longitude or latitude. No natural organized knowledge of the globe. The answer is clearly that they got this revelation directly from the oracles of God.

When we confess our sins to Him, they are gone forever, even from the infinite, omniscient mind of Christ. And it is in this process of expulsion of our sin that the remission of our diseased state, our healing, and our transformation and renewal lies. We are healed as we appropriate the pure, unblemished Mind of Christ through His word.

I cannot overstate the central importance of this in the lives of Christians seeking healing of spirit, soul, and body.

"For who hath known the mind of the Lord, that he may instruct him? But we have the Mind of Christ" (1 Corinthians 2:16).

But while we are on earth in the flesh, this is not a process of "perfection" but rather a process of "perfecting." It is not a finished work, but He is the "Author and the Finisher" of our faith. And make no mistake about it; faith is fundamental to this process. "Faith cometh by hearing the Word." It is all interminably intertwined.

Paul's first epistle to the church at Corinth makes it crystal clear that despite any of our pious religious activities, when we violate the Law of Love, "we are nothing."

"If I have the gift of prophecy, and know all mysteries and all knowledge; and if I have all faith, so as to remove mountains, but do not have love, I am nothing" (1 Corinthians 13:2).

Paul is describing a spiritual law here. When the apostle speaks of love in Corinthians 13, he is not talking about some airy-fairy, flower-child attitude of just being "a good person." He is speaking about the centrality of the Law of the Spirit of Life in Christ Jesus, which is a restatement of the Law of Love. Nothing in our lives works without it. Our spirits are weak and vulnerable to attack by the enemy; our minds are twisted, and our bodies are subject to sickness and disease, regardless of how many volunteer activities we attend, Bible studies we join, or cookies we bake for the church bake sale; how loudly we sing in the praise and worship; or how fluently we speak in the tongues of angels. When we're out of the love walk, we're in the sin bin, and the

Law of Sin and Death kicks in. Then the enemy can take us at his will. All of a sudden comes sickness and then comes disease and lack in every area of our lives.

Here's Chaplain Rock's restatement of the Law of Sin and Death:

"You do it, and it'll do you."

We have now zeroed in on the transformative healing process that the Great Physician performs on those who come to Him in faith, which worketh by love (and only by love). Past hurts, betrayals, doubt and unbelief, worry and anxiety, fear, and brokenness of every kind must bow its knee in front of the Lord, who inhabits our spirits and transforms us by renewing our minds with a most precious gift, His mind.

Our spirits are regenerated in an instant, but our minds are remade by a continuous process over time, in which our neurological plasticity permits Him to reconstruct our minds according to His image. This is because our spirits are independent of the dimension of time and space, but our minds as well as our bodies are very much tethered to time and space. Any renewal transformative process occurs over time, and the changes have a literal material substrate. Our neuroanatomy is literally changed and healed.

Because we have free will, we are free at any time to interfere or even stop this process. Of course, we do exactly this from time to time. Jesus will give you back the keys to driving your life anytime you reach for them out of rebelliousness. And He'll even take a backseat in your life, if that's the way you want it. Even Paul the apostle bemoaned the fact that he did what he didn't want to do and at times did not act in ways that he would have preferred to act. Every one of us can relate to that.

The key element that is different is that once we are born from above, we no longer run to sin but rather are convicted when we fall short or miss the mark. And we are sick about it. There is no creature so miserable as a born-again child of God who is out of fellowship with the Lord.

The legendary Christian evangelist Adrian Rogers once said, "I sin just as much as I want ... actually I sin way more than I want. But now I'm running away from sin whereas before I got saved I was running to it every chance I got, just like the rest of the world."

The unsaved world basically stays up nights figuring out how to sin more—lotto, Powerball, marijuana boutiques, alcohol-drenched spring breaks, internet pornography, and so on. Only they don't regard it as sin. It just makes them feel good, so it's okay. That is the logical result of moral relativism—prostitution, LGBT lifestyles, abortion, drug addiction, gambling, and so forth. These are all individual free will decisions.

But for those who desperately seek the Lord's fellowship and are struggling with sin that is hurting that fellowship with Him, it is critically important to understand that there is nothing—literally nothing—we can add to the operative work of Jesus, the Great Physician. We have to stop saying things like, "Jesus and I are working on that," when it comes to getting freed from some besetting sin in our lives.

The reality is, He does not need our help, and there is nothing we bring to the table, save one thing: faith alone. Remember, we are saved by "Grace alone, through faith alone, in Christ alone."

Faith worketh by love, but don't think for a second that we can self-generate the kind of love needed to smash strongholds. Satan has no power over us, but we build these strongholds, and the enemy is all too pleased to slap in a little cement to help us strengthen these bondages. Most of the time, the enemy uses fear to cement these strongholds—fear of losing something, fear of discovery, and, often the most dangerous kind of fear, free-floating anxiety, or fear not seemingly or consciously connected to a specific issue in our lives. Situational fear can often be dealt with by the human organism, whereas free floating anxiety is often crippling. Remember: fear is not just a feeling. Fear is a spiritual force and a faith disconnector.

It is His love, not our natural ooey-gooey, so-called love that is shed abroad in our hearts. The overwhelming number of unsaved folks who do good deeds do them out of selfish motives to glorify themselves in their own eyes and in the eyes of others. They do these deeds to make themselves feel better. And that is an abomination before the eyes of God, because it is a false salvation by works; that is, trying to show what nice people they are. It is a form of worshipping self. Practically speaking, it gets them nowhere because it simply becomes a boasting of how wonderful they are. It is toxic to the individual in the final analysis.

But the real God-kind of love, the love that flows from the throne room of God is another story entirely. Love that is born from faith in Jesus Christ of Nazareth. It's all about our faith and the object of our faith—Him.

He is indeed the author and finisher of our faith. But notice the Bible says "our" faith, not His faith. Not your believing mother's father. Our faith. It is a decision that is ours alone. He will never force us, and the Bible makes it clear that "it is impossible to please God without faith."

It doesn't say "without hope" or "without love." His word tells us it is impossible to please Him without faith. Every charitable work done outside of faith in Him is meaningless, vain, and self-serving. Good works can even flow from Satan, because he uses these kinds of self-serving faith to facilitate our self-love and to anesthetize us to sin.

So it's clear now that the Great Physician works only in the province where faith is in operation. That is certainly in line with what we know about Jesus's inability to perform any "great" healings in Nazareth, His hometown, where there was doubt and unbelief as to Him. Imagine that the incarnate omnipotent Creator of the universe in the flesh "could do no great works" there. Notice it doesn't say, "He would do no great works there"; rather, it specifies that He could do no great works.

Does that mean that He was not omnipotent? Not at all. It just means that His kingdom system works in a very specific way that He has designed, and He is a just, righteous Creator who is literally incapable of betraying His own nature and His own way of doing things. That is His righteousness.

Moreover—and here is where we can make the breakthrough—this tells us that the healing of all of our brokenness, spirit, soul, and body is a choice that only we can make. Remember this: it is always God's will for us to be healed, but He's not going to force it upon us, not any more than He will force salvation upon us. As Kenneth Copeland says, "You can go to hell if you want to, but you'd be foolish to do so." You can remain in your brokenness, in your bondage, in your sickness and disease, in your lack, if you wish. But you'd be foolish to do so.

Lots of Christians are going to disagree with the suggestion that it is always God's will for us to be healed, but they're just plain wrong. In the life of a Christian, He is never the author of sickness and disease. Never. He has already decided on our healing at Calvary. In fact, He already purchased our healing for us two thousand years ago at Calvary, where He literally took every one of our infirmities on Himself.

While He is the wellspring of all our healing, we alone must make the choice to believe and to drink from that well. Just like the woman with the issue of blood for twelve years said to herself, "If I but touch the hem of His garment I shall be healed," and as she headed into the press, she was healed the instant she made contact with the fringe of His tsitsis His prayer shawl. The totally amazing thing is that Jesus didn't even know she was there. He had no consciousness of her.

Now I hear some saying, "Oh, Chaplain Rock, the Father looked down from above and saw her and gave her a touch."

There is absolutely no evidence of that in the Bible. That's not what the Bible says, and nowhere in the Bible is healing dispensed as a "squirt" from heaven. No "little dab'll do ya."

Generations of well-meaning believers ask God every Sunday in church for "a touch." I hear it all the time, even from the pulpit. That is totally unbiblical. Jesus Christ of Nazareth did not die a criminal's death on a Roman cross just to give out healings in touches, squirts, and dabs. That's the kind of dispensation that pagans seek from Mount Olympus, not the kind of redemption that was purchased in full at Mount Calvary. We need to be like that lady who worked her way inexorably through the crowd. And furthermore, there was no power in that fringe on the hem of His garment. No power at all. That was nothing other than a trigger point for that blessed poor woman to release her faith. But the Bible indicates to us that trigger points are important. Remember, we're bridging the divide between the material and the spiritual, so it may well be important to discern constantly the points of contact, so to speak, for us to grab hold to experience the supernatural marvels brought about by faith. Don't wait and beg for Jesus to notice you and give you a touch. He's already done his part. Work your way into the press, Christian, and touch Him, for we know that if you but touch the hem of His garment, you shall be made whole! That little lady with the issue of blood didn't hang around the synagogue waiting for a "touch" from the Lord. She worked her way inexorably into the press to touch Him.

But let's examine for a moment where this lady got such faith. Where does such faith come from? From going to synagogue or church diligently? From singing in the choir? From mopping the church floor? From baking cookies for the bake sale or bringing in a covered dish? From doing good works? From volunteering in the hospital? No.

Those are all nice, but they're not about faith. They may be the fruits of faith, but more often they are about us working for our salvation and showing off what wonderful people we are as we collect adulation from those around us. Most of all, that is simply being a people-pleaser, and God ignores that. Worse still for many Christians, they are dodges or canards that well-intentioned folks in the church employ to avoid coming to grips with surrendering every aspect of their existence to Jesus's Lordship.

No, this blessed woman undoubtedly got her faith by "hearing" and by "hearing the Word." That is how the Bible tells us we get our faith, from hearing the word of God, or the Gospel.

Where could she have heard the Word? Remember, the New Testament was not even written yet. There was no Christian radio and no Christian books.

This blessed daughter of Israel heard the Word from the Word Himself, the Logos in the flesh, an itinerant rabbi with a rough, hillbilly Galilean backwoods accent, who'd never been to seminary. Faith took root, and in an instant her life was never the same.

So where does this leave us, two thousand years later? Remember, this woman got her healing through faith in an instant, and she wasn't even redeemed at the time because Jesus hadn't yet gone to the Cross! We should not be surprised at that because we know that Jesus healed many who were unsaved; but one thing was always at work: faith. Faith comes first. Certainly, we know that faith comes before salvation. Salvation and every facet of salvation follows: healing, abundance, joy, victory in every area of our lives. In fact, the anointed healing ministry today is unmatched in its facility to bring people to a saving faith in Jesus of Nazareth.

Faith is *not* a feeling. It is a the most potent spiritual force in the universe. We serve a faith God who looked out into the dark, cold void before the Creation and spoke words of faith. "Light be … and light was." And we can access this force by surrender to Jesus. Because of His finished work on the cross, we can access this faith without measure. Every single human need, affliction, disease, or lack was addressed at Calvary, and when we finally believe that this is true, we can finally access every bit of His atonement. Our faith puts us in position to receive every part of the atonement. Every part of His finished work on the Cross. Let's put it this way: Your healing is not a promise. Your healing is a fact.

Now, like that little bleeding, anemic lady in the street, go get your healing. Now!

The problem remains that because of faulty religious teaching and bad preaching, we are double-minded about accepting God's word. We say we're believers, but we, in actuality, don't believe He really meant what He said. We take things figuratively, say they are metaphors, reduce them to symbols, and spiritualize everything. The Bible says that "a double-minded man is unstable in all his ways." Worse, a double-minded man is in no position to receive his healing or anything else. That is why most of the mainline denominations are failing, and the great cathedrals in Europe and elsewhere are being made into discotheques. Their doubt and unbelief has stripped the power out of them, and they are crumbling as compared with good, solid Bible-believing full-gospel churches throughout the globe, where people are getting saved and healed, and even the dead are being raised.

So how are we going to get our bodily healing and the transformation leading to the renewal of our minds if we are double-minded and unstable? We're not, plain and simple.

But if we conduct ourselves with the same single-mindedness exhibited by that woman with the issue of blood for twelve years, we are going to get the victory. That woman was single-minded. She had made up her mind that she was going to get her healing. She put everything on the line when she committed herself to the proposition that when she got to that scruffy rabbi coming down that dusty street and grabbed hold of his robe, she was going to get her healing.

And she did. She wasn't worried about her reputation. She wasn't worried about Jesus's reputation. She was totally single-minded, and while Jesus is the proverbial Hound of Heaven, she went after him like a pit bull. No doubt she never even entertained the possibility that she was not going to get what she needed.

And that's the way we are going to get our healing as well. Through that kind of unwavering pitbull faith.

Now we know that faith worketh by love, and that's important to consider here. The Bible doesn't tell us that this single-minded lady was so determined to get her healing that she knocked three people over to get to the Lord. It didn't say she was angry or resentful or bitter. It just says that she had spent all her substance on doctors. She had every right to be discouraged, embittered, and cynical. She had every natural reason to not walk in love. She had every reason to feel condemnation. She had every reason to hold world-class pity parties. She even had every reason to visit spiritualists and witches and resort to the dark side. But no, she just worked her way up there through the folks, quietly and delicately. So quietly that the all-knowing Creator of the universe didn't even notice she was there. He was so clueless to her presence that He said, "Who touched me? I felt virtue [power] go out of me."

I daresay that her touch was the most loving and tender and hopeful and faithful touch the world has ever known. It was just firm enough to connect into all the power in the Kingdom of Heaven, but it was so tender that she could practically have picked our Savior's pocket right there in the street. For all we know, that's the way that poor lady might have made her living up to that day.

I spent many hours in the darkness of my prison cell over the years, meditating on that scene. The Lord has been so gracious with downloading revelation knowledge relating to those verses in order to let me know that there's a lot more going on in that scene than meets the eye. One thing, however, is clear. On the very face of this, it was all about her faith in Him. Not the size of her faith but the object of her faith. And interestingly, it did not involve His touch of her but her touch of Him.

Thus, receiving our healing is up to us. It's our decision. We don't have to beg the Lord for a touch or a squirt of grace. That's just simply not biblical. For those of us who are saved, unlike that anemic woman who was not, He's already done His part at Calvary. He did it all at Calvary. That's why we call it His "finished" work. We're way ahead of where she was, and she got her healing manifested in the natural, right away.

Look at it this way: if Jesus Christ of Nazareth came right through your front door and sat down on your sofa, smack dab in your living room, right at this very moment, what more could He possibly do for you? Make no mistake; just being in His physical presence would be a blessing beyond what we could imagine. But really now, what more could He do for you that He hasn't already done?

His work at Calvary was "finished" work. It wasn't just a good start or a preliminary project. It was fully complete and all-sufficient. Add to that, He's already given you His word. He's already poured out His blood for you, and on top of that, He's given you His Spirit to come and live inside you. He's also given you His name and adopted you.

Henceforth, it is absolutely critical for your recovery, your renewal, and your transformation, as it has been for mine, for you to accept that Jesus has already purchased your healing for you. We're in a much better position than that little lady was because we're redeemed from the curse of the Law, and that poor lady lived under the Law of Sin and Death. The marvelous thing is she still got her healing.

Read my lips: Our healing is a fact. It's not a promise; it's a fact.

Now it's up to us to step out in faith and love. And when we do, we too can declare with single-minded certainty, "If I but touch the hem of His garment, I will be healed!"

Let's take this a step further. As an extension of this single-minded faith, I want to assert something that the Holy Spirit has taught me—it has changed my life and allowed me to experience healing of my brokenness. I promise you that if you process this and apply it to your own special set of circumstances, you will never view the Gospel in the same way. This is one of the most important things you are ever going to read, and it will change your Christian walk forever. Here goes. Get out your yellow highlighter.

There comes a time in your life as a serious Christian when you need to stop thinking of yourself as the person who touches the garment, and start to think of yourself as the person wearing the garment.

I know that for some, that sounds pretty radical. I already hear the wailing and the whining. "Chaplain Rock, after all, that was Je-e-e-sus!"

Well, yes, that was Jesus, and I know you're just little old you, but Jesus told us that we're gonna do all these things that He did and greater things than these. We can take Him at His word. He was not speaking parables here, and He absolutely was not being hyperbolic. He was speaking plainly, and I firmly believe that if we do not take the Lord at His word, we do so at our own peril. Listen up, Pilgrim. We are either going to believe Him, or we're not. The first Adam paid a great price for not believing what the second Adam told him in the Garden, and Jesus paid with His blood to reverse the mess from that rebelliousness.

It's often said that if you want to keep something, you have to give it away. That's exactly what's operating here. Want to get your healing? Start giving healing away, so to speak. Start laying your healing hands on others who are suffering. Of course the healing doesn't originate from you, but it does originate from the spirit of life in Christ Jesus, who is living inside you. When you put your spirit and your soul and your body in line with that flow of Holy Ghost power, you start connecting with that power from the world of eternal life through the laying on of hands, as well as through the associated intercessory prayer.

Then, not only are you going to see folks receiving their healing, but you're going to experience that healing power yourself as it flows through you into others. You will receive healing of all of your sicknesses, all of your diseases, all of your brokenness, and all of your suffering as well. It cannot miss. Love never fails, and when you do this in faith, you have positioned yourself smack dab in that river of living water we hear so much about. Further, you're squarely in that love walk.

Christianity is not a passive belief system, as worldly, know-nothing secular philosophers, with their worthless PhDs, speak of it. Christianity is an adventure for the active and vibrantly alive, for the optimistic, the hopeful, and the courageous individual who is set on making changes in the world.

I once heard a well-meaning pop-culture rabbi say, "Prayer doesn't change things; it changes us." I have no idea what that ridiculous statement means. It's certainly not in the Bible. That is so sad to hear from one of God's "chosen," but it is not surprising, as when one does not have Jesus as the center of his life, no amount of religiosity, no amount of Torah study, and no amount of vain repetition of memorized prayers can substitute for Jesus.

Ultimately, without Jesus, all of the pious services and rituals become empty and worthless, and we become so divorced from God that we can no longer believe that He is who He says He is, or that He can do what His word says He can do for us. We become powerless, discouraged, and cynical. The final step is this descent into agnosticism, so common in mainstream contemporary Judaic culture. It is a reformation of the entire faith into humanistic babble, dressed up as vague, politically correct "spirituality," with a little something for everyone. Homosexuality is then okay, abortion becomes a civil right, and God is stripped of His personhood. Sadly, this is happening in our mainline denominations as well.

15

WORKING OUT YOUR SALVATION

IMPRISONMENT FOR A LONG duration, I discovered, can provide a great laboratory to experiment with putting the Christian life through its paces. In extreme settings, like prison and probably military combat, we can really take Christianity out on the open road, like a Ferrari, and put the pedal to the metal, in a manner of speaking.

First of all, there are lots of broken, hurting people. All the time. Seven days a week, twenty-four hours a day. Beside you. Behind you. In double bunks, they're above you and below you. You are never alone. For years on end, you never have any privacy whatsoever. Zero. Unless of course you get sent to the "box," which is prison-speak for solitary confinement, where you can enjoy all the privacy and isolation you can stand for weeks or months or even years at a time. That's a whole other problem.

But in general population, there's an unlimited, never-ending supply of suffering people for you to "work out your salvation with fear and trembling." Trust me; they are eager in most cases to receive because, like that bleeding lady, they ain't got nowhere else to go.

"Wherefore, my beloved, as ye have always obeyed, not as in my presence only, but now much more in my absence, work out your own salvation with fear and trembling" (Philippians 2:12).

Never were more apt words spoken of the prison experience. Not surprising, since Paul spent a good part of his Christian life as a prisoner, particularly in Philippi, as we know for certain.

The essential elements of prison life, two thousand years later, haven't changed all that much, I can state that from personal experience, and I suspect that I've spent as many, if not more, years in prison than did Paul did. I say this with no pride or satisfaction whatsoever, nor with any boastfulness. It's still about separation, deprivation, humiliation, and condemnation.

In a very real sense, it appears as if the prison experience itself is, for Jesus, a particular sacramental focal point. Jesus Himself spoke of being in prison, "and you came to me." His apostle Paul wrote a good portion of the New Testament while in prison. There are many other important references to imprisonment throughout the word of God and the paradoxical blessedness or empowerment that can flow into such an adverse individual predicament. We naturally must ask, "Why is this?"

I had plenty of time behind the wall to contemplate this. Even when you are released, the experience stays with you forever, and you emerge never the same. Not only are you dealing with the psychological aftermath of such humiliation, but you are forced to deal with fresh humiliations each new day that are foisted upon ex-offenders by a technological society that never, ever forgets. With the Internet and modern search engines, nothing falls off the radar screen, and an ex-offender never gets a chance at a new private life or a fresh start. So the disability is real and fresh each day. Further, in the digital age, particularly in the last decade, this has intensified.

It appears that the prison experience is close to the heart of our Lord, who came to save sinners, the worst of the worst. He was the Great Physician, and as He Himself said, it is not the so-called healthy who have a need for a physician but the sick. Being a convict in prison or being a parolee or an ex-offender makes it impossible for an individual to escape the reality of his sin, as those "good" or "nice" people in the world do. Simply, it's tougher for the convicted felon to continue fooling himself that he's a "good person." That's the first step to being redeemed, renewed, and transformed.

"And Jesus said unto him, Why callest thou me good? there is none good but one, that is, God" (Mark 10:18).

In the movie *Scarface*, the character played by Al Pacino is a hideous gangster drug lord named Tony Montana. In a ritzy nightclub restaurant, Tony becomes so high on the cocaine he is snorting at the table that he gets loud and boisterous and begins to shout at the well-dressed patrons—so-called respectable citizens, who think, of course, that they have no sin of their own.

In his thick gangster Cuban accent, Tony shouts at them as they stare at him, "Go ahead! Look at the bad guy!" That is what the world does to convicts.

All their judgmentalism and self-righteousness is cast on the offender. Of course, our Lord sees the hypocrisy of this and has a special place in His heart for the man or woman so afflicted. Such extravagant grace. We convicts sure don't deserve it, but He gives it to us anyway! I mean, ya just gotta love this Guy, the Son of Man.

The world thinks this is a crock and that we ought to just lock 'em up and throw away the key. We understand that judgmental reaction on the part of the self-righteous, because Jesus tells us, "They hated Me first."

But I have learned that any experience, no matter how adverse, can become a blessing if we allow it to do so. And like Paul, who led an active Christian ministry in prison, I discovered that this was a very fertile mission field, in which we can work out, not work for, our salvation. We work out our salvation in the same manner as we work out in a gym. In prison, likewise, I worked out my body in the huge prison yard by mini-marathon running three times a week. I also worked out my salvation through ministry according to Paul's model. The secret is that you don't need to be in prison to do this. You can do it right where you are, regardless of your circumstances.

I found over the ten years that I was imprisoned that there are tons of men who are desperate for healing of body and mind and for deliverance. Most important, they are seeking true meaning and purpose in their lives, lives that heretofore were characterized by fear, anxiety, addiction, sexual perversion, murder, and every other form of depravity and brokenness.

Yes, there are lots of opportunities and programs behind the wall for educational and vocational training, but one thing I learned very well is that if we take a criminal and give him a GED high school diploma but don't give him an opportunity to change his heart, all society gets is an educated criminal.

If we take a man who is a career criminal, with a rap sheet a foot high, and teach him a vocational trade but do not give him an opportunity to be transformed by the renewing of his mind, all we let out into society at the end of his sentence is a criminal who knows how to weld, or polish floors, or how to earn six hundred dollars a week in custodial maintenance. Not really a match for being even a street-level drug dealer who can make that in a day.

Criminality is not purely a socioeconomic problem of the economically disadvantaged, as most so-called experts in criminology would assert. This is something that the criminologists just never could understand. It's a "sick heart" problem. The heart of man is, in its natural, unregenerated state, is sick and incurably twisted. This the literal meaning of "wicked," as wicker furniture is made from twisted fiber.

But when Jesus, the Great Physician, comes in and does spiritual "heart transplant surgery," even the twisted and perverse become "the righteousness of God in Christ." The penalties that society imposes remain, and many born-again prisoners doing life will never see the street again, but Jesus is now walking with them, and He promises to "never leave nor forsake" them. Many born-again prisoners, even those doing life sentences, report that they feel "freer" on the inside, walking now with Jesus, than they did without Him on the street before they were locked up forever.

My own life and the shocking constellation of life problems that I have made for myself are dramatic living proof of the need for an all-sufficient Savior. I came from the best family, had the best education money could buy, practiced the most prestigious profession in the most prestigious institutions on the planet, and enjoyed adulation the world over—and I threw it all away because of the "heart" problem that Jeremiah described very well almost three thousand years ago, when he wrote, "the heart of man is sick and incurably twisted; who can know it." It wasn't until I realized the truth of that very absolute, politically incorrect statement and gave my twisted heart to the Lord in return for His perfect heart that I was able to see daylight. Before that, I could not even think about rehabilitation, and everything in my life was about loss and destruction.

Bottom line? Without Jesus there is really no hope for meaningful change in one's life. Oh sure, addiction programs, for instance, can change a person's behavior, and the person can stop drinking, but until that person reaches out to God and changes his heart, all you get is a dry drunk.

Angry men and women with poor self-esteem as a result of the way the were raised can engage in all kinds of philanthropic endeavors in an attempt to make them feel good about themselves, but their hearts remain broken, and the anger and hurt just bubble below the surface. Without accessing the healing of the Great Physician, there are no lasting changes, despite all their charitable works.

For me, prison provided a great laboratory to work out my Christian life. And because I finally came to realize that it's not about me, I worked up the courage to do for others what He did for me: That is, He "shed His love abroad" into my heart. Ultimately, I found that I could be the vessel and the conduit for His love to flow into the lives of others. I longed for this because I came to realize that this was the only way that I could become whole and sound for the very first time in my life.

It is where I became bold enough to preach the Gospel to hardened criminals, to lay healing hands on the sick and suffering and cast out demons who were ruining men's lives. I became determined to get my healing by giving it to others, by becoming the conduit for the flow of the power of the Holy Spirit to course through my spirit, soul, and body into the other men, regenerating their spirits, transforming their minds and healing their flesh.

I decided that I wanted to appropriate everything He purchased for me on the cross. I wanted "the whole smash," the full Gospel, leaving nothing out. I asked for all the gifts because I knew from His word that He is a God who freely gives all things:

"He that spared not his own Son, but delivered him up for us all, how shall he not with him also freely give us all things?" (Romans 8:32).

Sure, lots of other convicts, family members, and friends were dubious. That goes along with a broken life. Lots laughed at me and ridiculed me. That goes with the territory. And a few were openly hostile. My family turned their backs on me. That's the oldest story in the book, but Jesus just keeps whispering to me, "Rock, don't sweat it; they hated me first."

But there were many desperate men who received and got their healing, who opened their hearts to Jesus, who were able to begin, like me, the process of real transformation. I needed to do this for myself just as much as for them. No, it wasn't entirely altruistic; in fact, I am certain that I got as much out of it as they did, and I need it more and more as the years have gone by. Besides, Jesus doesn't put a whole lot of stock in so-called altruism. Atheists can be altruistic. The Bible never says, "It's impossible to please God without altruism." The Bible says, "It's impossible to please God without faith."

Ministering salvation, including healing, both spiritual and physical, is the way we get our healing. Even more important, it's the way we keep our healing. Keeping our healing through ministry to others as well as obedient living is the best way to get our healing and maintain the progress in our transformation.

You can experience this transformation as well. Trust me; preaching the Gospel, casting out devils, and laying on healing hands in state prison is a lot more challenging than doing this kind of thing in the real world, even on a street corner or a subway platform.

Out in the street, about the worst thing that is likely to occur is for someone to think you're a nut job. A Jesus freak. But that's okay, especially when we realize that we are Jesus freaks. Yes, we are literally "out of our minds and in the spirit," as Kenneth Copeland is fond of saying. And that's as it should be when we have our feet finally planted on the "solid Rock." After all those years of drifting and being tossed to and fro by the waves, we can finally find ourselves tethered to "the anchor of our souls."

And that is where our healing is positioned, no matter what you are suffering. Be firmly and irretrievably tethered to Him, and surrender so completely to Him that you allow Jesus to take you so far out into deep water that without Him, you realize you will drown, just as Peter began to drown once he stepped out of the boat. He took a few steps, and then he took his eyes off the Lord. Keep your eyes on the Lord, day after day, hour after hour, minute after minute, year after year. I found that there is no better way to live life at its fullest.

This is not a burden or a task, because eventually we find that we need this. It's the only way we can live. Like Peter, we come to realize that we can't ever go back to the way we were. And after time goes by, we begin to see the changes, the evidence of things hoped for and previously unseen. These are the works He has wrought in our lives.

I found out the most amazing thing: Christianity is true, and Christianity works. But make no mistake about this; Christianity isn't true because it works; it works because it's true. It is absolute truth. Reality in the highest. Every single one of us has heard from others, "Well, that's fine if it works for you." The fact is that it works for everyone if they will simply get over themselves and yield to Him. Sooner or later, everyone will surrender to His love.

"That at the name of Jesus every knee should bow, of things in heaven, and things in earth, and things under the earth; And that every tongue should confess that Jesus Christ is Lord, to the glory of God the Father" (Philippians 2:10–11).

As a physician trained at the Johns Hopkins Medical School, I realize the limitations of anecdotal clinical reports. They are not entirely scientific, but when viewed by well-trained physicians, they can be very instructive and valuable, and they can provide priceless insights that produce great breakthroughs in knowledge. Penicillin began as an "anecdotal report."

For instance, about four years into my sentence, one Sunday morning way up in the frigid tundra of the north country of New York State, just a few miles from the Canadian border, I was on the walkway with a much older fellow. We were on our way to Christian service at the prison chapel.

The north country where I was imprisoned is the New York State equivalent of Siberia, and one feels distant and forgotten. I noticed that the old convict next to me, way past age seventy, was limping along. I asked him what had happened to his leg.

"Oh, Rock, I twisted my ankle badly out in the yard yesterday. I didn't notice much when it happened, but when I got out of my bunk this morning, the swelling had set in, and now I can barely walk on it."

I could see that this poor, old broken-down convict could barely walk, but, praise the Lord, he was walking the half mile to the prison chapel with me in the bitter cold of a north country winter to hear the word of God preached.

I didn't say much, and we proceeded to church. As I sat in the service, the Lord spoke into my heart as plain as day. "Put your hands on his ankle, Rock."

I made believe I didn't hear Him. I tried to ignore Him. I tried to convince myself that it wasn't His voice. I tried everything. The service went on and so did the Lord's prompting.

"Rock, put your hands on his ankle," the Lord repeated deep into my soul.

Finally, I said to Him silently in prayer, *Lord, who am I to do something like that?*

The Lord answered me, "Hush that. You are a son of the most high God. Now put your hands on his ankle. Don't worry about it, son. You don't have to be an Oral Roberts. I'll back you."

After the service was completed, and we were sitting around the chapel, fellowshipping and waiting for the go-back announcement over the PA, I worked up the courage to walk over to my friend, the elderly gentleman with the bad ankle. He was sitting on a wooden chair with his leg outstretched, kind of nursing it in anticipation of struggling through the long, cold walk back to the cell block. I leaned over to him as asked, "Would it be okay for me to pray for you, Jack?"

"Sure, Rock, no problem. Thanks … of course."

He reached out his hand to grasp mine in prayer, but I lowered myself to kneel before him. He seemed confused.

"May I place my hands on your ankle while we pray?" I asked, kneeling down in front of him and about twenty other inmates, all dressed like me in state greens. I was not exactly sure I had the courage to do this, but I proceeded. I had never seen anyone engage in healing ministry, but I had read hundreds of books and listened to literally thousands of hours of teaching tapes from the most respected Christian evangelists and teachers in the world.

"I guess so. Sure, Rock, go ahead."

I cupped my hands around the convict's ankle. I was praying out loud, confessing his healing. They call Christianity the Great Confession, and at that moment, I fully comprehended what that meant.

"In the name of Jesus Christ of Nazareth, we stand in agreement, every born-again child of God in this room, and receive the healing that Your Son purchased on the cross at Calvary with His blood. And I plead the blood of Jesus over Brother Jack's ankle. We know that You took Brother Jack's sickness and disease; You experienced his injury at Calvary two thousand years ago, and You gave him Your perfect flesh. We receive that healing now, and we thank You, Lord, as we wait patiently and expectantly for his healing to manifest itself in the natural. In the holy and powerful and precious name of Jesus, we so declare him healed and every tissue and cell and compound and molecule restored to the utter perfection of architecture and design that You created for Jack before the foundation of the universe. We receive this in Jesus's name. Amen."

I took my hands off Jack's ankle and sat quietly in the chair next to him. It was getting close to the go-back, and I saw the C.O. glance into the room at us. I looked Jack in the eyes, and I whispered to him, "Jack, your healing is a reality … it's a done deal. Do not—I repeat, do not—ask for it again. It's not necessary to pray for it again, because it's done. If you think of it or you get a twinge of pain, just thank Him and praise Him for your healing. You got that? And another thing, Jack, just keep your big-blab mouth shut about this." I winked at him. "Don't discuss this with everybody because I don't want somebody to talk you out of your healing. Okay, brother?"

He knew I was totally serious, and he nodded, mumbling, "Okay, Rock."

"Another thing, Jack—don't pay any attention to your feelings. Your healing is a fact. It's not a promise; it's a fact. Feelings come and go. Just wait patiently, and you'll be as good as new."

I got up, turned my back on him, and walked out quickly as they called the go-back over the loudspeaker. I purposely did not want to look at him or check his gait. As far as I was concerned, he was healed, regardless of anything else, and I did not want to trigger or affirm any doubt or unbelief that he might interpret from my expression.

Since that moment in the prison chapel, over the past eleven years, both as a prisoner and as a free man, I have laid healing hands on hundreds of people. As far as I'm concerned, when I finish a service, walk off the platform, step out of the pulpit, or leave a hospital bedside, I believe in my heart that everybody got their healing and everybody who confessed Jesus got saved. My feeling is that there's more than enough negative in the world and more than enough people to put doubt and unbelief on us. They don't need it from me.

So I stand on the Word. Yes, I stand right up on the Word. We are to trust what the Word says, not our feelings. Absolutely nowhere in the scriptures does it ever suggest that we base our faith walk on our feelings.

"For we walk by faith, not by sight" (2 Corinthians 5:7).

We simply stand on the Word, regardless of how we feel, see, hear, or think or however the enemy may try to rob, kill, or destroy us by sending people into our lives who may stoke the fires of doubt and unbelief.

The next morning I saw the old fellow walking briskly, like a new man, down the walkway on the way to chow. I stayed behind him so as not to make a big scene out of his healing. Even that kind of self-consciousness can be twisted by the enemy to steal our healing. It was a done deal, and his wounds, along with his sin, were cast into a sea of forgetfulness. Best left there. And frankly, I didn't need the adulation. Spiritual pride is a major risk in affairs like this, and I am particularly susceptible to it, particularly in successful healing ministry.

The enemy will use everything he can get his hands on to corrupt one of God's ministers, and pride is his oldest weapon. Jesus Himself usually told those He healed to keep their mouths shut about it because He didn't need to be dealing with the adulation of men. Jesus knew well the importance of fleeing from temptation.

Remember, He was God, but He was also a Man, all God and all Man, and He was in all points tempted as we are, including in the temptation of spiritual pride. He told us to "resist the devil and he will flee," but He also tells us in His word to "flee from temptation." So it's a good idea to just let people get their healing, and keep it moving, fleeing from even the temptation to ask them how they're feeling. It really doesn't matter. They're healed. Jack was healed. That seventy-five-year-old convict got his healing manifested within twenty-four hours.

Speaking as a surgeon who was trained as the senior resident on the Bellevue Hospital Trauma Service, in the natural course of events, seventy-five-year-old people do not heal like that.

It was a done deal. As I covertly watched him smiling and hustling down the walkway on the half-mile walk to the mess hall, I left it alone, praised God, and moved on.

I engaged in ministering the Lord's healing in this way many times after that, but one thing I learned from being a surgeon was that no matter how many time we can successfully execute an operation or a maneuver and avoid the pitfalls, in the next instant we can fall into the same old trap and make the blunder, even the most elementary blunder, that we have avoided a thousand times.

It doesn't matter if you're a brilliant, world-renowned surgeon, a successful minister, or a Gold Glove second baseman for the New York Yankees who suddenly misses the simple throw to first base. The error you've consciously side-stepped time after time, you can commit before you know it.

I learned this lesson from time to time in the operating room, and I learned it again on the night before I was shipped home from upstate. It is interesting how crafty the enemy can be. Because I was slated to leave the facility early the next morning, I was placed "on the draft," which meant I was officially "outta here." That is, I was no longer carried on the official census of that facility in Albany and was considered in transit, even though I wasn't leaving until the morning. I was jubilant. Beyond jubilant. I was over the moon and, consequently, I was pretty much focused on myself. That's a perfect example of being subtly out of the love walk.

All of my property was packed and in the draft room to be loaded onto the bus before dawn, and I had been transferred to a different cell block for the night. I was confined to the block so I didn't do something stupid, like go out and break my leg in the yard, which would muck up their transfer paperwork, not to mention the unthinkable—missing my transfer out of there.

Corrections is an arcane system. I always said that Corrections was kind of like the military but, notably, without the honor, and of course nobody was shooting at you. Like the military, Corrections had their own unique way of doing things that never seemed to change.

Anyway, I was in my new cell for the one night before going home. I didn't know anyone on the block, but my mind was already a million miles away. For the first time in years, my mind was "in the street." Thinking about going home is something you learn to avoid until you're on line at the Greyhound bus station with your release papers, and everything you own in the world is crammed into a cheap clear plastic bag.

We weren't locked down, so I was walking past some other guy's cube, and he asked me if I had some antacid. I told him I was on the draft, so he knew all I had were the state greens I was wearing and nothing else. He said he was having some heartburn, and he laid his hand on the middle of his chest, indicating where his discomfort was. Otherwise, he seemed fine. Distractedly, I told him I was sorry that I had none of my property. I chatted a bit and moved on.

I recall distinctly hearing the Lord speak into my spirit. "Lay hands on him, Rock."

As an MD, I know there's a whole differential diagnosis for chest discomfort, but he looked fine, and I kind of sloughed it off. I hear the Lord's voice now, years later, as plain as day, prompting me to lay healing hands on that fellow. I did not obey his prompting. I think it was because I was so wrapped up in myself that I was going home in the morning. I didn't know the fellow. I felt reserved about going in that direction and resisted the Lord's prompting. I didn't agonize over it and went back to my bunk and lay down, feeling vaguely uneasy but not sure why.

I fell asleep and woke up a couple of hours later for the eleven o'clock count. After the count, groggily, I worked my way to the lavatory to wash up, and as I passed the cube of the fellow who had asked me for the Tums earlier in the evening, I saw that his cube was empty, his property gone, his mattress rolled up.

I asked his neighbor where he was and was told that about an hour before, they had taken him out on a stretcher to the outside hospital emergency room with chest pain, suspecting a heart attack.

On one hand, I was not surprised because I knew that early myocardial infarctions, or heart attacks, can present totally innocuously as seemingly garden-variety heartburn. In fact, it is heartburn, as the gastric reflux seems to be stimulated by the ischemic event occurring in the neighboring myocardium.

Corrections is pretty paranoid whenever anyone complains of chest pain, and fortunately, the C.O.'s are pretty quick on the draw in calling ambulances, especially when middle-aged men complain of chest pain or shortness of breath.

So obviously, this fellow's seemingly innocuous heartburn evolved into frank chest pain during the hour or so after he asked me for the Tums, and I was napping. Yes, the enemy caught me napping. As a physician, I probably wouldn't have done anything differently because you're not going send everybody with heartburn to the coronary care unit.

However, as a minister of the Gospel of Jesus Christ, I was disobedient to His prompting in not laying healing hands on that fellow. I suspect he did fine in the long run, but that's not the point, and that is an uncertainty that I will have to live with. I over-intellectualized it and differentially diagnosed it as if I was on the medical wards at Hopkins, instead of obeying the Lord's prompting.

Today, I am absolutely convinced in my heart, as unlikely as it might seem to some, that had I laid healing hands on him when the Lord told me to do that, he would have been healed, regardless of the severity of the condition that was underlying his symptoms.

I am totally convinced of that and resolved from that moment to offer to pray for anyone I might encounter who was experiencing any kind of illness or injury. I will never make that mistake of disobedience again. Lots of people appreciate my offer, and we pray over them. Others say, "No thanks." I don't take it personally and move on.

My obligation is to the Lord, and He has made His will clear to me personally, as well by His word. God is not the author of sickness and disease, and it is always His will that we be healed. The Lord does not use sickness or disease to teach His people a lesson. He uses the Holy Spirit to teach His people.

So I left Franklin Correctional Facility the next morning, somewhat shaken but wiser in the way of the Lord, resolved to never again resist His prompting. This was a great step in my personal transformation and the renewing of my mind.

Most important, I reached a point in my Christian life where I stopped thinking of myself as the person constantly crawling to touch the hem of His garment, and for the first time I saw myself as the person wearing the garment. Putting on Jesus, as we are exhorted to do. Becoming like Him. Speaking His words. Doing the things He did, "and greater things than these."

In state prison I found a marvelous laboratory to work out my salvation. And with "fear and trembling," I did so. But those opportunities are not limited to crazy upside-down places like state prisons. They are all over. The home, the office, even in elevators, reaching out to strangers who are hurting and hungry for God's grace. Every moment of everyday life, there are innumerable opportunities to live out the adventure of Christian life. We only need to be willing to step out of our comfort zone to reach out to others, especially strangers.

The Christian life lived this way is a life of true high adventure, and real adventure needs courageous believers. Real Christians, not wannabe believers.

It takes real courage to live life as a true Christian. Otherwise, the world would be full of them.

And let me tell you, living this kind of courageous life in Christ is living life at its highest level, regardless of one's circumstances. This courageous adventure in the Lord can be lived out in a penthouse at Trump Tower or in a prison. It can be lived in a neighborhood or in a nursing home. In a university, with one's life stretched out before him or her, or in a hospice for the terminally ill on the precipice of seeming oblivion. Putting on Christ every day and showing the world the fruits of our salvation, every day in everything we do, is living life at the highest.

It is the highest and best use of our spirits, souls, and bodies. It is living as the men and women we were meant to be before the foundation of the Creation. We find that we have become the human beings He conceived us to be in the Garden and in the fullness of time. He sent His Son to put the garden in our hearts and began the transformation process by giving us opportunities to renew our minds.

Being imprisoned for so many years was a great humiliation for me. I've left the worst out. To dwell on the past is not a good thing, and even a memoir should be forward-looking, using the past as prologue. Suffice it to say that losing my family was heartbreaking. Being homeless when I was freed and living in a welfare motel and then in the basement of a sober house for six months was, at times, deeply discouraging as well as perplexing. But it was all a blessing, as it empowered me to stay on the journey.

But in coming into the true presence of our risen Savior, I truly became a transformed person. I was not an embittered or broken man but rather the man I was always intended to be, a man made in His likeness. In His image. And throughout this seemingly endless catastrophe, when everyone else, including my family, turned their backs and walked away, He faithfully has continued to walk with me, all the while transforming me by the renewing of my mind.

We do not seek this kind of pain in our lives, but we know that life is painful in a thousand ways. But when we surrender to Him in love, and we walk according His purposes, even those long seasons of brokenness and pain can prove to be blessings, empowering us through His Holy Spirit to a level of greatness in Him that we could never have imagined.

For we know that in our utter weakness, His power is made utterly perfect. And that is a blessing indeed.

In closing, Matthew's Gospel speaks of the wise men, the Magi, on that early Christmas morning more than two thousand years ago. After visiting the Christ Child and realizing, in their wisdom, that they had been in the presence of the Creator God, sensing the fullness of God manifested in an infant in the humble midst of a lowly stable, Matthew writes that they departed and returned to their regular lives as different men, walking in a new way, changed in ways they could never have imagined. He describes it as their going home somehow different;

that is, they went back to their own country "another way." It is more than just taking a different geographic route; rather, it is metaphor for walking a new walk and living a new life, as men renewed.

"And being warned of God in a dream that they should not return to Herod, they departed into their own country another way" (Matthew 2:12).

Yes, like those visitors from the East, I too was changed profoundly, having met Jesus, having come to know Him intimately, having come to know His essence, which is white-hot love in its purest state. And like the Magi who previously thought they were so wise in the ways of the world, finally basking worshipfully in the holy presence of God in swaddling cloths, I too was finally set free from the prison of self.

I left prison before dark that morning so many years ago, picked up the pieces of my life, and departed, taking a new route home, taking the first step on a new, exciting journey of a thousand miles, one step at a time. I was starting a new adventure, walking a new walk.

I had "gate money"—forty dollars—in my pocket and a Greyhound bus ticket. I was a new man. No chauffeured Rolls-Royce; a long way from the plastic surgery operating room on Park Avenue or the Fifth Avenue penthouse in Trump Tower. He was transforming me into the man I was always intended to be.

Like the wise men who, after worshipping Jesus, chose a new route back, I came to understand that out of my brokenness, after all those years, I too had wisely chosen "the needful thing." I had finally found my way to a new home, setting out "into my own country another way."

16

IF I MET JESUS

HOW WOULD I KNOW Jesus of Nazareth if I met Him on the highways of life? In his great Christian treatise, *To Jerusalem*, Somerset Ward challenges us to "Behold, the Man!"

How would I know who He was? What would I notice about Him that would distinguish Him from the rest of the hustle and bustle of the world around us?

Would I be attracted to Him in some way? By His appearance, perhaps? I think not, as the Bible says there was nothing comely about Him.

Would I be drawn to Him by His conversation? Perhaps.

If I met Jesus, perhaps at the mall, what would I think of Him?

I'd like to think that I'd like Him, but I don't know for sure. I do know, however, that He spoke absolute truth. That is often hard for us to deal with during our routine day. Perhaps I might recoil or shy away from Him.

I wish it wasn't so, but it is a fact that barely a day goes by but that we do not indulge ourselves in useless, destructive rationalizations, blame-shifting and self-deceptions to avoid facing inconvenient truths about ourselves, our motives, our choices, and our behavior. I also know how poorly I can act when I'm out wandering the byways of life, and I could embarrass myself before the Lord.

Sadly, I know this is true, and it pains me.

If I met Christ walking the streets of this world, like the two discouraged disciples on the hot, dusty road to Emmaus, would I recognize my Master?

Most of the world who passed Him saw our Lord as a scruffy nonentity, a hillbilly from the backwoods of Galilee. Most of them missed His royalty. Only a few disciples and later a mercurial mob recognized Him as a King, paving His way with palm fronds as He passed by on a donkey. Even then, they allowed their tunnel vision of materialism and self-deceptiveness to blind them to the true nature of His kingdom.

Our Lord gave Simon Peter the nickname, ironically and humorously, of "the Rock," for at that point he was anything but a rock. Ultimately, the Rock saw the Lord for what He was as he bent his knee, exclaiming, "You are the Christ, the Son of the Living God."

Sadly, he lived up to the sad irony of his moniker, as a short time later, when he met Christ on the lanes and byways of his frightening world, Peter refused to recognize Him, even in the cold, dark courtyard of the high priest, denouncing Him thrice as he exclaimed, "I do not know the man."

But while we traveled and negotiated the twists and turns of the highways of the life, we did bump into Jesus, and as believers we were blessed because unlike Peter in the courtyard, we did "know the Man."

We did meet the Lord of glory, and we knew Him because we realized that He could be more intimate with us than any person we had ever known. With every other individual with whom we have come into close contact, there was always an incomplete union. With all the willpower we could exert, with all the human love and passion we could muster, with all the mutual attraction that can be experienced between two humans—a husband and a wife, a child and his mother—there was always a metaphysical boundary between us, and the object of our love could be only approached but never penetrated. And the more we tried to bridge it, the more conscious we became of this demarcation, and we realized this separation was real. The reality of human interaction is that there can never be complete and utter communion with another human individual.

However, with Him we could experience complete and utter union. There was no separation. We could experience a blissful communion only with Him that cleared away every other consideration, every pain and anxiety, lightened every load, and shattered every yoke. Only with Him, the object of our pure worship, could we feel utter acceptance, devoid of toxic jealousy or possessiveness. Our love was not of this world but of His. For the first time in our lives, our love for someone other than ourselves was precious and pure. It was all about Him and for the first time not completely, fundamentally about us. We surprised even ourselves because we reveled in the fact that we could love so selflessly, as He loved us.

We recognized Him because He knew us first. And when He told us that he would never leave us and never forsake us, we believed it unreservedly and were assured of this with every fiber of our being.

With every other person on earth, when it came to conversation. there was always a reticence on our part, a fearfulness occasioned by our concern that we would be judged or thought ill of. In our sharing with Him there was none of that because He knew everything about us anyway. He was tempted at all points, just as we are, and was never shocked or reproving. In fact, we came to realize that with our immanent Lord, no verbalization was necessary, as He could finish every sentence before we uttered it. Silent prayer and praying in the Spirit became a joy, as we could finally pray "the perfect will of God." After a time, praying in our heavenly languages became the most natural way to open the clear channel between God and us.

In our misery and our humiliations, in our afflictions and our depravity, He comes alongside us as a companion and regards the "hot mess" of our lives along with us, never shaming us, never embarrassing us. He kneels down with us, examining the filth we have made and whispers in a still, small voice, "I can clean that spot for you. I can make it as white as snow if you wish."

In my own life in Christ, initially as a prisoner with a fifteen-year sentence, all appeals exhausted, and having lost everything and everyone, I faced a realistic probability that I would never see the outside world again; I would, perhaps, succumb to a natural or a violent death behind the wall. This is not uncommon. Given the length of my sentence of commitment and the chaotic, unpredictable environment in which I would serve it, this was very possibly bordering on a life sentence. Simply put, I felt that my life was over, and for a very long time I could barely pick up my head. I suffered large and long in silence because there's not a whole lot of heart-to-heart sharing going on in state prison. On the phone with friends and family, they didn't want to hear it. Their hearts were so broken as well that I couldn't subject them to my misery in full, although they sensed it, undoubtedly. Overall, they ran the other way. I don't blame them and I apologize for the pain I've caused.

Having spurned sweetly enticing plea offers that would have me in and out in as little as six months, I stood on pride and, to some extent, principle and exercised my right to a trial by my peers. My attorneys, actually two separate "dream teams," believed firmly in my innocence. After three years of hearings and seven months of testimony, we lost. I blew trial and got slammed with the maximum sentence possible.

I beat myself up daily through fear and self-love because I had made a bad situation immeasurably worse than it needed to be. I gave up hope of life, and more than once, in my darkest hours in that pit, I would lie in my bunk in unbearable pain through the hours late at night, seriously contemplating whether the bracket holding the huge electric fan to the wall at the end of the cell block would support my considerable weight if I suspended a ligature wrapped around my neck from it. I had no belt but figured I could fashion something that would serve. Perhaps I would hoard shoelaces and weave them into a noose. Is that suicidal ideation? I suppose so.

I spent nighttimes more than once imagining what I would do to myself with a handgun if someone gave me one. Honestly, during the worst of times, it was fifty-fifty at best. Most of the time early on I could not imagine finding the strength to get through the next minute, let alone the next ten or fifteen years. I knew that I was drowning and concluded that I needed someone to save me. I knew there was literally no one in my life who could do that.

Out of desperation, for the first time in my life, I made my last willful decision. I decided to suspend my disbelief, and I grabbed hold of this figure people called the Savior of the world. On December 27, 2004, I was born from above.

At 8:30 in the evening, on my knees in my cell, I asked Him to come into my heart and save me from this living death. I had no idea how He could do this, but I knew that I couldn't handle this alone anymore.

I don't recall feeling anything in the flesh, but there was, for the first time, a sense of a glimmer of hope and optimism. I realized that in a very real but indescribable way, I had crossed a line, and I knew there was no turning back. I also felt a relief because I understood that I was no longer responsible for saving myself. I knew there was no way that I could do that, but I also knew He had promised to take over every aspect of my life, clean up the mess that I was in, and bear the burdens that were crushing me.

Also, I had a hunch that this was a person who I could hold to His word. Someone I could rely on and who wouldn't walk away because my checkbook was gone. More than anything, I was desperate and had nothing more to lose.

Feeling vaguely lighter, I climbed into my bunk, put my headphones on, tuned in the local Christian praise-and-worship radio station, the Mars Hill Network, and fell soundly asleep. This became my go-to-sleep routine, which continues to this day, many years later. It is on even as I write these words, a decade later and a million miles away.

I have the Mars Hill Network app on my iPhone, and I am constantly amazed that when I turn it on, I recall my prison experience but not with fear and misery. Rather, I am endued with a warm, homey feeling. Then I realize that it was in the midst of that upstate prison that I was able, for the first time in my life, to transcend my circumstances and cross over into the world of eternal life. And I realize now that it is something I need to keep doing, even as the memories of the years of darkness begin to fray around the edges. In a very real way, my spiritual journey in prison—an everyday, every-hour project—was the watershed experience of my life. It was a seminal experience, even more so than the years I spent in medical school and residency.

I cannot say that I knew Him personally in the beginning, but I knew myself and was quite sure that I could not go it alone anymore. The painful phone calls home, hearing the recriminations and the subtle "distancing" from me only added to my misery. At that moment I said to Him, "Jesus, here are the keys to my life. I'm going to sit in the backseat and let you do the driving from now on."

But over the succeeding months and years, as I continued in this commitment and immersed myself in His word, I came to want to know Him more. I wanted to be drawn into His life and out of my own life, a life of the living dead behind prison walls and razor-wire concertina.

Much of my spiritual direction in this pursuit came from Reginald Somerset Ward, the greatest Anglican spiritual director of the twentieth century. In his brilliant treatise on deep Christian spirituality, *To Jerusalem*, Ward aptly compares the world in which we exist to a prison, partly in a metaphorical sense but also in a very real sense to a worldly, material form of incarceration. His work was all-inspiring to me, and I've read this book hundreds of times. Ward played the role of .my spiritual director, and I was never separated from him or from my King James Bible. It is that way today as well.

I discovered his devotional writings while in prison, and over the long years I read and reread these passages, finding them to be unlike any

Christian devotional literature I had ever read—and by year eight I had read them all, many of them several times, from C. S. Lewis to C. H. Spurgeon, from A. W. Tozer to Oswald Chambers. Then I discovered Reginald Somerset Ward's insights, and I found a pragmatic way of working out my Christianity on a daily basis; that is, "working out my salvation with fear and trembling."

One particularly brilliant spiritual concept that came to mean so much to me had a great impact on my walk with the Lord. It made real the practicality of tangible communion with Him, and when that occurred, it changed my life in the Lord forever, as well as my life in prison and afterward. It provided me with a means of transcending the bondage I was in for blissful moments each day; it can do the same for anyone. It has given me a road map to physical and spiritual healing every day as a truly free man, regardless of my circumstances.

More important, it can offer every sufferer release from any kind of bondage common to man on earth.

When we consider the myriad possibilities for "adventure" in the interior everyday life of the Christian, we realize that our normal daily lives are similar, in many meaningful ways, to a prison.

We are incarcerated within the fence line of specific restrictions and requirements, rules, and requirements that seem to hem us in, as we are confined in the material realm at every turn. Alterations that we seek to make in our lives, when they come at all, seem to proceed at a glacial pace.

Each day we are faced with the seeming drudgery of requirements imposed by vocations, diet, and other cyclical physiological needs, producing a closed environment focused on survival, with opportunities for adventure seemingly absent. Even when we are not confined by bars, razor wire, or stone walls, as in the penitentiary, we are seemingly confined in our thinking by our illusion that our universe in measured only in three dimensions, forgetting that the fourth dimension, the spirit realm, is our way out to an exciting world beyond.

In all fairness, even we as believers are unskilled in the methods necessary to explore the spiritual realm. Worse, it generally seems as if we are discouraged from this exploration by mainstream religion. The miraculous, however, is not just for the apostolic age, as some would have us believe. Rather, supernatural opportunities wait to be experienced in our lives by the dozens. They need only a spirit of expectancy and the serious quashing of doubt and unbelief.

It also takes a devotion to purity in our lives, for the Lord makes this clear when He predicates our heavenly vision on this:

"Blessed are the pure in heart for they will see God" (Matthew 5:8).

This is a simple declaration, but that simplicity is deceptive because it is pregnant with meaning. In fact, it is a spiritual law. Conversely, without purity, we cannot even visualize God or the kingdom. Furthermore, the Lord is talking not merely about the great by-and-by. He is telling us that all of the opportunities for us to experience God and the kingdom are predicated on and facilitated by our growth in sanctification. Again, we are drawn back to the love walk.

However, not only does the Law of the Spirit of Life in Christ Jesus set us free from the Law of Sin and Death, but in so doing we are freed from the prison of the three-dimensional universe in which our souls and bodies exist. We are freed to follow our regenerated spirits—spirits born from above and now inhabited by love Himself. We are freed to explore the spirit realm and to allow ourselves to be drawn into and apprehend the world of eternal life, just as we live on this blue marble, floating in a celestial sea of alternating darkness and light.

Sadly, though, we've been tethered so long that we don't know that the circular earthly prison of our senses is merely a porous illusion and that the world of eternal life can be accessed through a spiritual door. That door is the glorified God-Man, Jesus Christ of Nazareth.

"I am the door: by me if any man enter in, he shall be saved, and shall go in and out, and find pasture" (John 10:9).

In and out? What in heaven is the Lord telling us here? Perhaps He is addressing exactly what we seek; that is, the entry point for us to enter into the world of eternal life in a way that we can be refreshed, healed, renewed, and transformed, returning to the world of the material as He wills it.

As Somerset Ward lays out, it is plainly axiomatic, from our fundamental understanding of Christian spirituality, that we can enter into the world of eternal life via three routes or mechanisms: first by prayer and meditation on the Word; second, when we go home to be with the Lord, either by earthly death or at the rapture; and finally, when He invites us to break the bread with Him and enter into the world of eternal life at the Lord's Supper. It is via this sacrament that we can escape the confines of the prison of this world.

It is at the Lord's Supper that He comes to us individually, not as He came at Bethlehem for all humanity but to each of us, gathered together, suffering, in pain, heavy-labored, and disaffected. He comes to us with compassion, condescended in perfect humility.

At the Lord's Supper, He visits us in our bonds in perfect compassion and empathy, for we are sick, and He visits us. We are in prison and He comes to us.

I first received this revelation years ago, as a broken man, alone in my prison cell. I was moved to tears. I was undone by the image of this manifestation of Jesus's love. Abandoned and broken, looking at heaven-only-knew how many more years of imprisonment, I sensed an ill-defined glimmer of hope in my life—the light at the end of the tunnel. A way out of my exquisite twenty-four-hour, seven-day-a-week pain and brokenness, an escape from my bitter desperation that I could access. I knew that I knew that I knew that this was real, and I gave myself over to Him, resolving in my heart that I would surrender in allowing Him to take me out into deep water, for I was drowning. In the tenth chapter of John's Gospel, Jesus speaks of a "door," an exit (and an entry as well) from my worldly prison of misery, and I was determined to find it. For on the other side of that "door" in the world of eternal life, He feeds us with the bread of Life and with His precious blood, and we are made whole.

In my cell behind two rows of razor wire, electrified fencing, and gun towers, I was determined to develop a personal relationship with our Risen Lord and would use all the tools He gave us to do so. As I studied and meditated on this metaphor, I realized that there was indeed a tangible way to enjoy a daily personal relationship with Jesus. Interestingly, I was not schooled in religiosity or denominational doctrine, but rather than shy away from personal practice of the Eucharist, I resolved to figure out the way to experience it on my own, through prayer, meditation, and contemplation of my devotional readings.

I resolved to break out from my worldly bondage into the bliss of the world of eternal life. I had sensed all along, in my spirit, that the Lord's dispensation in that upper room, the night before He went to the cross, was intended to give us a tangible gift, a way and a method, to experience true communion with Him as we labored here on earth, awaiting His return, toiling in loneliness and coldness and with little love.

Having been initially drawn to this novel concept of the true nature of the prison in which we all live, I lay in my cell in my state greens, not knowing when or if I would ever again see the outside world. And I was compelled to delve deeper into independent investigation of this experience with the Blessed Sacrament and how it permits us to transcend tangibly the chains of our ordinary natural existence. I wanted more than spiritual milk; I was determined to get the "meat."

"So let us stop going over the basic teachings about Christ again and again. Let us go on instead and become mature in our understanding. Surely we don't need to start again with the fundamental importance of repenting from evil deeds and placing our faith in God" (Hebrews 6:1).

By that time (and certainly since then), I had read or listened to the spiritual teachings of virtually every serious Christian expositor since the first century and found most of was elementary—Christianity 101, if you will. That is, a lot of milk, as the writer of Hebrews said, and little if any meat.

Most notably, I realized at that early time in my Christian infancy that our evangelical, born-again church practiced an abbreviated and tortuously constricted form of the Lord's Supper; in fact, not discerning the Body and the Blood of Jesus. Perhaps this was due to a reaction against the Romanism and its traditions of men that so twisted the true meaning of this blessed gift on the eve of the cross.

Regardless, I knew there was more to this, and I was able to discern over time that it would be an overly constricted view of God's grace and love to treat the Lord's Supper as simply a ritual with such a limited purpose as some sort of pious memorial service.

As I dug deeper, exploring the mystery of the Lord's Supper, searching for a way to practice and experience the presence of Jesus, the Lord revealed to me that during the Lord's Supper, there is a flowing of life from the world of eternal life that engulfs us like a wave. As my mentor, Rev. Ward describes: It flows as through an open door and floods those who are willing and believing to receive. Then, like an ocean, as God wills, the wave undertow pulls us out into the deep water of eternity, and then it recedes.

I was transported back to my early childhood, growing up at the edge of the Atlantic Ocean off Long Island, and the warm summers of standing in the turbulent sea as the waves broke around me. They nearly would engulf me in one instant and then, in the next, would draw me into the azure-green sea as the undulating waves receded.

This is happily an experience that is common to man, and this metaphor works beautifully. I was blessed to make the connection to the kingdom of heaven opening for us, engulfing us, and then drawing us in ever so gently and lovingly in blissful communion with not only our Savior but the world of eternal life from which He visits us in the prison of our world.

I believe that there are many today in the body of Christ, including evangelical believers, who know in their hearts that this is true, and they deeply and tenderly long to experience this. However, they are inhibited by church doctrine that trivializes the Lord's Supper by rolling out a tray full of the "elements" once a month.

So the question that faces believers who are desperately seeking this gift from the Giver is how to access it, apart from the measly corporate worship doctrine imposed by church bureaucracy, which stifles real seeking. Here are some guidelines to help grow in achieving the fullness of the spiritual experience of the Lord's Supper.

Firstly, this is not something that will be achieved overnight but rather by long, joyful, and gradual growth. It comes with maturity, devotion, concentration, and training. These, by the way, are all first-century Christian concepts that have generally been lost on our current church. I am not talking about hard work but about the real meaning of daily devotion and real worship, as opposed to the goose-bump kind of worship we associate with listening to over-produced praise-and-worship music on K-LOVE radio. There's nothing wrong with praise-and-worship music, except for the danger that it appeals so highly to the senses that it can easily crowd out all the other important Christian worship modalities that propelled the first-century saints to turn the world upside down in their ardor for a scruffy, itinerant rabbi who died on a Roman cross a few years before.

Importantly, I am quite sure that the presence of unconfessed sin will short-circuit the entire process and render it unfruitful—a mere dead ritual with no power to heal or otherwise transform. This low-expectation empty ritual pretty much sums up the experience of the Lord's Supper, as it is practiced in our evangelical churches today. What's worse, it's totally unbiblical because the failure to discern the body and the blood in the elements of the Lord's Supper is the reason, as Paul teaches us, that so many in the body of Christ today are sick and cannot get their healing. Further, in its own inimitable way, the Roman Church and all its mainline denominational offshoots have ritualized the Lord's Supper to the point of its becoming robotic and totally divorced from any spiritual reality. It is a mere skeletal artifact of what Jesus meant it to be.

Too many of those who take Communion, therefore, have no concept of what they are engaged in; thus, they are incapable of receiving.

"My people are destroyed for a lack of knowledge" (Hosea 4:6).

However, to the believer who takes the Lord at His word and is eager to receive, the most important element in this endeavor is true desire. This is the kind of pure desire that is always grown of love. It is desire that is focused on apprehending the Giver first and only secondarily on obtaining the gift.

Simon Magus, in the book of Acts, desired the power of the Holy Spirit as it was evidenced in the miracles performed by Peter and John. The Bible even refers to him as a "believer." Of course, it's easy to believe when you see the lame healed, the dead raised, and so forth, and Simon Magus was an example of this kind of "cheap" faith.

He was so impressed by the acts of the apostles, moving in the power of the Holy Spirit, that he offered Peter payment to get that power. Peter discerned that Simon Magus was indeed a believer of sorts but that there was no love in him; his faith was all about what he could get from the spirit of life in Christ Jesus. Thus, Simon Magus had the desire for supernatural things but not a pure, sanctified desire grown out of love for the Giver.

"But Peter said unto him, Thy money perish with thee, because thou hast thought that the gift of God may be purchased with money" (Acts 8:20).

Although the book of Acts does record that Simon was mortified by Peter's frank condemnation, we are left guessing as to what became of this first-century enterprising huckster. One legend has it that he followed Peter and Paul to Rome, whereupon he fell into cahoots with a Babylonian mystery religious cult, hijacked the fledgling Christian Church at Rome founded by Paul, then attempted to hijack Judaism along with it, and proceeded to grow the whole thing into what is commonly known today as the Roman Catholic Church.

But this is all legend and supposition.

Interestingly, the legendary Christian preacher C. H. Spurgeon, the greatest preacher of the nineteenth century, who regularly preached to crowds of fifteen to twenty thousand people in an era of no electrical sound amplification or lighting, tells of the time he was contacted by another "enterprising huckster," P. T. Barnum. The great promoter in America, hearing of Reverend Spurgeon's huge crowds that dwarfed anything else on earth, cabled Spurgeon and offered him huge amounts of cash to promote him. In true fashion, the great Christian preacher immediately cabled back to the impresario, P. T. Barnum, the exact words of Peter the apostle to Simon Magus, nineteen hundred years earlier: "May thy money perish with thee because thou hast thought that the gift of God may be purchased with money."

How apt that history repeats itself so elegantly. We have no record that Barnum was distressed in the least by Spurgeon's reply.

While desire is the beginning and not the end of building our foundation for experiencing the presence of the risen Lord in the Lord's Supper, desire grown of love is definitely a prerequisite. Out of this purity of desire comes devotion, and out of this devotion comes practice and repetition—not vain repetition but repetition grown out of burning love and desire. In material human terms, think of how often a young suitor would walk across the threshold of his sweetheart's door. He certainly would not look at it as a vain repetition or a duty but rather something that he could not do often enough.

This is the way we need to think about the Lord's Supper. Stop thinking of it as an empty ritual or a table we roll out once a month. Frankly, that is an abomination before the Lord.

Rather, we find that by coming to the table of grace constantly, by making it part of our daily lives, we come to the full experience gradually—imperceptibly at first but ultimately to all His fullness. First comes the definite acceptance of a presence, a belief borne of faith. Then our senses may become stimulated by an actual awareness of a communication at the height of the process. Slowly, over days, weeks, months, or even years, the presence is confirmed in its reality by our inner souls.

Ultimately, as the worshipper becomes more experienced and comfortable, less distracted by external stimuli, and more familiar with the road to be traveled, suddenly a door opens, the entry into the world of eternal life occurs, and, for some, an ecstatic communion with the risen Lord is consummated.

Words on a page cannot do justice to what I am describing. Each worshipper must develop this part of his or her spiritual life, utilizing this in two ways: (1) as a guide to how to begin and proceed; and (2) as an assurance that at the end of this loving worship, our Lord and the world from which He comes does indeed await us.

It is vital to reiterate that it is worship itself that is the essence of the process here. Thus, we seek Him in "spirit and in truth."

This revelation of the immense spiritual depth of the practice and centrality of the Lord's Supper made me realize what our evangelical churches were tragically missing. I knew that recovering this in the midst of my own nasty existence in prison would be central to accessing the healing of my brokenness that Jesus promised. However, I needed to establish for myself the methodology for this sacrament in my own devotional life. I realized that I wasn't getting it in my born-again church, but I was convinced that it was a central sacrament of our worship.

It was clear to me at last that Jesus had offered us this as a precious gift to use in our spiritual walks and not simply as the memorial ritual to which it has been relegated by our born-again churches. Our Lord was not speaking figuratively in John 6 and elsewhere. This was all over the New Testament and was not a case of lifting a single scripture verse out of context. This was something He intended us to use to nourish our spirits, our souls, and our bodies until He comes, much as the Lord provided manna in the desert for the wandering Israelites. I too was a pilgrim, wandering in my wilderness years in prison.

While there is no easy way to achieve the fullness of this spiritual experience, there are a few guidelines worth summarizing.

Patience is foremost, for we know from Luke's Gospel,

"In your patience possess ye your souls" (Luke 21:19).

Patience and perseverance will invariably flow from a purity of loving desire.

Patience is not something that we can develop. It is part of the fruit of the Spirit. It is a gift, and it is freely available to those who ask in faith, which worketh by love.

The authentic experience will be evidenced by an inflowing of the joy of the Lord and the resulting strength and power in our lives, not necessarily sensed at the moment of blissful communion. Remember we are dealing in a world of timelessness.

Accordingly, we notice that we are often we seized by inexpressible joy and invigorating vitality later on, at home, in our ministry, or even on line at Walmart. We will begin to enjoy moments of great spiritual clarity more and more frequently as we make the Lord's Supper part of our worship lives.

I know this from personal experience, and I also know that you can experience this as well.

It is my prayer for the body of Christ that what I have experienced and from what is written here, you will discover the open door and enter in, that you will experience the presence of the Lord and the life He brings. That you will experience His light that can illuminate the dark recesses of your soul and, if it be His will, a real experience of the world of timeless eternity from which He comes.

I have contemplated this expanded view of the Lord's Supper worshipfully over and over again, in tandem with my devotionals. Like Paul, in prison I became determined to know nothing but Jesus Christ and Him crucified. I wanted to know Him, the fellowship of His suffering, and the power of His resurrection. I came to realize that making a project of exploring the true meaning of the Lord's Supper was a pretty good place to start. It has become an important part of my testimony of healing, transformation, and victory over unspeakable bondage. Perhaps as much as anything else, I am moved to bring it to others, for I believe that it is critical to our victory in the Lord:

"And they overcame him by the blood of the Lamb, and by the word of their testimony; and they loved not their lives unto the death" (Revelation 12:11).

After much prayer and meditation on the Lord's Supper, more than a decade ago, shortly after I gave my life to the Lord, I stepped out in faith and began taking the Lord's Supper, alone in my cell, late at night while everyone else was asleep. The block was pretty dark. In the beginning, I used a vanilla Oreo-type sandwich cookie—I split it in half and scraped the icing off. It was a credible wafer of sorts, and it tasted good too. I didn't see any proscription against that in Luke 22 or in Matthew 26, for that matter.

Let's get something straight: they were eating bread at the final supper in the upper room that night before the cross. It was matzoh or unleavened bread to be sure on that particular night, but only because it was Passover night. The boys most certainly, however, were not eating dried-up, stick-in-the-throat communion wafers, a modern perverse interpretation of bread.

Jesus had introduced this radical new twist to the age-old blessing that the Jewish people traditionally said over the bread and the wine. As a young Jewish boy, I was brought up on this blessing in my Jewish ancestral home and in the synagogue. While this is something new and unique to my Gentile Christian brothers and sisters, as a Jewish Christian, I was weaned on this ceremony, as we have been doing this routine with the bread and the wine for the better part of six thousand years. It is central to our home worship life, although we weren't pretentious about it.

Only now do I see it as a figure of the Lord's Supper, and I feel blessed to have been doing this since I was a little boy.

This fact is incomprehensible to Gentile Christians. This is understandable because of their different life experiences, but it reveals a sadly neglectful and widespread ignorance of Jesus's roots. One absolutely cannot begin to understand Jesus of Nazareth without delving deeply into His Jewishness. This makes some Christians uncomfortable and has done for thousands of years. However, this rejection of Rabbi Jesus does nothing but retard one's spiritual growth. Jesus was Jewish from the moment of His birth, and He died on a Roman cross that Passover eve two thousand years ago, with matzoh in His teeth.

Long before I was saved, I was mysteriously drawn to Him. It was in the beginning of my travails, so I am not surprised that I was becoming more sensitive to the Hound of Heaven's pursuit of me. I began to read books about Him, largely books of the Jesus-project genre that explored the "historical Jesus." One in particular, *Rabbi Jesus*, by Professor Bruce Chilton of Bard College, caught my attention because it explored in detail the Lord's Jewish upbringing. I must say that although it is not to be relied on for sound biblical doctrine and is more of a historical tour de force, Chilton's works made me realize that first, Jesus was a Man who actually existed, and second, He was a nice Jewish boy, pampered by a Jewish mother who had a great belief in Him and expected great things of Him.

That was something with which I could personally identify, and I was hooked. It was a first step on my journey to the foot of the cross. Looking back, I find it fascinating how the Lord will use anything to reach the lost, the hurt, and the suffering, even the scholarly writings of an Anglican priest like Professor Chilton.

On Friday nights at Temple Avodah in Oceanside, after service, at the collation, called the *oneg shabbat,* our beloved, gentle Rabbi Charles Ozer would step up to the white linen-covered table and lift up in his hands a beautiful challah bread almost three feet long, every knot of the loaf shining. He would break the bread and pronounce the blessing over the bread and the wine in Hebrew, before the entire congregation assembled in the social hall adjoining the sanctuary:

Barukh atah Adonai, Eloheinu, melekh ha-olam
Blessed art Thou, O Lord, our God, King of the Universe

hamotzi lechem min ha'aretz. (Amein).
who bringeth forth bread from the earth. (Amen)

Barukh atah Adonai, Eloheinu, melekh ha-olam
Blessed art Thou, O Lord, our God, King of the universe

borei p'ri hagafen (Amein)
Who creates the fruit of the vine(Amen)

The Bible doesn't specify or distinguish what kind of bread we are to use when we do this. The New Testament doesn't specify what kind of fruit of the vine we are to use when we do this. Jesus simply says, "Eat my flesh and drink my blood and you will be part of me and I will be part of you." He just says of the traditional Hebrew blessing over the Shabbat or Sabbath meal, in effect, "When you do this from now on, remember what I just told you." That is the true meaning of His actual words: "Do this in remembrance of me."

This typifies Christian thought, in which almost every area of Jewish life, as practiced and prescribed in the Torah, is now assigned new meanings, in which Jesus is now the fulfillment of the precepts of the Law. To interpret the Lord's Supper as anything less than this is to relegate it to being merely an accessory memorial ritual, rather than a miraculous gift of His love and His infinite grace. Rabbi Ozer, God love him, taught us how to do this, although the poor man couldn't possibly discern the body and blood of Yeshua ha Mashiach, Jesus the Messiah. To him, it was only a ritual, a thanksgiving of sorts. There's nothing wrong with that, but to a Christian Jew—that is, a completed Jew—it is infinitely more. It is the *re-membering* of Jesus the Messiah. When I use the term "re-membering," it is critical to point out that this term is used in contradistinction to the term "dis-membering." So in the Lord's Supper as we *re-member* Him, we are actually experiencing His fullness bodily.

As Pentecostal believers, we pursue the "gifts' of the Holy Spirit in our daily lives, including (but not limited to) tongues, prophecy, and healing, never forgetting the Giver of the gifts in our pursuit. It is elegantly beautiful and so typically extravagant of God the Son, that in the sacrament of the Lord's Supper, the gift we pursue and receive is the fullness of the Giver Himself.

This is not just a memorial service honoring His memory. It is a spiritual meal in which we experience the presence of His person. We are not to concern ourselves with man-made explanations, traditions, or doctrines and theories of consubstantiation, transubstantiation, or other vain attempts to bio-theologically explain this mystery. That is a spiritual dead end that results in the error of man-made religion. We are to take Jesus simply and purely at His word. Nothing more and certainly nothing less than His word. Jesus said it; I believe it; that settles it.

So the bottom line of all this brilliant, complicated theology is that half an Oreo cookie works just fine because Jesus can handle it. Obviously, I had no access to wine, and when I could not get grape juice, I used Cranberry Ice Crystal Light. I liked this because it contained real juice solids so it satisfied being fruit of the vine, as the cookie was bread of sorts from the earth. Frankly, Jesus could handle Dr. Pepper, if that was all I could get.

Interestingly, part of the original traditional Hebrew blessing includes an accommodation for the individual life circumstance (for example, prison) that might be so restricted that wine or even grape juice is not available to the celebrant. It includes the following:

(if using other liquids)
shehakol nih'yeh bid'varo (Amein)
Who made all things exist through His word (Amen)

It is amazing because the Jews knew that the particularity of the emblems were irrelevant, as God could handle it. This is a spiritual meal, to be sure, but it is indeed a meal, and God, who is not bound by space or time, responds to real faith. He can make do with any elements, for we know, as did the ancient Jews, that God was He "Who made all things exist through His word."

Remember, Jesus, the God-Man, was a fellow who changed water into wine right on the spot at a wedding party, so we are either going to believe the whole Gospel or we're not. I choose to believe, and in the midst of the storm of my life in prison, belief was all I had left.

Later on, I developed a nice little technique for making my own Bible-style flatbreads. I rolled my own dough with flour from the prison commissary, water, and a little salt. I thought it would be a nice touch to add the salt because He tells us we are the salt of the earth, and I continue doing this today. I rolled it out and formed in my hands three- or four-inch patties of dough, which I then fried in oil. We had access to a cooktop, so this was easy.

The breads that I made looked as though they could have been on that Last Supper table two thousand years ago. They were delicious, and I looked forward to enjoying the mini-meal of the Lord's Supper. Really, if the Lord's Supper isn't delectable, even in its sparse simplicity, then what is? We should be enjoying everything related to our Lord without apology. Worship should be a pep rally for Jesus, and the Lord's Supper should be at least a mini-feast, delicious and satisfying in every way to the spirit, to the soul, and to the body.

I pronounced the *barukha* (the blessing over the juice) in exactly the same way Jesus did that night when He lifted the cup to his lips and drank. I said the same *barukha* I had been taught by my father over the bread. It was the same bharucha our Lord said two millennia ago. I received the bread and the fruit of the vine in the power of the Holy Spirit, in faith, as the body and blood of Jesus of Nazareth. I praised Him and thanked Him and confirmed it with a firm "amen," stated in faith.

I made this a regular practice every day. There were dark times in my life as a prisoner that were unspeakable. These were times when I practiced the Lord's Supper three or more times a day, because I was determined to put that Communion table between me and the enemy, and I rebuked him by stating, "Satan, you are not coming one step closer." I was fighting to keep my head above water at times. It worked.

These were many days when I was so greatly discouraged by fear, setback, and anxiety that I turned to the Word and the Communion table as my only defense. I clung to that Lord's table in the midst of the storm, and it gave me the focus to keep my eyes on Jesus. I gradually began to accept that there was no limit to how deep in the Lord regular practice of the Lord's Supper can take us when it is practiced in faith, in spirit, and in truth as a regular devotional meditation. In great weakness, because His power is made perfect, the table of grace is empowering.

He brought me through, and I continue in this, years later. I believe that the regular taking of the Lord's Supper is critically important to living the victorious life in Christ. In His blood, we are sanctified by His righteousness. In His perfect flesh is our healing—healing of our spirits, our minds, and our bodies.

In many evangelical churches, which I dearly love and respect, this thinking is most decidedly politically incorrect or at least it is outside the mainstream. So be it. It's not something we are going to break fellowship over.

But respectfully, I believe they are missing it unnecessarily.

Though well intentioned, the born-again church has totally missed the meaning of the Lord's table. They deny themselves the presence of the Lord in the elements. This is nothing but rank doubt and unbelief. Consequently, as Paul says, many are sick in the body of Christ, both spiritually and physically. I am sure that Paul could not have made it any clearer when he wrote,

"For those who eat and drink without discerning the body of Christ eat and drink judgment on themselves" (1 Corinthians 11:29 KJV).

"That is why many of you are weak and sick and some have even died" (1 Corinthians 11:30 NLT).

I am baffled by how our evangelical churches can read this, as well as Jesus's own words in John 6, and still fail to enjoy the true and full meaning of the Lord's table and appreciate how essential it is as a gift. It is a gift that the Lord Himself bestowed upon His church to nourish their spirits, souls, and bodies until He comes again to receive us, His bride.

Clearly, the rejection of the literal presence of the Lord in the Lord's Supper is the Evangelical Church's reaction against the excesses of Romanism. However, to reject on thin doctrinal grounds the central sacrament given to us by the Lord Jesus, out of His love and concern for us, is to simply throw the baby away with the bathwater. It robs us of our right to experience the spiritual meal of His perfect flesh and His sanctifying blood. For a church born of the Reformation, which distinguishes itself by its regard for the word of God as the literal, infallible, inerrant truth, this position is inexplicable and frustrating.

Of course, the New Testament clearly states that no scripture is subject to private, individual meaning. However, it is the Evangelical Church that is idiosyncratic in its terribly restrictive interpretation of the Eucharist.

Thus, I exhort those who are in Christ to bring their sufferings and their brokenness to the Lord's table and partake in spirit, certainly, but in absolute truth as well. When Jesus tells us, "This is My body and this is My blood," He is not equivocating. He is not exaggerating, and there is not a shred of evidence that He is speaking in parables or symbols. Many of His Jewish disciples left Him in disbelief as well, and never does the Bible indicate that Jesus ever walked back this teaching by saying, "Wait a minute, guys. You're misunderstanding this. I didn't mean it literally. You're taking it too seriously!"

No, He told them just the opposite. He doubled down on the literalness of the body and the blood when He admonished them by agreeing with them when they protested, "This is a hard teaching, is it not?" This is Good News.

> This is the bread which cometh down from heaven, that a man may eat thereof, and not die.
>
> I am the living bread which came down from heaven: if any man eat of this bread, he shall live for ever: and the bread that I will give is my flesh, which I will give for the life of the world.
>
> The Jews therefore strove among themselves, saying, How can this man give us his flesh to eat?
>
> Then Jesus said unto them, Verily, verily, I say unto you, Except ye eat the flesh of the Son of man, and drink his blood, ye have no life in you.
>
> Whoso eateth my flesh, and drinketh my blood, hath eternal life; and I will raise him up at the last day.

For my flesh is meat indeed, and my blood is drink indeed.

He that eateth my flesh, and drinketh my blood, dwelleth in me, and I in him.

As the living Father hath sent me, and I live by the Father: so he that eateth me, even he shall live by me.

This is that bread which came down from heaven: not as your fathers did eat manna, and are dead: he that eateth of this bread shall live for ever.

These things saith he in the synagogue, as he taught in Capernaum.

Many therefore of his disciples, when they had heard this, said, This is an hard saying; who can hear it?

When Jesus knew in himself that his disciples murmured at it, he said unto them, Doth this offend you?

What and if ye shall see the Son of man ascend up where he was before?

It is the spirit that quickeneth; the flesh profiteth nothing: the words that I speak unto you, they are spirit, and they are life.

But there are some of you that believe not. For Jesus knew from the beginning who they were that believed not, and who should betray him. (John 6:50–64)

Is Jesus lying here? I think not. Is He exaggerating here? Impossible.

If Jesus is not telling the absolute truth here, then perhaps He's lying in John 3:16, the central scripture of our faith.

Once we start to water down the Lord's teachings to mere metaphors, we embark on a slippery slope that we need to stay away from.

No, Jesus is not a liar. We can take our Lord at His word. For us to do otherwise is to do so at peril of our salvation.

"May it never be! Rather, let God be found true, though every man be found a liar, as it is written, 'that you may be justified in your words, and prevail when you are judged'" (Romans 3:4 NASB).

On the dusty, hot, depressing road to Emmaus two thousand years ago, a few days after the Crucifixion and the resurrection, Jesus met two of His closest disciples who, amazingly, did not recognize Him. In fact, they talked with their Lord at length and took a meal with Him but still did not recognize Him until He broke the bread at the table, whereupon He vanished. Their hearts, however, were burning with the recognition of His presence, and they were able to receive Him. It never fails.

This actually happened just as it is written. It is in the New Testament as a signpost, as it were, for it is an instruction on how we can also spiritually experience our Lord's presence in a real way in ordinary life, on the lanes and byways of our very own world—a way that we can repeat over and over again with expectancy and growing passion.

We certainly do not need a priest or a pastor. Jesus Himself makes the miracle happen every time. When we practice the Lord's Supper in faith, it will begin to happen for us every time, and like His heartbroken disciples on the sad road to Emmaus, our hearts too will burn with His love. Once each week or once each day. For that matter, whenever we are wounded and suffering, we can come to our Savior at His table as often as we are moved to do. We can bring Him our brokenness and our woundedness, and He will sit at meat with us, giving us His refreshment in His perfect flesh and His precious blood. We can give Him our sadness, and He will freely give us His joy, for we know this:

"Then he said unto them, Go your way, eat the fat, and drink the sweet, and send portions unto them for whom nothing is prepared: for this day is holy unto our LORD: neither be ye sorry; for the joy of the LORD is your strength" (Nehemiah 8:10).

And faith rules the whole thing. Not the namby-pamby concept of faith that the world seems to value. Not the empty faith spoken of in Hallmark cards. Not the weak-tea faith that passes as begging and pleading and hoping against hope that maybe, just maybe, God will finally notice us and give us a touch or a dab of grace. Not that kind of Swiss-cheesy faith permeated with doubt and unbelief. The faith I speak of is the "now" kind of faith spoken of in Hebrews 11.

"Now faith is the substance of things hoped for, the evidence of things not seen" (Hebrews 11:1).

A God-kind of faith. An expectant, assured kind of faith that has us believers sitting on the edge of our seats, waiting breathlessly for Him to make it to come to pass any moment. That's "now" faith. Not later, not maybe, but now.

"Thy will be done on earth as it is in Heaven."

God's will is already done in heaven when we pray, for instance, for our healing. It's a done deal. It was settled at Calvary. That's "now" faith. What remains is only for us to receive this reality and to patiently expect it to manifest in the natural. The biggest reason we do not receive our answered prayer is twofold—first, because we pray in doubt and unbelief; and second, because of unconfessed sin. Without turning our sins over to the Lord, there can be no forgiveness.

"Forgive us our debts as we forgive our debtors."

Interestingly, the Lord Himself, in the so-called Lord's Prayer, gave us the basic underlying formula for all of our prayer; that is, prayer that is made in belief, not doubt. That is prayer that changes things. Further, it's all based on the absolutely essential concept of "now" faith, as stated in Hebrews 11:1.

Too many Christians have been taught that the word "now" in Hebrews 11 is just a King James Version translational throwaway. Nothing could be further from the reality that real faith is in the "now." When we pray to Him in this kind of expectant faith, we know that He hears us and will give us whatever we ask of Him. His promises are realities in the spiritual realm, which is the highest reality. Whether He grants us healing, deliverance, or anything else, we believe that it has come to pass, and we wait patiently and expectantly for it to manifest itself in the natural. It is obvious that the Lord exhorts us to step out more boldly in faith than most of the body of Christ today is willing to do, for when He opens Mark 11:23 with the admonition "Verily," it is our cue to take what follows literally and absolutely, not figuratively. Do we have the courage of our convictions to follow Him?

"For verily I say unto you, That whosoever shall say unto this mountain, Be thou removed, and be thou cast into the sea; and shall not doubt in his heart, but shall believe that those things which he saith shall come to pass; he shall have whatsoever he saith" (Mark 11:23).

When we exercise, in obedience, this kind of faith—His kind of faith—then we will see things change. Verily, we will!

For although our tears may endure for the night, "joy cometh in the morning" and in this way, as we emerge from the long dark tunnel of our woundedness into the morning light of our new life in Christ, we will no longer have to live in regret, resentment, and defeat. Sitting at His table, spiritually enjoying His body and imbibing His blood, buoyantly and expectantly, in "now" faith, we will confidently shout, no longer "If I met Jesus" but "When I meet Jesus!" At the Lord's Supper He yearns for you.

Moreover, as I sat for years at the Lord's table in a darkened prison cell block on the edge of my bunk, the Lord revealed something more that I want to share with you, as I share it every day with those broken, wounded, hopeless, and near the end of life to whom I minister in nursing homes and hospices.

As you practice the taking of the Lord's Supper more and more in faith, gradually you will find, as did I, that the emblems begin to taste less and less like mere earthly bread and wine. They will acquire for you a different but very distinctive taste entirely. It takes some time and regular practice and dedication to this devotional, but the results are worth it. The Lord Jesus is for everyone, but He is an acquired taste.

As you take Him into your body, even in the midst of the terrible storms of life, you will ultimately come to acquire that taste for Him with every fiber of your being. For the first time in your life, you will sweetly savor and know the heavenly taste of real victory.

For Jesus, the Great Physician, truly becomes the divine taste of victory. He is the taste of the Lord's Supper on our spiritual palates. Once we come to His table of grace in this way and taste the honey sweetness of His victory in every area of our lives, it is truly a spiritual delicacy that a Child of God will never give up.

The glorified God-Man waits for you to enter into the gate. Take His perfect flesh into your broken body. He shed His blood so that we may nurse on the fruit of His riven side. Drink of eternal life. It is nourishment on which we, as children of God, are dependent. It is a heavenly drink from which we shall never be weaned.

Enter in, child of God. Enter in, for all your healing awaits on the other side of the threshold.

The Doctor is in. The Great Physician neither slumbers nor sleeps. The heavenly healer is on call for you, twenty-four/seven.

Forever, world without end.

All your joy, all your strength, all your peace, all your victory is in Him.

Come in, child of God, from your hot, dusty, broken hearted journey on your own road to Emmaus. There is room at the inn, and the table of grace awaits you.

He has prepared a feast before you in the presence of thine enemies.

He breaks the bread, and He pours the cup.

Your cup runneth over. Drink deeply.

Your heart burns with recognition and loving desire.

Softly and tenderly, Jesus is calling. Calling to you and to me.

He spoke out your name at Creation, and the sound of His voice literally echoes today, bouncing off the corners of the universe at this moment. Nothing lost.

In fact, He has a white stone for you, overcomer, with your new name inscribed on it. A white stone. Your ebenezer from the Lord, Himself.

"He that hath an ear, let him hear what the Spirit saith unto the churches; To him that overcometh will I give to eat of the hidden manna, and will give him a white stone, and in the stone a new name written, which no man knoweth saving he that receiveth it" (Revelation 2:17).

Tarry no longer, child of God. The Great Physician has been waiting for you and loving you since before the foundation of the universe.

Go for it.

In faith, in spirit, and in truth—go for it, Pilgrim. Behold, the Man!

"Blessed be the LORD God of Israel for ever and ever. And all the people said, Amen, and praised the LORD" (1 Chronicles 16:36).

17

JUST AS I AM

JUST A FEW MONTHS before I received my MD from Johns Hopkins, I sat in the sumptuous office of the great surgeon in chief at the world-famous Columbia Presbyterian Medical Center, the ivory tower high above upper New York City. Across the desk from me sat the famous man.

Columbia was recruiting me vigorously for my internship after medical school, as were a number of other hospitals, and I was kind of taking a "victory lap" after a rather stellar stint at Hopkins, the mecca of the medical universe.

I did not know the Lord at the time and was very full of myself and way more immature than I could ever have appreciated at the time. I was totally clueless as to life in so many ways and would remain so for many years. In summary, I was twenty-four.

The great man leaned forward and looked at me intently.

"Dr. Dombroff, in thirty or forty years, what do you want to have accomplished?" he asked.

I did not expect that question, but I remember exactly what my answer was. I mulled it over for a moment, but it was not hard for me to answer, because interestingly, it had been on my mind for a long time as I had gone through the Ivy League, medical school at Hopkins and had engaged in cardiac surgery research that later turned out to be groundbreaking.

I suspect that my interviewer asked this question regularly and expected answers something along the lines of brilliant surgical achievements and so forth. I wasn't thinking in those terms.

"I want to look back and be able to say that at some specific point in time I changed someone's life in a profound way for the better that would not have happened had I not been passing through his life at that moment," I answered. I really didn't know exactly what I meant by this at the time but I knew that it was more than saving a life. That's what surgeons do. Uncharacteristically and not even fully understanding the answer myself, I blurted it out.

He looked quizzical, and we moved on to touring the wards and seeing some patients at the world-renowned medical center. However, I never forgot the encounter because unexpectedly I'd revealed something about Richard to the great man; more significantly, I learned something about myself. Actually, I was a little embarrassed at my answer because it seemed as it was a little "airy-fairy." Especially for a surgeon.

There's no question that in life we gain so much as the years pass, but life is also often characterized by loss. Things are taken from us in the natural course of human existence. Often, we throw things away, not reckoning the cost.

In Oliver Stone's brilliant cinematic treatment of professional athletics, *Any Given Sunday,* the protagonist, played by Al Pacino, is an aging superstar football player-turned-head-coach who addresses his superstar players in the locker room one last time before the championship game.

He talks about how life is often about loss, how life takes things from us, and how we squander so many of our blessings ourselves. He then goes on to tell the young stars, "I blew away all my money and chased away anyone who ever loved me."

Obviously, that is a common story, and it pretty much sums up my storied existence—but only up to a point.

These days, as a nursing home and hospice chaplain, I tend to make rounds in a way that is very similar to my years in clinical medicine and surgery at the great hospitals of the world. I have certain patients who are on my list to see, and also I poke my head into rooms to say hi to new patients, introduce myself as "Chaplain Rock," and ask them if there is anything I can do for them.

As happenstance would have it, I came into the room of a young man who was dying with cancer that was widely metastatic to all of his body, including his brain. I asked him cheerfully, "Is there anything I can do for you?"

"Do you have anything for terminal liver cancer?" he asked.

I do not get into discussions with sick people about the details of their specific conditions because that's not my job, and also there are more than enough doctors and others who are more than willing to entertain endless blather about sickness, disease, and death. Even in Christian healing prayer services, well-intentioned believers often spend more time testifying about the intricacies and minutiae of disease and death than they devote to speaking healing and life over themselves or others. They don't need me to add to that critical mass of deadly doubt and unbelief.

The long and short of this was that after chatting with this young man with metastatic liver cancer, I prayed with him, something he had never done in his life. I then asked him if he would like to get things "right with God." He said he would, and I guided him to a saving knowledge and confession of Jesus Christ of Nazareth. We took the Lord's Supper together at his bedside. We hugged each other. I congratulated him, and I told him I would see him next weekend. I will always remember that he smiled an amazing little sly grin as I left the room.

I have found that when people are at the precipice of death, they are often freed from the bondage to traditions and cultural inhibitions learned from family, communities, and life experiences. In short, they are desperate for the meaning of their lives. All the bankrupt philosophies of man that they may have been taught while growing up and with which they have been inculcated often don't amount to a hill of beans at the end of life. They seem to develop a sixth sense for truth and have no appetite for lies.

That's where the Gospel comes in.

This young fellow was no different, and like many others, I have been privileged, as an ambassador for Christ, to bring him to the only source of true peace and meaning in his life, the living God-Man, Jesus of Nazareth.

As I left his room, in my spirit, I could hear the angels singing in the throne room of God. I love that sound. I've heard it many times.

"Likewise, I say unto you, there is joy in the presence of the angels of God over one sinner that repenteth" (Luke 15:10).

I put him on my visitation list and proceeded on with rounds. I do not recall his name, but that is of no import, because I knew that the Lord had his name tattooed on the palms of His hands from before the foundation of the universe.

"Behold, I have graven thee upon the palms of my hands; thy walls are continually before me" (Isaiah 49:16).

The following Sunday, as I was making my rounds, looking at my visitation list, I entered this young fellow's room and absentmindedly exclaimed, "Hiya, brother. Chaplain Rock here!" I look up from my list

He lay in his bed, comatose, surrounded by family—a sister and a brother. They looked up at me with initial surprise but then with welcoming grins, similar to the amazing smile I remembered the young man had given me the week earlier.

His sister jumped up and came over to me. I was half afraid that I was going to get scolded for something. That's an occupational hazard of getting into so much trouble in life.

She took my hand and said, "Chaplain Rock, my brother told me about you praying with him, and we are very grateful. We were raised Jewish, but we're not religious people. Thank you so much. It meant a lot to him. He's in a coma, and he's going now."

I hugged her and walked slowly to the right side of his bed. This was the side from which I always ministered. It was a habit because we old surgeons always do our best work from the patient's right side of the operating table.

I took his hand and anointed his forehead with oil. He was semi-comatose, and his breathing was stertorous. I prayed out loud, in the natural as well as quietly in tongues, for when we pray over someone in tongues, we pray the "perfect will of God" over his life.

We joined hands around his bed and prayed as well. They knew he was at the end of his painful journey. I assured them truthfully that their brother would be in heaven with the Lord forever. We had settled that last week.

"I am the resurrection, and the life: he that believeth in me, though he were dead, yet shall he live" (John 11:25).

When we were finished, we sat in loving silence all together for a while. Their brother and I had sung praise-and-worship songs together when he had come to the Lord last week. So we all sang together, or at least, I kind of sang and those nice people kind of followed along. But they liked it. Just before leaving, I leaned way over the young man's right ear, without any assurance that he would hear me. I knew his spirit would hear it anyway. I kneeled down by his bedside, and I sang to him quietly one last song, my favorite:

> *Softly and tenderly Jesus is calling,*
> *Calling for you and for me;*
> *See, on the portals He's waiting and watching,*
> *Watching for you and for me*
> *Come home, come home,*
> *You who are weary, come home*
> *Earnestly, tenderly, Jesus is calling,*
> *Calling, O sinner, come home!*

It evoked no immediate reaction from him, but just as I finished, he turned his head ever so slightly to me, still on my knees in prayer at his bedside. He squeezed my hand gently, and, eyes still closed, he evidenced that famous family grin I now knew so well.

Then, finally freed of his bonds, he went home to be with the Lord.

I realized at that very moment that I had finally fulfilled the elusive life ambition I had so unexpectedly articulated in that pretentious surgical internship interview forty years earlier in New York. Changing a life profoundly. The goal that had eluded me for nearly six decades. I had accomplished what I had set out to do in life but in a way that I could never have dreamed possible as a young, hungry man in a rush. But after all the triumphs and all the adulation, after all the gains and losses, despite all the pain and sorrow, it had been worth the trip.

Today, I have a very sweet, modest, and rather solitary life in ministry, as well as some speaking, teaching, and consulting projects, just to keep my "hand in." My life, of course, is very different than I could ever have imagined.

I can see the evidence all around me that I am different as well. That "man in the mirror" from olden days is gone. I live comfortably and quietly. Alone. All the money that I have in the world is in my back pocket. However, for the first time in my life, miraculously, I seem to save money every month. The Lord is so gracious.

Loaves and fishes, loaves and fishes.

I possess none of the trappings of past worldly wealth or greatness, no more yachts or private jets, no more Rolls-Royces or penthouses in Trump Tower. They are memories. Some wonderful, some not so. However, now, dancing ridiculously with wheelchaired patients, as David danced unrestrainedly before the Lord, or when ministering on my knees to the sick and suffering, I sometimes get flashes of realization that I have finally become, in the Lord, the human being I was always intended to be. It is those times that I see how amazingly miraculous the new birth really is.

My family members, all raised culturally Jewish, do not return my calls, and I spend most of my holidays alone. As I have become more active and recognized in Christian ministry, most of my family will no longer acknowledge that I even exist. My children, whom I adore, for the most part have not seen me for years. I understand that I have two grandchildren, neither of whom I have ever seen, except on Facebook, where, late at night, I occasionally work up the courage to sneak a peek that warms my heart and breaks it at the same time. I am sad to say that these youngsters probably do not know my name. Their mother, Nicole, my firstborn, the light of my life and my soul mate for so many years, has not spoken to me in eight years, not since I have been born again and have become more prominent in the ministry.

Of course, of everything that I have gained and lost, these personal human losses pain me unspeakably, and they are the hardest cross to bear. Sometimes I cannot lift up my head, contemplating this. I have had to turn this over to the Lord, because only the Great Physician can heal this. I believe He will do so because I believe it is His will and because I know that the Great Physician is "board certified" in reconciliation.

I am healthy and robust, and, although I do not know what the future will bring, I do know that God is not through with me. I pledged my life to Him as a sacrifice years ago, when He delivered me from my prison chains. I spoke with him just this morning. I am still "the apple of His eye" (Zechariah 2:8).

I believe that He will continue to work out His plans for my life in His service. Like the apostle Paul, writing from the Philippian jail, I am confident of this.

"He which hath begun a good work in you will perform it until the day of Jesus Christ" (Philippians 1:6).

I do sometimes think I see dark clouds of uncertainty ahead, and every once in a while, like the discouraged prophet Elijah, fresh from his triumph over the prophets of Baal, I want to just go sit down "under a juniper tree" and weep. (1 Kings 19:5). They would not be bitter tears, however. Perhaps bittersweet.

Like everyone, I do not want to die alone. I know we are mere blades of grass and that our lives are as a vapor, but life today in the Lord is beautiful. Above all, I know one thing for sure:

Because He lives, I can face tomorrow.

Just as I am.

BRIEF ANNOTATED READING
LIST FOR SERIOUS DISCIPLESHIP

This is an abbreviated list of some of the seminal works that have assisted me in my growth in the Lord. Many of the great, enduring literary works produced over the ages are not included simply because they are so monumental that they are generally recognized as required reading for the serious disciple of Jesus of Nazareth. Those works include such major-league titles as *Augustine's Confessions*, *The Pilgrim's Progress*, Oswald Chambers' *My Utmost for His Highest*, and too many others to include. I urge you to make them part of your personal library. There is a reason why everybody knows them.

I have tried to fashion a reading list of perhaps some lesser-known or some less fashionable Christian manifestos, devotionals, and scholarly works, as well as a variety of wholesome, masterful, and enjoyable works of fiction suitable for the sanctified life. New works of greatness are constantly produced that sometimes older works of surpassing greatness can become overlooked or relegated to the bottom shelf or fall out of print. What they all have in common is the fact that each and every one of them are works that I cannot live without. Each author has enriched me beyond measure, and I am certain that each will change your life if you give them a chance to do so. My prayer is that you will find them so enjoyable and enriching that you will conclude, as have I, that you too cannot live without them.

FOUNDATIONAL READINGS

The King James Version of the Holy Bible. There are many translations of the Old and New Testament, and I recommend that you read every one of them, as each has something to offer in opening up God's revelation knowledge of His word. However, I am convinced that the serious disciple should become fully conversant in the utter beauty and serious scholarship inherent in the authorized version, which, in my opinion, most accurately and faithfully conveys the true meaning and intent of our Lord. For the record, let me state categorically that the most important parts of these preceding pages are, by far, the scripture verses. The rest is merely window dressing.

Any work by A. W. Tozer. His works define passion in matters of faith and are a critical reading experience for every saint. Works such as *The Pursuit of God* will assist the serious disciple in growth in the faith by providing both the new Christian as well as the mature believer with a glimpse into the life of true devotion to God. Ravi Zacharias's collection of Tozer's essays, titled *The Radical Cross*, will turn your life upside down spiritually and give you new goals in the walk with the Lord.

Any work by Charles Howard Spurgeon. Particularly beginning with Spurgeon's landmark devotional, *Morning and Evening*, in its original edition, the serious student of our Lord will be treated to insights and understandings of the Word and of the nature of the object of our faith that cannot be gleaned anywhere else. Spurgeon, the writer, was every bit as monumental as Spurgeon, the preacher. Everything Spurgeon committed to paper was gold.

Any work by Andrew Murray. This great saint lived about two hundred years ago, but his writing is forward-looking and applicable to the needs of the contemporary body of Christ. He is the godfather of our modern charismatic Pentecostal movement, and his numerous works are treasures and a pure joy of discovery. There is never a time that you will pick up any one of his inspiring works that you will not marvel at some gem of new understanding it has afforded you.

Alfred Edersheim's *The Life and Times of Jesus the Messiah*. Edersheim, the brilliant nineteenth-century Oxford professor of biblical studies and Jewish convert to Christ, has given us a timeless and monumental work on the life of Christ that has stood the test of time. Ninety-nine percent of every other biography of the Savior of the world pales in comparison. You will realize, moreover, that what makes it so great is not only Edersheim's meticulous scholarship but, more important, that he believed fervently in Jesus as his personal Lord and Savior. This stands in stark contrast to so many other works on Jesus and the Bible written by brilliant scholars who are either non believers or frank apostates with divinity degrees. It is in two volumes and promises a lifetime of treasures on virtually every page that will give you new and better understandings of our Lord and the times in which He walked the lanes and byways of this world.

To Jerusalem by Reginald Somerset Ward has been so inspirational to me and I owe Rev. Ward a great debt of gratitude for fundamentally shaping my view of real Christianity and all of its possibilities.

ESSENTIAL READINGS

Rabbi Jesus by Professor Bruce Chilton

Seven Story Mountain by Thomas Merton

The Purpose-Driven Life by Pastor Rick Warren

Mere Christianity by C. S. Lewis

Life of Christ by Frederic Farrar

Any work by Max Lucado

The Cost of Discipleship by Dietrich Bonhoeffer

Jesus Calling by Sarah Young

Battlefield of the Mind by Joyce Meyers

The Mitford Series by Jan Karon

Anchor for the Soul by Pastor Ray Pritchard

The Valley of Vision by Arthur G. Bennett

The Aubrey/Maturin Series by Patrick O'Brian

Come Away, My Beloved by Frances J. Roberts

What the Bible Says to the Minister: The Minister's Personal Handbook

The Imitation of Christ by Thomas à Kempis

Practicing the Presence of God by Brother Lawrence

The Starbridge Series by Susan Howatch

Any work by Kenneth Hagin

Any work by E. W. Kenyon

Ben-Hur: A Tale of the Christ by Lew Wallace

The Greatest Story Ever Told by Fulton Oursler

There are too many others to include but this is a great start. I have every confidence that you will hunger for Him more and more as you immerse yourself in the Word of God and Godly readings. You will be richly blessed.

CPSIA information can be obtained at www.ICGtesting.com
Printed in the USA
BVOW08*0213171016

465218BV00003B/8/P